IN THE SWEET

......Surviving in the Coal fields of the Appalachian Mountains in Harlan County Kentucky

By Joyce Osborn Wilson

Joyce Romine Osborn Wilson

Emily Nancy Howard, Romine, Smith

In The Sweet by and By

By Joyce Osborn Wilson

Sweet Memories,

Sad Heartaches,

Sweet Teen Years,

Sad Old Years,

Sweet Memories, Stay Forever

Sad Memories Linger Always

In The Heart, In The Mind,

In The Sweet By and By...

Editor

Laura Burke and Joyce Osborn Wilson

A special thanks to Chad Bryant for his expertise in designing the cover of this book
and the many hours he devoted to getting this book published

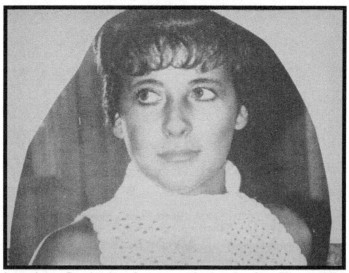

My precious sister, Carol, taken from us at the hands of her Foster child January 17, 2000

DEDICATION

My mother and I dedicate this book to Carol, beloved sister and precious daughter. She was savagely taken from us January 17, 2000 at the hands of a foster child. We'd also like to dedicate it to my sister Shirley. She was my idol, my hero and my confidante. A special thanks to my daughter, Kimberly, for believing in me.

MY INTRODUCTION

It is said, though it can't be proven, that ninety-five percent of all southern Howards can trace their family tree back a thousand years. Howards can trace their line directly or indirectly to the first Duke of Norfolk. Some can go back farther still, to the Saxon line, known as Hereward, first seen in 957, during the reign of King Edgar.

This story began when mother asked if I wanted to read her life story. "Of course," I said. She then went to her bedroom closet, pulled out an old metal flip top suitcase and brought out a spiral notebook she had written her memoires in. When I read her sweet notes of how hard her family had lived, her mother having 16 children, and none dying a natural death, I felt compelled to write her story. Her name is Emily, and her mother and father's names were Martha and Milty, short for J. B. M. Howard. It is a very poignant story.

My research took me through a little more than forty years of sitting for hours in genealogy centers, libraries, the Tampa Mormon Research Center, writing letters and talking to people in Harlan County, KY. From Emily's little memories comes the story from my mother's heart and soul. There were many tragedies, her own words of how each of her siblings died and with each funeral singing the sweet song, "In the Sweet By and By." In short, it is her life, her happiness and her sufferings of such poverty, no words can describe. In reading about it in her words, and in retelling it here, I feel that it has become a part of me. It has made me proud of my beginnings. From it, I have learned that it is not a sin to be born poor, but it is a sin to never try to do something to better ones self.

Undoubtedly this ability comes from the fact that the Howards hold such a prominent place in history, one of the most illustrious families in the world. Included in this line are Dukes and Duchesses, military heroes and husbands of queens. There's even a saint in the family, and the Howard name has held the English title "Duke of Norfolk" since the late 1400's. This Dukedom carries with it the office "Earl Marshal of England," which is in charge of state ceremonies such as coronations and royal funerals.

So much for living in interesting times. As for my mother's family, we hail from Kentucky. My line hasn't seen a Duke or a Duchess in generations. No castles or forts graced the land my people hunted and farmed, unless you consider that each house was a fortress against weather and hardship and starvation.

It would seem that my mother's people were nothing special, nothing worth noting to the outsider. But just as those Howards across the sea struggled, just as their fortunes did wax and wane with the shifting political sands of the times, so did my mother's people. And just as they struggled to survive and improve their lives, I think it makes for a story worth telling. It is in the struggles they faced that you see lives that are more than the sum total of their parts, more than simply what they grew each year or what they hunted or how many children they had. They lived simple lives, but ones filled with sweetness and promise all the same.

The Howard family was much like that of the Whitfield's and McCoy's, often fighting for land rights or bootlegging claims setting boundary lines. This was a clannish hillbilly way of life, fighting and making up. It was a backward way of learning respect for each other in this remote country. We were taught to stand up and fight for our rights.

My mother's family's story begins in the 1790's in an area of Kentucky that hadn't been settled yet, long before the present county of Harlan even existed.

That's where my mother's great, great, great grandfather, Samuel Howard lived. A native of central Virginia, he was a hardened Revolutionary War veteran before he was 21. Familiar with rivers and rolling hills, he found Harlan when it was still called Mt. Pleasant, and set about to build a better life. He was already well on his way when the county was named Harlan in 1819.

The place is rugged, mountainous and remote, with fertile soil and thick forests. Mountains border the county on three sides. The highest part of the State of Kentucky is at Black Mountain, which is 4,150 feet above sea level, in Harlan County on the southeastern boundary line. The hills hold springs of clean fresh cold water making it a haven for homesteading and a place to hide. The town appears to be cut off from the outside world, desolate and almost forbidden to strangers. The Cumberland River runs through the area as well, sometimes violently. During its frontier history, Kentucky was a place where you could wander for months and not see another living soul. It was a place where buffalo once roamed. It was a haven for frontiersmen and scoundrels alike.

Samuel was one of those who made Harlan. He married and raised a family. He lived under a cliff until he could build a cabin. His third son, Samuel, Jr. married Elizabeth Ann Brittain, whose father was General George Brittain who served under General George Washington. The name Brittain would be passed on many times. He took directly from the land and its wild plants, animals and herbs before he could tame a garden from the thicket. He helped build the first log courthouse in Harlan in 1808. Later his own great grandson would serve as County Clerk there.

Samuel planted deep roots in the Kentucky soil. His son James Howard lived his entire life within Harlan County, marrying and raising twelve children. James' first son, Dallas Dudley Howard would do the same. And his wife would contribute in a special way to my generation, with both her name and her spirit. Her name was Emily.

Emily Jones married Dallas in 1862, and gave him eight children before dying of the flux sometime around 1881. Before she died she took it upon herself to provide for her youngest son, who needed all her help.

James Milton Brittain Howard was born in January 6, 1878. A weak child, he was struck with infantile paralysis at age three. He would spend his entire life on crutches. However, Emily saw that he was a child of strong will. She believed that he would flourish with the right care, and she spent her last days making sure he would get it.

She summoned her sister-in-law Susan Howard. Susan was her husband's sister and was the second wife of John McCreary. As John's second wife, she was mother to his children from a previous marriage. Now Emily asked her to raise her youngest son Milty.

Susan gave her word, and when she gave her word she always kept it. Milty did learn how to survive. He became a talented musician and a great outdoorsman, and lived to serve a continuous 29 years as Magistrate. He loved and married Martha and with her had sixteen children, twelve of whom lived to adulthood.

Through all this, Milty never forgot the sacrifice his mother made for him, or that she loved him and believed in him before anyone else. He would choose one daughter to bear the name of his mother Emily, perhaps because he saw in her that same strong-willed spirit that would not accept the lot that was given to her, but would struggle to get the best out of life.

My mother was that young girl. Her name was Emily Nancy Howard. She lived in the mountains of Kentucky all her life. This book is taken from her diary, and tells the story of her people.

Mother's people were born into poverty most cannot imagine. They endured backbreaking work, cold, starvation, fear of childbirth at a young age and loss after loss. Despite this, their lives were rich and interesting, and echo the stories of so many mountain families. They are a proud and strong people. I am delighted to share their spirits with you.

Mother's 6th Great Grandfather Samual Howard, Sr
the only known picture of him. Kentucky's first Revolutionary Soldier

CHAPTER 1: The Courtship of 1895

The place where my people are buried is a hill near heaven. Outsiders would not go looking for it. The people there are left alone.

I can stand in the middle of Kitt's cemetery and imagine that I too am gone, except for my spirit wandering between the graves. It is not a field, or a flat place that one would think of when they hear the word cemetery. Mountain people tuck their loved ones into hills that are remote and sacred places. They chisel names into the stones or rest them under small wooden crosses. It is quiet here. There is no town, no animals, no machinery, and no conversation to break the stillness. After the visitors leave, there is no weeping. All that is left is the wind.

Listening to the wind is like listening to the voice of God. His voice softens the silence and fills the open spaces, rustling the trees. People are often buried under the trees. They must rest in the roots, and use them to climb to the sky up to heaven. I think that maybe it's the wind carrying them up.

The cemetery can only be reached by walking up the steep path from Kitt's Hollow. That's the rough side of the mountain, with room for only the smallest wagon trail. If you don't own a wagon and your kin has to be carried up there, men have to rest several times along the trip.

Aunt Susan told me that many people whispered things about my grandmother, Emily. They said she could have beaten the bloody flux if only they'd had more food the winter before. She went without when the children needed food. She worked hard and was tired. Many women had died in childbirth that year, being so close to starving when they tried to give birth.

Aunt Susan said she remembered when it started, the fever and the cramps that would double Emily over as she did the washing. She'd try to rest, but sitting there she'd shake and sweat like it was a mid-summer day.

Aunt Susan had seen it before of course. She'd had it herself the season before and it had put her low for a few weeks. But my grandmother wasn't strong that season. The harvest had been poor. She worked long hours to take care of the children and the garden.

All those things made it impossible for her to fight it off. When she called Aunt Susan to the house days earlier, she cried, realizing that Emily was on her deathbed, asking her to tend to her youngest son. It was wrong; much could have been done. She could have used Castor Oil or Epsom salts or ipecac to help her vomit, or fed her apples boiled in milk. She would have aired out her room and kept her sheets and bedroom washed and applied blisters to her wrists. But by the time Susan discovered Emily's problem, no mountain cure was good enough to save her.

When my Pappy went to Aunt Susan, she held him in her arms like the new mother she was, and she knew that his sense of loss was as profound as her own. It didn't have to happen. They would mourn together, for now he belonged to her.

It wasn't unusual back in her day that when men were widowed, they'd remarry quickly, or send their younger children off to be cared for by a woman's hand, often a mother or a sister, until they were grown. Many people just didn't think it was right for a man to care for a small child, especially if it was a girl. A man just couldn't teach a girl child what she needed to be a mountain wife, and it just wasn't fitting. But Grandmother Emily wanted something more from Aunt Susan. She wanted Aunt Susan to take up the raising of my Pappy for good, not just until he was grown but forever.

That was on account of Pappy's being crippled from polio at the age of three. My grandmother knew that her husband Dallas wouldn't be able to handle the needs of someone like that. He wouldn't be comfortable raising a boy with a crutch.

Pappy had one short leg. He would need to wear two different sized shoes for the rest of his life, and that was when finding just one pair was often a struggle. I'm sure she just knew it would be safer to give Pappy's care over to a woman who would always be there, instead of figuring on a stepmother to come in and love him like a real mother.

But Aunt Susan was always quick to point out that it wasn't hard to love my Pappy. Where many people saw only his handicap and his crutch, she saw a beautiful child, one with dancing sky blue eyes, golden blonde hair and fair skin. And he was always smiling. She had a choice; she could raise him as a cripple with special privileges or she could raise him as a mountain woodsman. Because of her, he acted like all the other kids. He went whenever and wherever, putting his good foot down first and giving his body a shove with his crutches as he ran. He could leap like a deer. No one could use the old saying, "walk with a cripple and you'll end up with a limp" with him.

Aunt Susan and Uncle John were wonderful parents. Aunt Susan was gentle and soft-spoken with Pappy and Uncle John poured the mountain into him like milk over cornbread. Pappy could never get enough, learning to fish and to hunt and to take care of himself. After the day was done, Uncle John and Pappy spent their evenings telling Aunt Susan about what they had done that day and what they planned for the next. No matter the weather, the two were out exploring the countryside and learning its ways.

Aunt Susan worried when my Pappy first wanted to carry a gun for hunting. She finally got over her worries when she realized that he got around as well as anyone with two good feet. Uncle John was a good teacher for him too, showing him not just how to shoot, but the things that would keep him alive. He taught him that red squirrel was bigger and tasted better than gray squirrels. It was a rare day that they didn't bring home three or four for the frying pan.

Aunt Susan loved to have a good meal for them when they returned, making fresh apple cake and iced tea to go with whatever they caught or killed. I know for truth that you'll never leave her table hungry. If they caught brim or catfish or bass, she'd roll the fresh fish fillets in meal and drop them in a pan of hot grease to fry to a golden brown. When they returned with squirrel, she could make great squirrel gravy to cover biscuits that came out of the oven brown as a berry. Then she'd use the meat for squirrel dumplings, which was a particular favorite with the family. When they brought home a possum, she'd place yams and onions in a deep baking pan and bake it to a golden brown in the old coal stove. When she finished, the meat pulled away from the bones.

Next to the mountain, Uncle John's passion was music. He loved the fiddle, which belonged to his father. "Our music will keep the family together," he'd tell Pappy firmly. Music did bring mountain people together. They would travel for miles whenever there was a chance to get together for music. Most men played some instrument, and dancing was the best way to meet other boys and girls. Pappy knew he'd best learn how to play or he'd miss out. Dancing would be awkward with his crutch. But he'd go one better and play the music that led the dance. He'd lead the dance in a different way. He told his Uncle John that he liked banjo music.

"Well Milty, if you could play any instrument that you wanted, I'm figuring that you'd want to play the banjo, am I right?" Uncle John offered one day. Pappy nodded slowly, and added, "That five-string banjo of Mr. Madden's is fine. I've always enjoyed watching him play it, how his fingers just dance over the strings.

Uncle John said nothing and when Pappy turned around to look at him there was a banjo propped against the leg of the table. He was amazed, because it was obviously used, but in really good condition. The strings looked almost new and the skin over the bottom of it was clean and tight. "Now how did you afford an instrument such as this?" Uncle John kept his expression even, but Pappy could tell that he was pleased with himself. "Well, I guess that will stay my secret," was all he would say.

He knew the value of that banjo and practiced it nearly every night. He quickly became a good player. Aunt Susan would often boast how it wasn't long at all before he could pick out a tune, and after a time he was good enough to call off barn dances tapping out the rhythm with his good foot. He was quite popular with many of the surrounding communities and before long he was playing barn dances nearly every weekend.

One of the biggest and most exciting aspects of mountain life is the barn dance, hands down. People gather from all around to listen to fiddles and banjos and dance. Once a barn dance gets moving, it would amaze you to see the dust that fills the air from all the foot stomping, hand slapping and dancing that goes on.

But the dance isn't really that loud. You can hear the shuffling of feet on the ground as the music plays. Some dancers liked to add their own twist to things, but it would be small. The group dance was more important than what each person wanted to add to it. And the caller would speak to the crowd but never yelled, just spoke to them like he was having a conversation out in the yard. Everyone was orderly, moving in time. Everyone was so happy to be together, so happy to be alive, so happy to hear the musicians play and feel their music lead them that they let all those feelings wash over them. Most everyone would be grinning from ear to ear.

Pappy couldn't dance, but truthfully he was as much a dancer as the rest of them. He was always connected with them as he played, always watching them move as he played. He would watch them line up in formation, noticing how experienced they were, how old or young. Were the dancers connected to him? Were they listening? Did they know the dances he was playing? He listened for the sound of their feet hitting the ground and he guided them along. If they needed him to go more slowly he would, but slowly he'd take charge of the dance, slowly bringing up the pace until everyone reeled and whirled along at the pace he chose. He was the leader of the dance.

And it was on just such a night that my mother first saw Pappy. As she told it to me, I can see that night in my mind like it was yesterday. I could see the smile in her eyes and his both when he said that this was the night that he spotted the most beautiful girl he had ever seen.

Mother was petite and lovely then, young and fresh in a dashing red, green and black checkered gingham dress. It was high necked with long sleeves and the skirt was full and brushed the tops of her black button-up shoes. Her hair was thick and shiny and she wore it loose so that it fell below her hips and swayed when she walked. People called her pretty and were impressed with her flawless skin, olive-colored like an Indian maiden. There were many Indian tribes in Kentucky back then, and her mother was part Cherokee and part Sioux. She was stout built, had black hair which was done up in the back and olive colored skin. She had high cheekbones and she had full shaped lips like mothers.

That night her mother had her eye on Martha just in case anyone showed disrespect. Back then it wasn't right for a girl to walk up to a man and start talking to him. And it wasn't right for a man to do that either, which didn't stop them from trying. But the respectful way was to go through a girl's mother.

So she pretended not to notice Pappy that night, but oh, he was hard to miss. He was the center of her attention, even when he wasn't doing the calling. At one point, his uncle tapped him on the shoulder and he mouthed the words, "Your turn." Pappy was wonderful at calling. Mother watched him the whole night, even after his uncle took up the calling once again.

Pappy asked his aunt about "the fat lady on the wagon and the young girl." He meant Grandmother Mary, who was short and stocky. Aunt Susan told him that this was Mary Whitson and her daughter Martha. Many people in the area knew them because my grandmother was an Indian who'd married William Lee. My grandfather and many people thought that when my grandfather died and she'd remarried a man named Sam Whitson that she'd really married the mysterious drifter Jesse James.

Many stories about this man circulated throughout Kentucky and college turn papers were written about the story. Sam Whitson stayed very mysterious until the end of his days, and kept everyone guessing. He was buried at the base of a Chestnut Tree in an unknown grave.

Rumor has it Sam Whitson was the mysterious drifter "Jesse James." Mary and Sam

Pappy found a clever way to meet Mother at that very first dance. When he saw her disappear up the road with her mother, he hurried quickly through the woods so that he might come out into the road ahead of them, then slowed his pace to a near crawl, knowing that they'd soon catch up with him. When they did, he spoke to my grandmother. "It's quite a lovely evening," he offered.

She grunted. "Yes, it is." Mother couldn't get up the courage to say anything to him, but she looked anxiously at him when she thought he wouldn't see. He introduced himself and told them that he lived with his Uncle John and Aunt Susan McCreary because his mother died.

I loved hearing Mother describe him back then. Was he ever handsome! His hair was so shiny and fair, nothing like hers. It was so nice to stare at his crisp light hair and his beautiful blue eyes. They reminded her of a sunny sky after an early morning rain.

Mary said, "Yes, I know." What was she saying? Oh yes, she knew all about Pappy, had gotten his story from one of the other mothers. Thankfully she sounded friendlier when she said that, so she must have heard good things about him. Thank goodness. That or she was soft on him because she was reminded of her own first husband when Pappy told her about his mother.

He asked where they lived and she said, "We live on top of Coxton Mountain, which is a very long ways. It is above Magazine Holler." She relaxed a bit and told of our life on the mountain. She told about Sam Whitson, her husband, who would be waiting for them over in Coxton Camp, which was a small mining camp. "Sam has his mule and sled with him," she said, "to haul me around and whatever supplies we need. Martha and Sam can walk it back up the mountain, but as you can see, I am a bit too heavy for such a long walk." Mother could see him eye her, and turned before she could notice his expression, because grandmother must have weighed close to three hundred pounds. She finally found her voice, saying, "Sometimes we spend the night with friends and then get an early start for home the next morning."

"Yes," Mary said, "and I'm afraid that is what we will have to do tonight for dark will surely catch us before we can get home."

Pappy asked Mary if he might come and visit them. She hesitated for some time as if giving the question lots of thought. But she liked him, and was just trying to make him worry. Slowly she said, "I guess perhaps it will be alright." When he asked how old Mother was, Mother spoke up quickly again. "Mother, I will be thirteen in May." Mary said nothing to that just smiled and walked on. Finally she said, "We are almost to where Sam will be waiting, so we must hurry."

"It's getting late and I too must go home."

They all said goodbye.

"And what did you do after that, Pappy?" I would ask the question even though by now I already knew the answer. He loved to tell that story and we all loved hearing it.

"Your mother's house was a small two-room log cabin set back on the mountain. I knew that because I didn't go straight home that night. In the darkness, by the moonlight, I hiked forever through trails up from Magazine Holler and found that house so I'd know where it was. I didn't want to have to hunt for it that Sunday; I wanted to go right to it."

"So that Sunday next I dressed in the best clothes I had and went courting up Coxton way. When I got there, the hunting dogs told the whole mountain that I was there, and I was afraid I was a goner before I'd even gotten to the house. But Sam, your mother's stepfather, came out yelling at the dogs. They came up to him slinking, then shot off when he fussed at them. But then he fixed me with this tight stare until Mary came out. She recognized me immediately but didn't say a thing. I realized much later that this was their way of having fun with me, but I didn't know it then, I can tell you I did not!"

Sam asked, "Milty, you are a long ways from home aren't you? What brings you way up here? You're dressed like you should be in church."

They enjoyed it completely when this made me nervous. I stared at them but didn't say a thing either. Finally Mary came to my rescue. She said, "Sam, I asked Milty to come see us."

"Inside the cabin, they had one fair sized room where everyone could gather. Like most families, they did everything in that room but sleep. A scrub broom made from hickory sticks sat in one corner. A gourd used for water dipper hung on the wall next to the enamel water bucket. An old churn for churning butter from their milk cow sat next to a handmade wooden table. A large wooden box sat near the stove filled with firewood and kindling. All the pots hung on the wall. The shelves nailed to one wall were stacked with quilts and homemade canned goods. Jars of jams were stacked neatly on the lowest shelf and a large bowl of fresh apples was on the table. Cooking smells filled the air. String beans were hanging from the rafters of the ceiling. I knew then that Mary was a good woman and a hard worker, and that she was willing to do whatever it took to get her family through the winter. I was pleased because I bet that her daughter was just the same. It was a house in good order."

This was always the place in the story where Mother picked up, and we turned to her automatically. She smiled, put her hand on Pappy's shoulder, and continued for him.

"I was so nervous that day! I stood in the next room as he came in, running my hands along the lines of my dress, hoping that I looked all right. I had chosen a different dress for today - a deep blue and white checkered dress with a high neckline and long sleeves. The skirt was full and long. I had brushed my hair away from my face. I thought the dress was beautiful and I hoped that he would like it.

Sam and Mary told him to have a chair. When he sat down, I walked into the room. Mary said, "Martha look who's here." I tried not to, but I couldn't help blushing. My Mother and Sam laughed and mother said, "Milty, she is very shy but she will talk when she gets used to you. We hardly ever have anyone to visit us way up here."

"We sat for a while and they talked. Sam asked about his Uncle John and Aunt Susan. Finally mother told me to take your Pappy outside and show him around our small farm. So he grabbed his crutches and followed me outside. The whole time we walked, your Pappy would not take his eyes off me. He made me feel like the most beautiful girl in the world. Mother stuck her head out the cabin door and said, "Now, don't stray too far from the cabin. Dinner will be ready pretty soon."

"We walked around looking at the hogs and the cow. There was little to see, but we looked at things as slowly as possible, so that we could talk as much as we wanted. Slowly we made out way over to the pasture where we kept the plow mule standing near a group of trees. He listened as I talked, but I couldn't help but think that he didn't have his mind completely focused on what I was saying. I showed him the sled we used to haul Mother and our supplies up the mountain. In the middle of showing him this, he said words I've never forgotten."

"You are beautiful, Martha," he said simply, "and I have wanted to be alone with you from the first moment I saw you." Then he asked me what I did to pass the time up here so far away from other people. He said it so simply and quietly that it took me a second or two to realize that he'd asked me a question, and another few seconds to find my voice again. But I wasn't uncomfortable with him and I didn't feel shy."

Mother told him about helping Mother and Sam with the chores and about the big rock around the hill which was her favorite place. "Sometimes I build a playhouse on it and sometimes I just like to sit and daydream. I love to watch the birds and the little animals play. About once a month, I get to go with Sam and mother off the mountain to the store," she told him. "That's the best time of all. I get bored a lot."

"Martha, would you mind showing me your favorite rock?" he said. By this time she realized that he really wanted to be out of sight of the cabin, and that sent such a lovely thrill through her stomach to the tips of her toes. "Oh come on, I would love for you to see it," she said.

The rock was large and flat on top for easy sitting. One side was slanted making it easy to climb onto. They climbed it and sat down. "No wonder you like it here," Pappy said. "It is peaceful and serene. The mountains can be seen for such a long distance and the quietness of the surroundings make you feel you are near heaven."

Mother knew right then that she would have a life with him, no matter the cost.

The moment wasn't lost on him either. She could see him struggle to be graceful while adjusting his crutch so that it was out of his way but still close by. But when he leaned over to take her hand, she felt the strength in his grasp, and the tenderness that he used because he was holding her hand, because it was the most precious thing in the world to him. "I have very warm feelings towards you, Martha," he said quietly. She could feel every word he said passing right from his hand into hers. She smiled again, and wondered what it would be like if he kissed her.

Too soon Grandmother Mary called them to dinner.

He spent the day with them and stayed just as long as he could, leaving barely in time to make it off the mountain and back home before it got too dark to walk. Days later he returned and asked Sam if he could go for a walk with him. They walked across the clean swept dirt covered yard, past the barn and near the pasture.

"As I watched them leave, I had the feeling down deep that he would be asking Sam for my hand, and I was right. Sam fought with him for a while."

"You've known each other for less than two weeks, how can you be in love, Milty?" he said.

"But your Pappy would not budge. He told Sam that he'd fallen in love with me the first time he saw me. I think Sam realized there was no way around him, and anyway I know that Sam liked your Pappy a lot. He gave his blessing and they returned to the house. There they sat and talked to my mother and me."

"Martha, I have asked Mr. Whitson for your hand in marriage and he agreed that it was okay and if it is okay with Mrs. Whitson I would like to marry you and make you my wife. Mrs. Whitson is it okay with you?"

Mother smiled softly, "Well, Milty, if it's okay with Sam, I guess it's okay with me, but have you asked Martha?"

There was a silence. I could feel him looking at me, but I held my head down, which seemed the only decent thing to do. Milty handed me a note he had written himself, and I looked at it as the worn paper touched my hand. After a brief hesitation, I unfolded it and read the contents.

YOU ARE THE *ONLY* GIRL IN ALL THIS WIDE, WIDE, *WORLD* THAT *SUITS ME.*

WILL YOU BE MY SWEET HEART?

LAST NIGHT I HAD A BEAUTIFUL DREAM, AND IN IT YOU WERE THERE, BUT MORNING CAME AND I AWOKE TO FIND MY DREAM WAS BARE. ALL MY HOPES WERE SHATTERED. NO MORE LOVE I'LL SHARE. UNTIL I HAVE THIS DREAM AGAIN, AND MAYBE YOU'LL BE THERE?

I looked up at last and saw those beautiful blue eyes staring at me. I knew my answer. "Yes, it's okay with me, I will marry you Milton." I had to say nothing more. The wedding was set. Your Pappy and I married in 1895. I was thirteen and he was seventeen.

Martha and Milty, the only formal portrait of them

CHAPTER 2:

Sleep, Susan, Sleep

That barn dance changed my parents forever and completely. From then on, their lives were all about family. But it wasn't just a romantic thing with flowers and music, living together and raising our family would be about surviving the hard times and living through months of cold and near starvation. But they didn't know that in the early days. The early days were just about being man and wife, and managing in close quarters.

Right after the wedding, they had to live with Mother's parents. In a cabin with a cold, damp floor a table laden with enameled chipped dishes and dented forks, small coal stove where all the cooking was done, and a feather bed covered with handmade quilts.

It was a bit hard to consummate their vows with an audience. And Mother tells me that Pappy wanted to be with her all the time. It embarrassed her in the beginning, she said, because she wished for more privacy. But she could only think about him, and her parents were really quiet about it. Sometimes, she said, she'd see her mother share a private smile with Sam. Things like that helped her relax about the living arrangements.

And they also loved being out in public together, because they made a striking couple. Mother had coal black hair, hazel eyes and wore a size 2-1/2 shoe. Pappy had golden hair, the bluest eyes that twinkled like stars and was tall and lean. They stood out.

Sometimes on Saturday nights they would go to the barn dances. She never would dance without him. She preferred to sit beside him while he did his calling, watching the others dance. I can imagine how they looked together, with her next to him with her hair curled upon the floor around her ankles.

But they didn't need a barn dance to have fun. When work was done for the day and supper over, Sam played his fiddle while Pappy picked his banjo and neighbors gathered in from all around the mountain. Everyone had such a good time. Young girls would make eyes at Pappy, and often there would be boys flirting with Mother, but it didn't matter. They only had eyes for each other.

They'd only been married a few short months when Mother noticed a change in her body and a queasy strangeness in her stomach. Hot sweats and nagging heartburn kept her awake at night. She tired easily, making it difficult to get through the days. Grandmother Mary watched her dresses get tight.

After a few months, she said, "Martha, I have noticed you sure are gaining weight."

"Well I don't know why," Mother said. "I can't eat a thing that stays down."

Mary paused, and then remarked quietly, "Well, I think you are with child."

No one had ever told Mother about childbearing. At the time she was barely fourteen. But everyone had heard stories, and knew of women who hadn't survived childbirth, or had lost their babies before they reached a year old. Being pregnant was a happy event for a mountain woman, but not an easy thing to go through.

Doctors weren't always available in the mountains. Midwives were often called granny women, the women in the community we trusted to help us with the birthing of the children. The best ones were the ones who inherited the duty from their mothers, who would bring them along and teach them the right ways, baby by baby.

Grandmother Mary never explained this Mother. After she told her that she was pregnant, she just stared at her for a time, then laughed, picked up her hoe and walked out to the garden. That was the mountain way.

Pappy was just the opposite, and her love for him grew like wild roses in spring. As the baby grew inside her, she'd catch him watching her closely with those deep blue eyes, and a soft smile that gave his face gentle creases that she loved to touch.

As the weeks continued, Mother would recall having vivid dreams about the child growing inside her. "Those dreams were terrible," she say. "I'd wake from a deep sleep. In my dream, I was running through the woods as fast as I could, holding my belly in pain. I could tell something was wrong with my baby and I had to get out to my favorite rock. The wind was crashing around me from a storm, whipping my hair and making the leaves slippery so I fell over and over again trying to get out there. When I finally made it, I was exhausted, and I crawled to the top of the rock on my hands and knees, calling out for Milty again and again."

This story always scared us when she told it, and by this time we were listening to every pause she made. Dreams were messages, sometimes from the Lord and sometimes from the Devil. From the hair standing up on the back of my neck, I felt sure this one had been sent to Mother by the Devil himself. "And lightning crashed all around me," she'd continue, "and Milty would never come. I was alone with no one to help me and I started having that baby. You could never imagine the pain I was in, screaming to the heavens to let me die. I was sweating drops of blood I was in so much pain, rolling around on the top of that rock. But the worst thing was that I couldn't get up, and I could sense that I wasn't alone. There was a mountain lion in the shadows. I could see his eyes just at the edge of the rock, afraid to come out into the storm, but just waiting for me to deliver that baby, and in my weakness steal it away from me for good. I would scream for your Pappy, and I would scream to try to scare the mountain lion. But he would just scream back at me, because he wasn't the least bit afraid of me. I would always wake up at that point, and be unable to go back to sleep for the rest of the night. I felt certain that my dreams were a vision, but I never told your Pappy, because I knew it would make him worry."

I can only imagine the fear that Mother must have felt when, one day close to her time, Pappy decided that he needed to visit his Aunt Susan. She'd been feeling poorly, and he wanted to see her before the baby was born. Why she didn't tell him about those dreams I'll never know, but she was probably trying to be brave, and not worry him about her fears. Well she shouldn't have been so brave, because later in that very day she was struck with pain in her back. She told her mother that she was feeling bad and needed to lie down. Alone in her bed, the pain became unbearable.

"I realized then that I was going to die," she always told us.

"I immediately thought of my dream, with the pain and climbing out to the rock up the hill, and I realized that my dream wasn't about having the baby, but about dying. I had always said that when I died I should be laid out on that rock, and I realized that in my dream I had gone there to die and save everyone in the house from hearing me scream and cry in pain. Lying in a pool of sweat, it all made perfect sense to me. I took my mind off the pain imagining all my neighbors and my sweet young husband weeping over my body, which had been washed clean and dressed in a clean beautiful dress of sky blue. My poor mother had been all alone with my father when he died. I would hate for her to find me here, without even Milty around to comfort her. For her, I could haul myself up and go to my rock to die.

Quietly I left the cabin and headed for the woods. I just felt certain that when I turned up missing, your Pappy would understand where I had gone. I would go to my rock and lay myself out as was the mountain custom.

Much later, when I had made it all the way out to my rock, the pain had just gotten worse and worse. For my part, I had given into it with screaming and sobbing. And that's how my husband and my mother found me, curled up in a tight ball. When I explained through my choking sobs what I was doing, my mother just laughed at me."

"You foolish child," she said. "You are not dying, you're in labor. It's time for your baby to be born."

"I couldn't understand this, but I was in too much pain to question her. They gently eased me up off the rock, took me back to the house and tucked me back in bed. Mother told Sam to hitch up the mule and get the midwife as fast as he could. He rushed out while she began heating water on the stove and collecting clean ragged towels to prepare for the birth."

I could imagine the whole thing in my mind. Their cabin had no indoor plumbing and little heat for the new baby. Pappy must have sat on the side of the bed comforting her while she clutched his hand. Mother was just fourteen years old. He would have made a dozen or more trips to the door watching for Mr. Sam and the midwife, clicking a rhythm with his fingernails on his crutch handle like he always did now.

Finally, he would have seen them coming up the mountain, and would have told Mother. He'd go out to meet them and return with the midwife, carrying her bag. She'd have entered the room, knelt down beside the bed, then would have said softly, "it will be some time yet little one." She'd have turned to Sam and Pappy, saying, "We must get this cabin warmer or the child will freeze before it is delivered."

Mother told us that the labor dragged on for hours. The midwife would ease Mother up into a sitting position, and even a standing position to try to encourage the baby to come, but nothing seemed to work and eventually she was too weak to stand. Often she would check the position of the baby with fingers she'd greased with some homemade mixture that smelled of herbs. The afternoon stretched into the night and into the wee hours of the morning.

"I still remember your Pappy's eyes," Mother said quietly. "I was young, but I understood that there was fear in them. He thought I was going to die. I do not remember much past the morning. They told me that my labor continued into the late afternoon. Finally the midwife told Mary to sit in the chair and had Sam help get me into a sitting position on mother's lap to make the birth a little easier. I do not remember this, or the three hours that followed. But I do know that I gave birth to a beautiful baby girl with a head full of your Pappy's golden hair."

With this great thing accomplished, it was time to pay the midwife. Sam killed a chicken, scalding the bird and picking feathers then handing it to Mary to cook. She made a large pot of chicken and dumplings and a pone of cornbread. The midwife sat down with the rest of the family then and ate like it was the best meal she'd ever eaten. The blessing of the child calmed everyone, and they relaxed in the warm cabin and spoke in quiet, happy tones. Later she accepted some dried shuck beans and two cans of apple jelly, and rode away with Sam into the snow and freezing temperatures.

When she woke, Pappy was the first person she saw. He leaned over to kiss her as he laid the baby with her. "It's our very own baby girl," he beamed.

"One day, you will understand this, Emily," she always says. "But I stared at the gentle face, quiet in sleep. I knew, even though I was new to this child and these feelings, that I would give my life for this daughter of mine. Your Pappy knew that I almost had done just that. I'd do it again. That feeling is what it means to be a mother. I hugged the baby, then looked up at my own mother and asked her why she didn't tell me about babies and prepare me for it." She said only that she knew I would learn of it on my own soon enough. I felt tears behind my lids. I was hurt, but I knew that my mother meant no harm. She was an honest woman and she was right. There was no sense in explaining what couldn't be explained, in explaining something that had to be lived. I kissed the forehead of my child and I knew we'd never speak of it again."

Pappy wanted to name the baby Emily after his mother, but Mother begged him to name her after his Aunt Susan, so Susan Dewey Howard she was.

She was a beautiful girl. She had mother's olive skin, and she was very tiny, weighing four and a half pounds. And she was a healthy, happy baby who made everyone around her happy. Sam and Grandmother Mary were crazy about her. No one paid much attention that year to the things they had to do in order to survive. Nothing seemed as hard that year, because they were soaking up the joy of that little girl and enjoying her company and everything that she learned and everything she did as a little baby. The days seemed warm and happy even when it was cold outside. By the time the weather warmed, she was crawling, but strangely she did not get into things like most babies. She seemed to take after Sam a lot, even though they didn't share blood. Her eyes watched every movement he made, but missed nothing that anyone else did either.

She had sky blue eyes like her father, and the same smile. She was a spring flower and we were just like a family of honeybees buzzing around her.

"Oh you just don't know what that year was like for us. It's so hard to describe because it went so fast. I didn't want to go to sleep at night because I was afraid I'd miss a second with my precious girl. And I was growing up and learning things everyday about what kind of wife I wanted to be. We settled into the life of a real family."

One thing I learned besides how to make my Sudie smile was that I loved to garden. The garden was important to our way of life; a bad crop one year and we'd have a disaster of a winter. That year I noticed just how black the soil was when the horse and plow turned it up under foot. And that season I stepped in the dirt with my bare feet and I could feel it so cool between my toes that it was like wading in a stream. It smelled fresh and alive.

Our main crop that year, as in years to come, was corn. We cut it off the cob when it was fresh. We used the milk from the cob for creamed corn. We ate it in corn pones, corn fritters, corn pudding and succotash. With the corn harvested at the end of the season, we'd dry it and then grind it for corn meal.

It could also be used for the chickens and the hogs to make the meat taste sweeter.

But I also grew other things as well, grew things year round while the weather held out. In the early spring we planted cucumbers, English peas, lettuce and onions. After Good Friday we would plant tomatoes, watermelon, okra, radishes, beans, field peas, squash, peppers, zucchini and pumpkins which would be harvested in the summer. By July we were so busy canning and pickling, stringing beans and making jelly, sauerkraut and succotash that we could barely keep up.

As the garden grew, so did Sudie. By two years old, she was trying to pick up a hoe just like me. Sam loved to peel apples and give her slices to suck on and she giggled as she stood by Pappy's chair, clutching her apple and holding onto his crutches. Everyone talked about her beauty and how sweet she was.

By three she began showing her responsible side. She always put away her few handmade toys and tried to help out around the cabin. She kept us so busy, but she was the air we breathed. Sharing the same house with my parents made it easy to care for her. She honestly had no favorites among us, giving equal attention to everyone near. We lived in a beautiful dream that revolved around our precious daughter."

Mother almost always stopped talking about Sudie at that point. She liked remembering the good times they had with their sweet little daughter, and not the terrible part that came later. She must have been between three and four years old when it happened, just before New Year's Day. Grandmother Mary's favorite habit was smoking a corncob pipe. At late evening she'd lean over and light it by the fireplace, then listen to our stories or tell some of her own while puffing on that pipe. I had seen many neighbor women do the same thing at the dances. She made Sudie a little pipe patterned after her own. Sudie loved that pipe and carried it with pride. She loved to pretend that she was Grandmother Mary, sitting on the floor next to her rocking chair. She pretended to smoke along with her, watching the smoke come out of her mouth. Sudie laughed and blew make believe smoke spirals from her mouth and listened to bedtime stories.

No one ever knew exactly what happened the night of the fire, but I can see her little body in my mind's eye, sliding out of her bed and bouncing softly over to the fireplace in the early morning light while everyone else slept. Then she'd lean into the grate, trying to light the pipe just like her grandmother must have done. And that would have been when the edge of her outing gown must have caught a spark. The fire would have quickly turned her into a live torch. She must have run screaming toward the door when she felt the fire on her.

"I will remember that scream for the rest of my life, Emily," Mother says to me when she remembers that day. "I think the mountain itself must have heard her screams. Screams that echoed throughout the mountains. The air was cold, the wind was blowing and the gown was completely engulfed. Our Sudie fell in the yard. Sam got to her first, rolling her on the ground to put out the flames. But it was much too late. Her skin stuck to the gown as he lifted her into his arms. She was lifeless, her blonde hair burned, her face blistered from the fire, her body limp, her long lashes singed and her face smudged with smoke. She was still clutching her little pipe."

It makes me cry whenever she tells this. Sometimes Mother cries along with me, for just a day earlier her life had been picture perfect, only to have her child ripped away from her so cruelly.

"Oh your Grandmother Mary screamed and shook her hand at God that day. No, No, No," she screamed, "why did he take our precious baby? You did not need her! She screamed to the sky as if God were peering at us from behind the clouds."

It was January 1, 1900, and it was a sickening and horrible New Year's Day. Anguish filled the cabin. Grandmother Mary wanted to die, as she knew in her heart that it was the corncob pipe that caused Sudie's death.

"Oh the anguish I felt, Emily." Mother would always hold me close when she spoke of it. "I wanted to crawl in the box right next to my child so that they would bury us together. Our house, which had only the day before been so happy, was now a funeral home. I could not speak the words of my pain."

Neighbors soon flooded the house when they heard of the tragedy. They came from throughout the mountains bringing food and comfort. The wooden casket that held Sudie was set up by the window and the sun cast a golden glow of light on her face as she lay there, looking as though she were asleep. Her long eyelashes were scorched, but her blistered lips smiled. People would whisper around her, as she was now in heaven and would never have to tiptoe when she walked anymore, for she now had wings to fly.

I think sometimes that I can see Mother with Sudie. She says that she stared at her for a long time, trying to memorize her baby's face. She knew that she was going to have to remember how beautiful Sudie was for the rest of her life. There had been no pictures taken of the little girl, and once she went into the grave, she'd never be seen again. The minister tried to speak words of comfort, but nothing helped.

Sudie was dead.

"The four of us huddled together as the casket was lifted and carried out to the wagon. People walked behind it single file as it pulled away with its precious treasure."

The graveyard was a ways out on the side of the mountain. It was a windy day and walking was hard as we silently stumbled over the hard rocky road leading us to that cemetery. Mother told me that Pappy had a hard time holding onto his crutches and at the same time trying to comfort her.

And so when I stand again in the cemetery and look across the field, I see where Sudie was buried, not far from her Grandmother Emily. Today it is like it must have been that day, with the wind blowing hard against the grass and the trees, making it hard to walk, pushing the people away so that the dead could be left alone. The sound of that wind would have just barely been pierced by the sound of feet stumbling over the hard rocky road. Standing silently, I can just imagine Mother moving slowly because she was walking with Pappy, and he was struggling to make it up the mountain with his crutches. They were both struggling inside though, bent over in their grief. Sam would be holding Grandmother Mary's arm and she would be puffing because she was so large and it was difficult for her to make it up the steep hill.

And I can see the gravediggers standing beside the fresh hole, dirt as black as night in a pile next to them. They would stand quietly until it was time to shovel soil back in place over Sudie's new home. The small crowd that had followed the family would begin to sway and cry out and sing.

We shall sing on that beautiful shore
Th' melodious songs of th' blest
And our spirit shall sorrow no more
Not a sigh for th' blessings of rest

In th' Sweet by and by
We shall meet on that beautiful shore
In th' sweet by an' by
We shall meet on that beautiful shore

I imagine the wailing tones of Mother's favorite hymn floating up, tangling in the tree branches and then climbing all the way to heaven. I get trapped for a time in the sadness. I sit down next to my sister's grave marker and scoop up a bit of dirt, letting it slip through my fingers. I can almost feel the pain that must have wept on that soil all those years ago. Life without their Sudie must have seemed too pointless.

CHAPTER 3: Blackberry Magic

After the death of Sudie, the family became familiar with the ways of silence. The year 1901 brought days of emptiness and grief. Poverty was bad enough, but death made life more difficult. Nights were the longest. Bedtime prayers were short, and at mealtime talk was brief. They didn't talk much in those days that followed. Mother was trapped in a deep grief.

But it is the same with all loss. Slowly you have to go on. It came sooner for them I think because they had no choice. There was no way to crawl into the grave with little Sudie and tell the world to go away for a while. Death stands on the doorstep of a mountain home and asks to be let in every day. And every day you must shoo it away from the porch or invite it in.

So, either they would survive or they would die. Making the choice to survive, even briefly, moves you back into the world of the living. You start to accept life again, even if you don't know how to handle all the pain in your heart.

January was usually the coldest month in the mountains, and the hardest to endure. The family had the added burden of Sudie's death, and the cold that settled around their hearts competed strongly with the weather that blew around them as they saw to daily chores. Each day they accepted the duty. Mainly they stuck it out because they had each other. If one person was going to get up and get started that day, the rest might as well. Keeping death away from the door was a family affair. Everyone was needed to survive the weather, the snows, the house that never felt warm, the food that never seemed to last.

They ate what they had stored from the earlier planting season. They ate what they had because there was nothing else to save them. They cooked things that would fill them up and convince death to look elsewhere. And when they felt like they couldn't eat from the same cellar one more day - when they were so tired of the same thing one more night they couldn't even feel grateful for the blessing of food - they'd add one little something different to it, just to make it new again.

So January and February were the months of dumplings. They tried tomato dumplings, blackberry dumplings, strawberry dumplings and apple dumplings. It was the month for trying white gravy, followed by tomato gravy, meal gravy, squirrel gravy and chicken gravy. Next they went through the beans, from soup beans to green beans, which they abandoned for the navy beans and then the shuck beans. They had biscuits, which isn't all the different from a dumpling but feels different when you call it something else. So for a while they'd have biscuits in the morning, cold biscuits for lunch with a fresh green onion, sometimes sugar biscuits with sugar and butter on the cold biscuit or a little honey.

They ate everything until they were sick of it. Fried cabbage, hot biscuits, gravy and a glass of milk completed many suppers. Sometimes they could afford to have a pudding, either with a little nutmeg and cinnamon, or just plain made with just milk, flour, sugar, butter, eggs and vanilla poured over hot cakes.

As the mountains began to thaw with it came sprigs of green and spring. Poke salat was picked, parboiled and cooked by adding scrambled eggs and served with cornbread. With poke salat also came the "runs" making quick trips to the old outhouse.

During hog killing season there was a lot of meat, but that time of year they only ate it every once in a while, as a special treat. There was no hunting to be done until it got above freezing.

You wouldn't imagine how it could happen unless you'd lived it, but in that hardship when life was so hard, that's when my parents remembered life again and how precious it was.

Later came March, and the mountain started to thaw. The woods drew Pappy out as they always did. He loved them in all seasons, and as it got warmer he could spend more and more time out there with all the familiar sights and sounds. As the early spring turned into late spring and early summer, he would watch as the birds came back to the forest. He would watch for the squirrels and the mountain lions to move again through the trees. He would gather his fishing gear and head for the streams. He would sit under the stars and play his banjo. Eventually, he was able to convince Mother to explore the land with him. And they found healing in the magic of blackberry season.

Mother was still very down, but each day he would coax her to walk with him after the work in the garden had been done and share in the bounty of their mountains. With patience, the walks got longer and longer and she found more and more things to smell and taste and see.

Blueberry season is always a little different each year, which is part of the appeal, but the result is the same. Ever since mid-April, you've been planting things in your own garden. You've been waiting for the last big frost of the year to pass and hoping that you've gotten your garden in with enough time to produce all it can, but late enough that you've missed any cold snap that would rot the seeds in their beds. But by June, the flurry of the planting season has died down a little, and in that lull between planting and July harvest, you realize that nature has done some planting of its own.

That when you catch sight of the blueberry crop. It's a treasure hunt. You look around while you're walking and you notice blueberries weighing down the vines like jewels dripping off the arms of Egyptian princesses, begging to be scooped off with delicate fingers and eaten where you stand.

The woods wrapped themselves around their silences that had started in January. It filled in the things they couldn't say and gave them some peace. Then they could begin to speak again.

"You know, the old-timers say there's gold hidden in this mountain?"

"There isn't!" Mother knew the story and had heard the old-timers herself, but she said it was so nice to hear his soft voice like a breeze stirring the wind. He'd start his favorite tale with a big opener that would have you waiting for the rest of the story.

"Oh yes, everyone knows about it! It all came in when they were fighting the hard war, armies tracking gold in here to hide it, or to move it to a safe place, no one can be sure. But you know flatlanders can't handle hard weather like we can. You know most of them riding through here didn't make it through the harsh weather."

"Well I guess that would make logical sense."

"You're right, it does."

"Where's the gold then?" She asked quietly, knowing the answer. He sighed with great drama, leaned against a tree and tugged a blueberry vine down to her height so that she could draw her hands over it and retrieve the berries.

"There's just no one that knows that for sure, Martha."

"Could it be in the cavern up past the Hoss Hole?"

"Now that's a nice one, I'll grant you," he said quietly, plucking a few berries off for himself. "But I think most people have looked through that one before. Now as I hear it, one day many years back, a group of boys took one of their friends way back in the woods, farther than they had ever been. And do you know what they did?"

"They didn't leave him, did they?"

"Have you heard this story?" he looked at her with mock suspicion. She shook her head solemnly and popped another berry in her mouth. He smiled down at her and went on. "You have great insight into the wiles of young boys Ms. Howard. Yes, they left that little fella out in the woods. They took him someplace he'd never even seen before, and you know how far boys can wander when they're hunting."

"So what happened? Did he find his way back?"

"Well this boy wasn't too bright you see. He didn't even realize he'd been left for quite some time. He played and played in the woods, hiding in caverns, thinking his friends would come back and not be able to find him while all the while they had gone back down the mountain and were fishing the day away."

"Terrible. I hope they got a good seat lickin'."

"Well I should hope so too, Martha," he said with the straightest face he could manage. "So while he was crawling around in those caverns, he happened upon a big stash of coins. Well you see, not being too bright, he didn't even know what those things were. Must have thought they were kids toys or something. He sat for hours and flipped them down the hill with his thumb."

"He didn't."

"Yes, he did! He told his pappy that when he made it home."

"Oh, he made it home, that's so good, you know he could have gotten killed by some mountain lion." He looked at Martha then and brushed a lock of hair away from her eyes. "Mrs. Howard, I just don't think you're paying attention to the point of this story."

"Absolutely. He came home safely and his mother rejoiced." He hesitated a second, but there was no sign of pain in her eyes, just a light teasing. To be safe, he said, "Well now I'm sure there was a load of relief in that woman's heart, but even better than that, there were a few gold coins in that boy's pocket. He had put some of them in his pocket just to bring back, and though it took him all night, he figured out how to get back to familiar territory, and he walked into his house pretty as you please. He told his parents that he'd been out playing and had found some toys that must have been carved by Indians. Then he pulled out those coins and dropped them on the table like they were nothing. I mean, you should have seen the look on their faces when he did that." He sounded like he'd seen the look on their faces himself.

"So have you seen these coins?" she asked. He drew back and looked at her with an open mouth. That was clearly not the point of the story either, and she chuckled.

"Well now, Mrs. Martha I know someone who says they've seen them. But don't you see? There's gold hidden in this mountain, someone just needs to know the deep back woods and go out there scouting for it."

"Sounds as likely as finding a sang root with ten prongs, Milty. I'm not saying it couldn't happen, but I wouldn't let the garden go to seed looking for it."

"You've got no sense of adventure, girl."

"You're right."

As they climbed they would pick, and Pappy would tell Mother stories about things he'd seen in the woods and animals he had encountered. They would laugh and pick blackberries and learn to be at ease with each other again. Pappy helped her come alive, and they found tender enjoyment in walking together deep into the hills.

Blackberry season brought the case of the "chiggers." Larger berries were deep in the mountains. Everyone knew the nights treat was Blackberry Cobbler. Nightfall brought misery from those little critters, a tiny red mite causing an itch that would not go away. A little grease or coal oil did the trick for curing the itch.

Pappy would continue his stories with Grandmother Mary and Sam listening in, sharing in the healing.

"Have I told you the story about the Big Toe?" he asked one night. It was a beautiful perfect night, and they had all gathered around in the yard next to the door, lounging after a full day of work and a full meal of fish Milty had caught, cooked up with some crisp potatoes and beans.

"I don't believe I've heard that story, Milt," Sam said with a grin and a pull on his pipe. Daddy had a way with stories and it always made people happy to hear him launch into another one.

"Well, it was spring of the year and this old-timer; he began getting the garden ready for planting. He hitched up the horse and plowed the earth tender and soft so the newly plowed dirt squashed through your toes.

So his old woman was real happy with his hard work, and as she laid out the rows to drop the seeds, she came across something in the fresh dirt. She picked it up and looked at it for the longest time, just wondering what it could be. She asked the old man, and he didn't know. She asked the old-timer up the hill and he didn't know. She asked the woman who washed and mended clothes for a living, but she didn't know either!" With this explanation, Milty had gotten to his feet, pretending to walk up the hill like an old woman to ask about this thing she'd found. Knowing he had everyone's attention, he gave Mother a wink and went on.

"Well the old woman took it to the house, placed it in the kitchen by the window and went about cooking her evening meal. But that thing just called to her. It seemed like such a waste to let it sit there. So being a thrifty mountain woman, she washed it and put it in the pot of beans she was cooking for their supper."

"She didn't!" Mary shrieked with a laugh. Everyone laughed then, and Milty slapped her lightly on the arm. "Why yes, Mother, she did. She washed it up and it seasoned the beans that night. Those beans were tender, spicy and delicious. In fact, the old man said they were about the best beans he'd ever remembered tasting, and his wife was a fine cook.

So when they'd finished the meal, the old woman pulled that thing out of the pot and put it back on the kitchen windowsill. See, she was thinking she could use it again the next night to cook the beans, because it hadn't fallen apart or anything, it was still quite good and whole.

And that's just what she did. The next night they had beans again, and weren't they just the best beans in the world again, and her old husband ate those things up and asked for seconds. Well the old woman was just thrilled. She was thinking this was some great new root she'd found, and she was going to really hunt in the ground for more just like it.

By the third night, it was clear that this was the best thing they'd ever found. It was going to change their marriage. She was about as happy as she'd ever been. She laid the thing on the windowsill again, and they washed up and went to bed."

"I think something is about to happen," Mother said quietly, adjusting the sewing on her lap and pretending not to care. But she was as interested in the story as everyone else, and wanted to hear the end.

"You'll never believe it," Pappy cried out. "Long about midnight the old lady was sleeping so peaceful, when she heard a tapping at the door, and someone said in the clearest voice you'd ever want to hear, I want my big toe!" All three of them screamed with laughter. Sam and Mary looked at each other and tears were streaming down their face.

"I want my big toe! That's what she heard. Well she nudged her old husband and he just grunted and pretended hadn't heard a thing."

"Don't you just know he did!" laughed Grandma Mary.

"Well she was so scared she nudged him again. Nothing happened. Her husband would not move." Milty waited as they call calmed down, and let it get real quiet outside before he went on.

"Well the old woman stayed real quiet too, she was just going to pretend that she hadn't heard a thing. Just as she was about to drift off to sleep, out of the darkness, she heard once last thing before her heart gave up the ghost." Pappy would get real quiet and lean over near Mother then, for the greatest effect. He'd get close to her ear so that she could just feel his breath and the hairs on the back of her neck would stand up. Then he'd growl in the meanest voice he could make, "I want my big toe and if you don't give it to me I am going to come and get you!"

And more and more often, the nights would be filled with the sound of storytelling and laughter. Mother would sit with quilt piecework in her hand, while Milty would tell stories or play the banjo. She would exchange new smiles with him. They grew up together that season. They learned how to move on.

This quilt is over 100 years old and handed down to Emily Howard from her Aunt Susan. The Daughters of the American Revolution asked permission to put it in their Museum of Art. Permission was not granted by the family for fear something would happen to the quilt. It belongs to Joyce Osborn at this time and will continue to be handed down and is a beautiful work of art. The Howard Women were known for their exquisite handwork.

CHAPTER 4: The First Train in Harlan, 1911

Two seasons came and went. It seemed only yesterday when Sudie was running and laughing. As their pain faded and life took on a sweetness yet again, they got the sign that another baby was on the way.

Pappy found work scarce. Working in the mines was the calling for most mountain men who had to leave the hills and make money. Trading and barter were replaced with earning a living wage, or at least trying to. But Pappy couldn't work in the mines with his leg, so he took to hunting the hills for ginseng. He became an experienced "Sanger" which is what mountain people called those who picked the plant.

Ginseng is an ancient plant. People have been using it for as long as anyone can remember to improve health, remove both mental and bodily fatigue, care for pulmonary complaints, dissolve tumors, and prolong life to a ripe old age. It tastes darkly sweet, like licorice.

Ginseng loves to grow wild in our mountains. All the streams that cut through the rock in make deep cuts in the rock layers. Once the river gets through, it rests in deep dark coves. That's what we call still water, and that's where you are sure to find the ginseng plants, just waiting for someone to find it and dig it up.

In the spring, ginseng sends up a stem with a cluster of leaves at the end. Later it makes a flower of yellowish green. The flowers mature through the year into a pod of bright red berries, and that's what the Sangers look for in the fall.

The best thing to dig sang with was a "sang hoe." You make your own hoe, because no one sells such a thing. Pappy made a nice one, with a blade for cutting through the brush and a flat end for digging. He could also use it as a weapon against the snakes. He bragged at how light it was, but I never knew what he used to make it.

Sang hunters are legendary, because ginseng doesn't always do what you want. Finding it takes a lot of skill, and just as much luck. It's pesky, because it doesn't send up shoots every year. And everything loves it, from squirrels to birds. So really, just about everyone and everything is looking for that sang when the season is right, and there isn't always enough to go around.

The older the roots get, the more prongs they make, and finding a root with lots of prongs is a big prize. If you could find one that had been missed all those years, so that it had four or five prongs on it, people would know about it when you went to sell it. Then people would quietly try to follow you around for days, thinking that you'd found a new hunting spot for the plant.

Pappy would tell me about all the things he used to look for when he searched for sang. He'd talk about finding the biggest plant he'd ever come across, only to realize when he examined it more closely that it was cohosh or sarsaparilla, which the old men called Fool's sang. He had special trees that he'd look under, and often he'd gather the pods and sprinkle them closer to home, or in a secret place that he could monitor for years in the future, to make the plant easier to gather with his bad leg and crutches.

I couldn't blame him for that. It was backbreaking work, and Pappy found it very tiring trying to hold onto his crutch and pick ginseng. When he became extremely tired, he sat on the ground and pushed his crutch ahead of him as he scooted along the ground picking. He'd go out for a week at a time in the early days, picking until he couldn't carry anymore. Then he'd head down the mountain to a man who would pay for the ginseng straight out, or let Pappy trade for supplies that we needed. That man would sell to a traveling ginseng buyer, a man that Pappy would try to find while he was wandering through the hollers on horseback, so that he could sell to him and get a better price.

Even with all that work, they were barely getting by. My mother and Sam and Uncle John and Aunt Susan helped all they could. It made being with child a little scary. But living on very little was the mountain way, and they were so excited about the new baby. They decided that if it were a girl this time they'd name her Emily. To their disappointment, in the early morning of May 4, 1902, they had a boy.

He was still a blessing though, and Pappy named the boy John Garrett after his Uncle John. Johnnie looked a little bit like both Mother and Pappy, with her black hair and his blue eyes. He was a beautiful boy and immediately captured Mother's heart.

By this time they had moved from Coxton Mountain and lived for a time with Uncle John and Aunt Susan who nearly took Johnnie over for they were so wild about him. He was the pride and joy of their lives.

Johnnie helped lift Mother's spirits. After a time of taking care of him and watching him grow, she decided that it was safe to love him. He made her feel like laughing again and gave her a new life simply by making his own life a gift to her.

"That boy is growing fast," Pappy said to her one day they sat near the fire, watching their son playing with a small carving that his father had made from a piece of oak. "Soon he'll be old enough to go with me into the woods when I go hunting and fishing."

"He's ready to go as soon as you think he is. He is all boy," Mother told him. Sure enough, they looked over at the boy who had stopped his game with the carving. He had heard them talking about the idea of taking him into the woods with his father's adventuring, and that had immediately gotten his attention. It was all he wanted to talk about from that day forward.

Other good things happened for them around that time as well. They were able to move away from Uncle John and Aunt Susan's house, and into a small framed house in Harlan. It was a great stroke of luck that they were able to get the house. Pappy would tell us proudly that he'd not paid one cent on it, but had gotten it in trade for an old hog rifle.

And it was nice for the new family to have a place of their own. Pappy picked up odd jobs taking in guns for cleaning and repairing and making handles. Carving wildlife into the handles was his trademark. As it became productive enough, he spent less and less time picking ginseng.

And my brother Johnnie was growing like a weed. He was never in trouble and just loved Uncle John and Aunt Susan. Since they were like parents to my Pappy, he naturally thought of them as his grandpa and grandma, and that's what he called them.

Strangely, for all his promises to take the boy under his wing and show him the ways of the mountains, Pappy wasn't as close to the boy as he had been to Sudie. Mother did her best to understand that, because she knew how hard it had been on herself in those early years, waiting for him to get past the age Sudie had been when she had died. She didn't realize how hard she'd counted those years until she passed them and felt such a sense of relief, like she knew only then that he was going to live and that she deserved to be a mother.

To be fair on Pappy, he was very busy in those days, struggling just to feed his family. He was always out looking for work to bring in more money than the ginseng and the gun cleaning. Meanwhile, Uncle John and Aunt Susan and Mother kept one eye on Johnnie and one eye on the garden. Soon they had their third child to prepare for.

Again the birthing was difficult. But mother had been in good health and the food had been plentiful enough to give the baby a healthy start too. So on October 30, 1904 another boy made his way into the Howard family, despite their wishes, but he was charming, with fair, curly brown hair and hazel eyes. He was named after the Honorable Geoffrey Howard M. P. son of the ninth Earl of Carlisle, Castle Howard, Yorkshire, England. A name passed all the way down to us from England.

Mother told me of her strong disappointment over having another boy. Pappy didn't let her dwell on it though. "Martha," he said, "I thought this child would be another little girl to replace our lovely Sudie, but we will love him as we did her. His face shows the face of a strong, intelligent, good child. We will be proud of our son."

"Of course he would feel that way," Mother confided in me. "He had another son to look after and be proud of. A girl was different, she would be the one to understand my life and how I lived in a way that a son couldn't. She's the one who would belong to me the way a mother and a daughter are like shadows of each other. I would teach her things, so that all my mountain secrets would live on in another heart."

Geoffrey and Johnnie became like shadows, playing hard and learning the ways of the mountain men, with Uncle John and Pappy with them all the way, teaching them all their ways. It was like a second childhood for Pappy, who would listen to their laughter filled shouts and just smile the biggest smile.

Mother would get quiet whenever she recalled those years. She'd start off with a story or a memory, then end up staring off into space like she was no longer with us. I'm not sure why, but I always get the feeling that she wasn't very happy during those years. Sometimes in a very quiet voice, she'd say, "The more children we had, the more alone I felt" But then she'd seem to shake herself, smile and hug me before going back to whatever chore she was doing at the time. "My children were good to me," she'd explain. But I could tell that she thought of all of them as little men, and had never lost the dream of having a daughter again. "There was just no end to us having boys. It didn't seem too much to ask that we'd have a little girl again. I could hardly

54

keep up with them the house was so full of them. We were beginning to be like an ant farm. There were busy boys everywhere."

She said herself that her moods were hard to control back then. I know from Pappy that she continued to have rough pregnancies. For a while there was a child every year or every other year, so it must have seemed that she stayed sick or pregnant most of the time. With a growing family, food would be scarce at the table. Pappy had to go back to hunting sang, though that didn't help him during the winter when the ground was hard. Then they had to depend on people buying his gun handles, which was never a sure thing even in the best of times.

I could tell that she doubted herself a lot during that time. She must have asked herself why she felt so angry with him when there was nothing he could do about her babies, any more than she could. "I loved him so much and I hated him so much," she told me one night as we sat, shoulder to shoulder looking into the night. "This was the man who had fallen in love with me the first time he had seen me at a barn dance. He still loved me, and I knew I still loved him. He was trying so hard for his family, despite his own obstacles. I knew how hard it was for him to keep his family together and fed. I also knew that the single desire of his life rose out of his love and sorrow, to do something of courage for his family." She shook her head and looked away from me so I wouldn't see the tears in her eyes. "I would have to leave the room and go to bed early those nights, Emily. I realized that I was being a terrible wife to him. He deserved better."

And still the family got bigger. Dallas Delmer arrived January 6, 1907, on Pappy's birthday. Another two years brought Murphy Cornett, named after the doctor who delivered him. Murphy had shiny black curly hair, big brown eyes and a quick smile. He was nothing but a live wire. June 11, 1911, they had Samuel George Lee Howard.

The family seemed to be on a roll having boys. They were popping out like a blooming football team. Live wires were running around everywhere, slamming doors, getting into everything that boys get into. Mother knew she had her hands full.

That very year Mother got a new lesson in just what life might be like without Pappy. That was the year of the terrible flu epidemic in Harlan. It seemed to wring the life out of a lot of people, and the whole family discussed the doomed families in quiet tones. As much as they worried for their neighbors, they worried for their own fate and stayed alone as much as possible.

Many people died that year. Every day as they went about their chores, they would stop silently and bow their heads as wagons passed, loaded with the dead. And then the worst happened. Pappy became ill.

Mother always talks about that flu like it was the devil. Listening to her describe it, I think she became ill right along with him, as wild as she was with fear. Like all the others before him, he quickly lost weight and became so weak that he couldn't walk. And day after day she had to watch him wither before her eyes until she could see his bones through his clothes. He could hardly hold his pants up, and she had to make extra holes for his belt. As Pappy suffered, she fasted and prayed, asking God to let him be well again, and make her more into the wife that he deserved. And when he took to his bed for good, she made sure to move the bed away from the window so he could not see wagons loaded with the dead roll by the house.

But she was determined that he would get better. She fed him with things he loved to eat, and while he didn't take an interest in food she kept at him until he took it. It took more days than she could count, but he began to improve under her care and began feeling some better. Uncle John and Aunt Susan would bring in food but leave it on the porch and go away again. It made Mother feel alone, but she understood. There was no way the family would survive without Uncle John and Aunt Susan, especially if Pappy died, which Mother didn't even want to think about. She made even more effort to keep food in him. She kept the bed sheets clean and aired out daily, refusing to let them sour under him, because Aunt Susan had told her that it would help keep away the flux. And luckily he never got the flux.

Something about that epidemic gave Mother a new life. "I remembered back when Sudie died and I felt like God was the cruelest god alive," she said. "I couldn't understand why he'd take away my child, the greatest little precious girl that I loved so much. But as I struggled to feed your pappy, to keep him comfortable and to keep all the other boys from getting the same illness that their father had, I found strength in my struggle. I felt God coming down on me with his love, giving me the strength I needed to keep going, and letting me know that I could have my husband back at full health with just hard work and by not giving up hope."

Change was in the air that year, and Pappy's recovery happened the same year that the L & N Railroad made its debut up Powell Valley on the south side of the Cumberland Mountain. Going through Pineville to Harlan up Clover Fork, it passed through Black Mountain to Virginia. It was very exciting when the first car of coal was shipped from Harlan, and everyone spoke of it. It also made the papers, and Mother clipped that page and saved it until this day. She'll pull it out every once in a while and I can read the faded writing and still feel a thrill of what it must have been like to see it for the first time. The first box of coal was shipped August 25, 1911 on L & N car No. 64326.

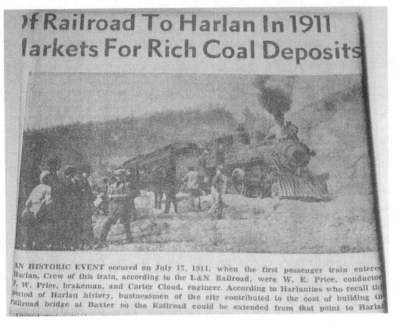

)f Railroad To Harlan In 1911
larkets For Rich Coal Deposits

AN HISTORIC EVENT occured on July 17, 1911, when the first passenger train entere
Harlan. Crew of this train, according to the L&N Railroad, were W. E. Price, conductor
J. W. Price, brakeman, and Carter Cloud, engineer. According to Harlanites who recall thi
period of Harlan history, businessmen of the city contributed to the cost of building th
railroad bridge at Baxter so the Railroad could be extended from that point to Harla

The first train coming into Harlan. This photo was taken from the
original paper.

So both Mother and Pappy were there when it happened. They sat on the front porch to wait for that shipment of coal to leave the mountain and make its way down the tracks through the mountain passes along the Cumberland River. They'd never seen a train and Pappy was really excited when he realized that the train would pass right by their house, rumbling and shaking the ground as it chugged down the tracks. They sat for some time straining to hear the sound of the whistle. When it came it carried with it the sound of the iron wheel of the train. At the first sound of the whistle blowing, Mother explained to me how she decided how Pappy could see the train making history in Harlan County. Working her tiny body under Pappy, she pulled Pappy up and onto her back and gently carried him to the door so he could watch it pass. She described the billows of smoke, all black with sparks flying from its stack with steam spewing from this giant train that came rumbling along the tracks right past our house. Mother laughed as she told how the large freight car wheels pounded the tracks as the engineer blew the whistle. Oh, what a lonesome whistle, trailing through the mountains, leaving its echo behind. They waved and smiled together s the whistle blew and rumbled on past out of sight.

The thought of riches filled the people's minds. They could feel the mountain open up to share its potential with the world. They felt strongly that it would bring progress and change into this place like the sunshine of morning. And people talked about this future into the early hours of the morning, spoke of it in hushed excited tones like they were dreams that would delicately land on the people lucky enough to sleep on a night like this and invade their sleep. For days, whenever and wherever people gathered, talk would turn to the advancements the rail would bring, the people, the inventions, the progress, the hope. It was going to be so good for Harlan. It would start a boom in the town. It would bring money into the area as coal was sold. It would create new jobs. Pappy had, for many years, made a living on ginseng. He still wouldn't be able to work in the mines, but if the mines flourished it would bring more people into the area to buy from him.

The whole family was ready for change. It was time to start a new life in the land of opportunity.

The very tracks that held the first train through Harlan.
Cumberland River is on the back side of the house.

CHAPTER 5: In the Shadow of the Mountain

But seasons passed us by, our clan continued to grow, and the expected prosperity did not come. The only thing our family was truly able to count on was struggle.

"We don't have an enormous estate to pass onto our children," Mother says one morning as we're in the kitchen together. "That may have been the case for the Howard Clan in Europe. Those stories that came down from your Aunt Susan and your grandmother were fancy, but they don't apply to us. The wooden floors were cold, but cleanly swept. The stove held skillets filled with half-melted fat for daily cooking and leftover cornbread was never to be found. The woodwork of our home has never even seen paint. Our doors looked neglected because they've gotten lots of use. I made drapes from torn sheets, and the windows had cracks that let in the cold damp air and kept us always on the edge of sickness, coughing the morning to get the night air out of our lungs."

Mother often wept out of frustration. She was born in the heart of Appalachia, the armpit of poverty and knew she was strapped to the ways of the mountains. She wanted better schools for us, but it was hard to find teachers willing to sacrifice coming to this part of the country where life was mostly about large families living in poverty.

"We never have leftovers, Emily. Clothes and shoes were hard to come by too. We wouldn't have made it if it weren't for the Salvation Army and the Red Cross."

The mention of Salvation Army shoes took us back to the early days. If you've never experienced Salvation Army shoes, count yourself lucky.

Salvationists were new in our part of the world in those days, having just come over to the Americas from England. They quickly took hold in the north though, and spread to our area of the country providing spiritual conversion and relief to all kinds of poor people in the mountains. I think they called themselves an army because lots of people didn't like them, said they were offering shoes and clothes in exchange for salvation, and that it wasn't real to come to God because you needed clothes more than forgiveness. They were actually kind of competing with the American Red Cross in the early days. People in our area seemed to trust the Salvationists more than the people with the Red Cross because the Salvationists always talked about God while the Red Cross just talked about helping people. The American Red Cross was really new, and so many of us had no idea who Clara Barton was and why she wanted to help us. It wasn't until the outbreak of the First World War that we understood what they were really about, so it was all up to the Salvationists to provide our family with shoes that would keep us from getting frostbitten during the winter.

The thing I remember most about those shoes is how we never got shoes that fit us. They were always too large or too small. I guess I had it pretty easy, because my foot was so small that the shoes were usually too big. That was painful enough as the shoes slipped around on my feet, or had to be worn with bits of old rag stuffed in the toe, but I felt bad for the boys who had bigger feet and had to make do with uncomfortably tight shoes. They were always taking them off at night to look at the damage those shoes made. It was no surprise that we always had a bad feeling about shoes and hated to wear them unless it was just freezing cold. We all had the toughest feet you could imagine.

But we were grateful. When winter came, you'd wear anything rather than get your feet frozen.

Those years before I was born, life was extremely hard. Like I said, the expected boom didn't really come. Oh, people did come into the mountain.

Big business wanted all that coal, see, and they weren't too concerned about what they did or who they stepped on to get it. Some things they brought in helped us, but mostly they were just stripping the land of trees and coal now that they could pull it down the mountain on the new trains. Fewer and fewer people could barter amongst each other for the things they needed. You had to have money, and that meant you had to work in the mines, or work for mine company money, which they called scrip. Before I was born, this lifestyle was just beginning, it didn't become a major way of life until I was older, but it started affecting our family early, I guess because we lived so near Harlan, which was a big area for mining.

No one in our family was a stranger to work though. They all worked. As soon as the children were old enough to have chores, they took on their responsibilities for the family. There was the garden to take care of, working the soil to make it ready for planting, keeping the animals out of it while it grew our precious harvest, and then bringing in the harvest as quickly as possible to set up absolutely everything we could in preparation for winter. Everyone took a turn at the garden. Even though Pappy was crippled, he would take a turn at the hoe, wrapping his short leg without any feeling around his crutch to keep himself steady.

If there wasn't the garden, there were the animals to keep tend to, either hens or cows. We'd have a hog to fatten for slaughter if we were lucky. The boys would hunt and fish, which wasn't just entertainment but a way to keep us in fresh meat. There was sewing and cooking to do every day.

Our family never saw the great riches that flowed out of Harlan into the pockets of people we'd never met. Many people made money from the coal that was pulled from our land, but in those days it really didn't seem to mean much to our lives. Mother wanted so much for her children to have an easier life, and often wept in frustration. The family was strapped to the ways of the mountains. We depended on it for survival, and often the shadow of our mountain shielded us from the worst that life had to offer. But sometimes it seemed that the shadow of the mountain also kept out progress, and kept us from really having any sort of easy life at all.

Mother wanted so much for us to have good schooling for instance, but it was hard to find teachers willing to sacrifice coming to this part of the country where life was mostly about large families living in poverty.

"I wish we had more to offer you children than our love," Mother would say often to me. "Love can be cold comfort when you're starving."

But don't feel sorry for us. Everyone lived like we did, and plenty of families had it a lot worse. And it really was a blessing in disguise that Pappy didn't work in the mines. I'm glad that they wouldn't take him on account of his leg. It kept him from so much of the trouble that affected other families. He didn't get that terrible cough that took so many of our good men, husbands, brothers and fathers alike. It kept him from the dangerous conditions that would kill our men too, the poisonous gas that would trap them in the shafts and kill them. It kept him from the fights that broke out later when the men wanted unions that would improve their conditions. It also kept us from owing all our check to the company's store. Yes, I had my father for a long time, working hard but alive, and for that I am very grateful.

Yes, our life did have sweetness. Mother tells me often how much she thanked her children for the sweetness that life gave her.

"When I saw nothing in our life but rags, you children would turn rags into toys. You'd tie them into knots and make balls that you'd sail through the air. Whenever plowing was done, the boys would search for worms and use them for fishing. Your Pap would hunt with them, and for fun he'd set up cans and bottles for target practice, teaching the boys how to shoot. The laughter that floated over the mountain through the trees would sweeten my days."

"And I'll tell you, we provided for our needs as we could. We had cows. I could always count on washing their nipples with warm water then filling a gallon bucket with their warm frothy milk. From that milk I could take a gallon, strain it, and set it up to clabber for the churning. We had a sturdy churn with a hole in the top for a long handle to slide through. At the end was a wooden paddle, which I'd have to pound for an eternity. But when the butter began to make we'd scoop it from the churn and have buttermilk for storage in the cellar and butter to pour into molds."

"The fall garden gave us pumpkins, and we used them not only to make pies but to carve into jack-o-lanterns for Halloween. We also had turnips, potatoes and sweet potatoes, which we loved. Turnip bulbs could be sliced thin, rolled in cornmeal and fried to a golden brown in a skillet. Potatoes could be put into the coals of the fireplace and roasted until done. The first harvest of everything was eaten fresh, and there's nothing better than that. Then the second picking of things like cucumbers, peppers and cabbage could be pickled and kept in the cool of the cellar below the house."

"When the vegetables came in I would wash and bleach out feed sacks and carry them to the garden to hold the harvest. We filled them high with corn or beans or whatever, then I'd hoist it onto my back and carry the load home. I'd work late into the night putting up the vegetables, canning to prepare for the winter months."

Milty built a grape arbor and the vine grew on it thickly. Grapes would hang from it in thick heavy clusters. I loved watching you children crawl under it and eat like kings until you had stomachaches and still have plenty left for jam."

"And then there was also the matter of Milty's bees. Robbing bees was a serious business, but as I look back, I can't ever remember a time when Milty ever got stung, because he was so calm with them. To find a new swarm, he went searching the bees out and when he found them, he'd do anything to get a good cluster, even sawing the limb from a tree where they'd built a hive. When he'd done this, he'd use a stick of firewood to smoke out the cluster and get them to fly into the top of the beehive that he'd brought with him.

Once he had them in their new home, he'd often search out the queen and clip her wings so she couldn't fly away. Then we just waited, and when it was time, he'd cover his broad brimmed hat with a net that would protect his whole head, then tie a string around his shirt sleeves and his pant legs. Then he'd light a brush torch and use the smoke to calm the hive while he robbed them of the sweet, precious harvest. And oh but that was a great treat. I could use the honey in cooking and you children chewed the wax of the honeycomb like gum."

That was our way of life. Mother and Pappy raised us up around it, and though it was hard, it was honest. I'm proud of that. We did not become moonshiners to make a living. We used what the Lord gave us and what he did not see fit to give us, we learned to live without.

But there were times when this was very hard to accept. In 1912, Mother recognized the old familiar body signs. Soon there was a whole new cycle again as her body prepared to give birth. Again came another round of night sweats, nausea and lack of energy. But this time there was no happy ending. She gave birth to a stillborn boy followed by another sad and painful funeral. She had tried desperately to save this child, pushing and straining to deliver quickly even as she knew her long labor would lose him. She listened for the cries from him, but none came.

For hours she stared at the rafters of the ceiling. Again, God wanted another one of her children before she was ready to let go. Accepting God's Will would always be the hardest task for a woman who loved Him as my mother did.

The year the child was stillborn was also the year that the town was renamed. Mount Pleasant officially became Harlan when the board passed on April 1, 1912. They got the name from the Revolutionary War hero Major Silas Harlan. Major Harlan came to Kentucky from Virginia in 1774. He was killed while commanding troops at the Battle of Blue Licks, in 1782. It seems to me that Kentucky honored him because he died for a cause. Mountain men trusted men who had causes. They always like to say that there was a cause for this or a cause for that or a cause for something or other. To me, the changing of the name didn't seem to make a difference in our lives at all. It's hard to see what people get so worked up about. The seasons just rolled on like they always did whether we called the community Mt. Pleasant or Harlan. It didn't change whether the family starved or not, and in fact it didn't change whether Mother was pregnant or not, which she was again in short order.

Birth control was unheard of in the Appalachian Mountains. Pappy had a lust for Mother and, as the old saying goes in the mountains. "She stayed barefoot and pregnant."

And before the end of 1913, there was yet another stillborn boy. The news shot through the family like a bullet. And, too, another sad funeral, another tiny wooden casket, waxed flowers and sad songs sung by the mourners. At home, the strain and tension floated on the air seeming to have a stagnant presence of that all too familiar scent of death. The house smelled of death. Mother blamed herself, and all those years she had wanted a girl so bad that she regretted when a boy child was born.

"Oh I hated my own pride," she said in a quiet moment. "I wanted to reach back in time and smack the regret from the lips of that younger, stupid me that I was. I would do anything to take those feelings back. Often, God teaches us lessons we never wanted to learn."

There was no birth control in those days for mother to turn to, and it was impossible to prevent pregnancy. That had always been the case, but the second stillborn child really pulled at my mother, because she knew she had not been ready for the birth, and could see the disaster before it happened, seeing the eventual death of that child loom before her. She hadn't been ready for another birth so soon, and didn't even feel like fighting for the baby. Her strength was gone. When she slept she had nightmares about her dead children, or didn't sleep at all. When the baby was born dead, the midwife knew immediately that she would take the childbed fever and she did. She told Pappy that Mother was a goner.

She stayed gravely ill for a long time, which I think was just a part of being so exhausted. There's no way to deal with grief that deep and keep your head about you. Life floated around her and she didn't care who came or went, or if she lived or followed her children to Kitt's cemetery. She stared out the window for hours, if she even bothered to get out of bed. The children kept the house going then, while Pappy did what he could to bring money in and keep the house together.

But even in her bitterness and sorrow, it was the thought of her family suffering that wouldn't give her any peace. As she lay there day upon day, she realized that Pappy would have to go get work soon. He had not worked much while Mother was recovering, and even then was by her side day and night. But the longer she took to recover, the harder he would have to work to catch up, and there were other mouths in the house to feed and other lives to consider.

That is when she gave up her sorrow. She knew from experience that the longer she sat in sorrow, the more chance there was that it would bring more death to the family. And that is when she started to recover.

"I started again with my garden, planting, hoeing and canning as all mountain women had to. The family needed my care. Times became tighter than usual, and many nights I went to bed half starved. I comforted myself with prayer. I was making up for all the times I had said I didn't want a child unless it was a girl."

"After those babies died, it was a big relief when Woodrow Roosevelt was born on January 17, 1916. His birth reminded me of Sudie, who was also born on a cold harsh winter day. He was our new sign of good luck, and he came into the world screaming his lungs out. He was born during the Roosevelt years and Milty named him Woodrow, because one day he could be a president himself. I loved when he said things like that. It lifted my spirits and made me laugh again."

Mother loved Woodrow so much and he was as happy as a promise too. She tried really hard with him, to show God that she would never feel sorry for any child He gave her. Like all the others, this childbirth hadn't been an easy one either, but for some reason Woodrow gave her the will to live. He was just different. She recovered more quickly than she ever had before, listening to his coos and laughter.

Uncle John and Aunt Susan also spoiled him. He was special to everyone. I think everyone was so weary from losing the other babies too, and it made everyone's bond with him special and sweet.

By this time, Pappy wanted another place to live. Land was very cheap, but money was hard to come by. Ginseng was getting harder and harder to find. He had to make long walks deeper and deeper into the mountains to gather enough to sell for food.

"Martha, we need to sell our place."

"Why, Milty? We're happy here in Harlan."

"We could sell our place here and invest the money in another place where the land is cheaper. We could have more land and possibly even a bigger house for all the children." They talked about it for a time and finally agreed that it was a good idea. Still, Woodrow was nearly two years old before Pappy started looking. He and Uncle John began to correspond with friends they knew out of town. They both heard that good land was selling for $5.50 an acre in London, Kentucky. So he packed up and left to check out the new town for both families to move. Uncle John agreed to stay behind and care for us.

"I think next to losing the children, being without your Pappy was the hardest thing I'd done up to that point. It was a long trip to London, and there was such a long time when we didn't see him. Adding to that, he was gone for months and still could not find a suitable place. He kept traveling around staying with friends, but could not find anything. It got harder and harder for us to make things work without him."

Eventually the family had to move in with Uncle John and Aunt Susan.

Mother still remembers that time with regret and a few tears. "I kept telling myself that things would get better when he returned and we were a family again, but I cried when we sold the house and had to give it over to the new owner. I had loved that home. I had become a real mother in that home with a real house of my own that belonged to no one else. It was a home where I didn't have to share a bedroom with my parents when I wanted to be with my husband. Suddenly I had to watch my husband's uncle pile my few handmade possessions onto his porch. There was no room in the house for it and barely enough to hold both families. We had to sleep three to a bed."

"I'm pretty sure my letters were hard on Milty, because I was so terribly unhappy. I told him over and over to just get any place so he could get his family back together. The whole family was feeling the strain. Aunt Susan was getting older and couldn't handle it all. She became ill under the strain of so many living with her. I couldn't even find land for a garden. Winter made times even harder. I'd get out around four o'clock in the morning with the chill of cold air hitting my face. The floor was always the coldest, and it was miserable relieving yourself in the chamber pot before dressing to cook breakfast. It was below zero and icicles hung from the porch. We feared that the milk cow would freeze to death, and then we'd be in big trouble because the cow made it possible for us to have plenty of milk as well as butter and all the things butter could make. Living without the cow would surely devastate us."

"Oh Emily, I am glad that you hadn't been born into all that yet. I was so very depressed, as I think we all were. In the meantime, Pappy tried to keep us up to date on his progress. He'd heard of some land in Blake, Kentucky, but the deal fell through which meant even more time looking. Times were becoming harder and harder for Uncle John and Aunt Susan. The children were growing fast. There were six boys plus us adults. The house seemed to sag from the weight of all of us. A kerosene light gave the only light throughout the house, and food was rationed. The children seemed to be satisfied with their meals, but the adults ate just enough to get by.

I knew we were imposing, though John and Susan never said a thing about it. My heart was so heavy in me. I often thought of my mother back on Coxton Mountain with Sam and my childhood in that small cabin, poor but well kept. Then as I crept into bed with four children tucked around me I wondered where your Pappy was sleeping that night. Those were the nights when I cried myself to sleep."

But finally Pappy sent the news they'd all been waiting for. He decided to go to Livingston, Kentucky where he found a place and went on to say land was cheap enough that Uncle John and Aunt Susan could also buy a place near them. He was soon back in Harlan packing everyone up and preparing to move to the new town along the Wilderness Trail.

Mother's sorrow lifted from her like a cloud drifting across the sky. They were overjoyed to be together again. A short time later Uncle John and Aunt Susan left Harlan and found a place in Livingston within walking distance of the new house.

And the house was wonderful. It became Mother's new pride and joy. It sat on a hill overlooking the highway. Uncle John bought a ways over on the other side of the highway. Pappy started selling shoes. He was given a large leather saddlebag that he could throw across his shoulders to carry his sample shoes in. He really adored that saddlebag, made of leather and built to carry lots of things in. He loved to come home with all kinds of stories about the people who tried to buy it from him, and how he wouldn't part with it.

"Martha, I am good at meeting people," he'd tell her at night.

"Yes I know you are," she'd agree.

"Thing is, I end up selling them a pair of shoes sometimes, but mostly they let me in the house to see my bag."

"Your bag?" She smiled, playing her usual part in his story.

"Oh yes, Martha. I have a fine bag. It holds a lot of things, and this is real leather. People love to see it and how much it holds. The farmer in the next hollow offered me a hog for it."

"Did he? And what did you tell him?"

"I told him I wouldn't take three hogs for it. It has made my life lots easier, I can sling it over one shoulder and carry things I wouldn't have been able to carry with my crutch." Mother was very happy then, able to have her family with her most every night, and so proud of Pappy and how this new work was helping him and the family out so much. The whole family quickly settled into the new routine.

There was a place for the garden again, on the side of the mountain in back of the house. The yard was also large enough to plant flowers in, and she'd go hunting wild flowers in the woods to carry back to the yard.

As the family gathered up their life again, Mother started having dreams about a new baby girl. She began to think maybe the thought was being given to her by God, and that Sudie was sending her blessing on it, along with the blessings of the other stillborn babies who were in heaven with her. Where before her dreams about babies had been nightmares, these were soft and comforting and sweet. Even after all these years, she was still secretly hoping to have a girl. She was blessed with boys it was true, and unlike before she didn't regret a single one of them. She loved raising them too. By then there was Johnnie, Goff, Dallas, Murphy, Sam and Woodrow. They were strong and happy boys, and they were her pride and joy.

But there were more surprises in store for Mother. Because in the year that Johnnie turned sixteen and started working in the mines, she got that feeling again. She was with child again.

Sam was the only boy who enlisted in the armed forces. The other boys
Worked in the mines.

CHAPTER 6: Emily, 1919

Word spread like a sage grass fire when they heard about Mother's tiny new baby girl. The curious and the skeptical came from everywhere. People from ridges and hollers far away formed lines up the steep mountainside to take a peek at her. People walked miles, making their way up the rocky, weatherworn path to our cabin. They huddled in small groups of three or four in the clean swept yard where no grass grew, rested on the half-rotten steps and the porch sparsely furnished with four worn ladder-back chairs and two heavily used rocking chairs. Finally, they lined up single file at the door, waiting for their turn to come in the house and see what all the talk was about, and if it was true.

"They said she weighed only two and one half pounds."

"Could she be a midget?"

"Will she live?"

"How big is she? Can you even see her?"

"Well of course you can see her. Kittens are smaller than that."

"Kittens? Are her eyes open?" Some brought food along with gifts of clothing, dolls and handmade crochet dresses patterned from doll clothes because they had heard that we were so poor and had so many mouths to feed.

The year was 1919, in Rockcastle County, Kentucky. On the third day of September Mother gave birth at last to her very own girl child. At last, the wish she'd held deep in her heart ever since Sudie's death had come true. She was a mother again to a little daughter. A two and one-half pound baby girl after eight boys and too much heartache. Her name was Emily. She was me.

"Emily is a good name," Pappy said. "We've waited a long time to have this child and she will be special." Mother held me in her arms, sat in one of the old beat up rocking chairs and opened the homemade blanket so that all the visitors could take a quiet and respectful look at me.

"You were a quiet baby," Mother said, "with the beauty of a fair-faced doll. Your ears were plastered to your sweet little head, and you had a faint touch of light brown hair, so soft, it felt like cotton candy. Your short fingers curled tightly and we just knew you were determined to make it. Other than your size, everything was proportioned. You were just a perfect baby."

Giggles came from those standing near. "She's the size of a good melon," one whispered.

"She's strong," said Woodrow. "I will always take care of her. We will run and play in the mountains and I will teach her things."

"Yes," Mother said, "She will be strong." And this she knew with such a strong pain in her heart that she could barely breathe.

"Emily is a good name," Pappy repeated. "She will stand tall and proud and have strength of the Howard's. I named her after my Mother, you know," he said smiling proudly as he leaned against his crutches, his short leg dangling against his good leg.

"Oh Emily, you had your Pappy's heart wrapped around your fat little finger from that minute on, because your lips lifted up in a smile. He grinned from ear to ear and pointed at you, like you knew what he was saying, like you just agreed with him. He always thought you were smart. You were different. A good child." The two of you were peas in a pod from that day forward.

The boys flocked onto the porch waiting turns to look at me. It was like a three-ring circus. We had been a yard full of people, standing with their gifts waiting for their turn for a peak of a baby the size of a gopher rat. Mother placed a teacup over my little head to show the people how small I was. The teacup came down over my shoulders.

The people who had come to look at me gave the family more than they realized. Having just the bare necessities, they had provided lots of clothes and toys. Mother packed them into barrels because we had no other space for them, but we used them for months later.

Pappy nailed the many dolls we'd received to the walls of our cabin, because room was sparse and we didn't have shelves. They hadn't expected such a tiny baby, and odds were against me. But they did what Aunt Susan did when Pappy came to her. They treated me as if I was going to live forever.

They pinned my clothes to a pillow to prevent irritation and to keep from losing me in the blankets. It also meant they could hold me without fear of hurting me. I slept in a dresser drawer. I was a good baby and the family took special care of me. More than anything, they hoped and prayed that I'd live.

My stomach could only hold small portions, but I ate well. I was a fighter from an early age. I was a Howard.

"Child, I'll never forget what a fighter you were the first time you got sick," Pappy says all the time when we're thinking about the old days. "When you were just three months old you took the worst case of pneumonia. The fear of losing you was just more than we could take. We had the memory of little Susan and all the stillborn boys still raw in our minds. It was nearing Christmas. Your mother turns to me, with as much calm as she can get up and says she has to take you to the doctor. Well I just nodded with her, because I wasn't going to argue. But I could barely look at her I was so scared."

"You weren't scared," I protested.

"Oh yes I was. I could hear you just struggling to get every breath you could. It made my heart just sick, knowing there was nothing at all I could do for you. All those weeks leading up to Christmas we had focused on caring for you and not on presents. We had kept you at home because there were no hospitals around and the doctor was a good hour away through rough mountains."

"So what did you do to try and get me well?"

"Oh you know how I feel, Emily. Most of the time a good home cure is better than any doctor visiting. But you were so small. I was worried to give you coal oil and sugar, which is what my mama taught me. I thought it would be too strong for you."

"But don't think I didn't try. When you first started getting sick, I boiled vinegar on the stove with you sleeping next to the vapors, to clear out your chest. That made you sleep a little better, but it didn't stop you from getting sick. Then when you had such trouble breathing I tried all kinds of soothing drinks, some with honey, some with honey and onions that my mother showed me."

"Honey should have done the trick," Pappy interrupted.

"Well of course it always had. And then when that didn't work, I made a paste of crushed garlic and rubbed it on your chest to try and help you fight all the germs, but there was nothing to it."

"Well your mother was making herself sick trying to get you well," Pappy said. "In fact now, when your mother said she couldn't take it anymore, the first snow had already fallen, so a trip to the doctor would be even harder, but she was right. She just had to go."

"Why didn't you take me, Pappy?" I asked, already knowing the answer.

"Well Em," as he often called me," I stayed with all those boys to protect them. It was wild living up there in those days, with all the whiskey runners out and about. The boys were still many of them too young to take care of themselves. I sent the oldest boys along with your mother and you."

"Dallas and Murphy."

"Right, Dallas and Murphy went along with you and your mother. She wrapped you up real good in blankets, then put a thin scarf and the only coat she owned over herself before stepping out into the sleet and howling wind outside."

"That was such a bad night," Mother said, taking up the story. "I held you in my arms as we scrambled through the dark along the trail. I don't care how many times I've walked that trail. It was so rocky and dark outside; we had to feel our way with our feet so as not to fall. Dallas and Murphy came after me, Dallas carrying the oil lantern to light our path."

"And you sure were quiet, child. The night wind was rising and I could hardly walk against it. Dallas and Murphy took turns holding the lantern and we just kept walking in silence. Sometimes I stumbled over the rocks and almost fell, but I managed to keep hold of you and regain my footing each time. Soon everyone's ears burned from the cold and our hands were numb without gloves."

"Then what happened?" I asked quickly. This was the best part of the story. "Oh, well suddenly we heard men's loud slurred voices. Bootleggers," Mother said softly, for effect. "We were afraid of them, but could not turn back. We picked up our pace past them, while the men yelled a few obscenities."

"Hey, lady, whatta ya doing out here?"

"Whatta ya holding in that thar blanket?"

"Hey lady, you got something to eat with ya? Are those your boys?"

"You boys think you're big enough to stop us, huh?"

"Well I was no longer conscious of any pain from the cold. I kept my eyes straight ahead and held onto the boys to keep them from looking around too.

We never answered as they continued drinking their liquor and we continued walking. Finally we passed them."

"I hate bootleggers," Dallas said venomously under his breath.

"Well by that time the doctor's house was near. When I finally saw it, I made my way up the steps, onto the porch and knocked hard on the door. The doctor's wife opened the door as the doctor stood behind her holding a lantern and a rifle, to see who was at their door at this ungodly hour."

"Why, Martha Howard, what are you doing here at this hour?"

"What did you say, Mother?"

"Well he had a rifle on his hip, I told him as quickly as I could that you had pneumonia and asked if he could please help," she said with a chuckle. "The boys and I stepped inside the room of the small log cabin. I could see the sparsely filled room from the dim light of the lantern and the light from the fireplace. There was a crude bed with quilts turned aside and table with a candle. A few chairs and that was all they had in the world. They were as poor as us. The doctor charged what the people could give, which was often food, a quilt or a smidgen of pork. Days later I would pay the doctor myself with a jar of jam, which is amazing considering his medicine saved your life."

"The doctor walked across the room and picked up a black bag. He took out a bottle of medicine and a dropper then gently held your mouth open and dropped a few drops of the medicine down your throat. You gagged at first, and then settled back into my arms. He gave me the rest of the bottle and instructed me to you two drops every four hours. Then he carefully cleared your air passages. I still remembered how you struggled and fought against his large hands, then eased into a restful sleep."

"So it worked?"

"Oh yes, child. Your breathing was immediately better. I thanked the doctor and turned back into the night to face the ungodly drunken bootleggers, but thankfully by the time we reached the side of the mountain where they had been drinking they were long gone. As we made our way home I whispered a prayer thanking God for our safety."

"And I was waiting for them as they came back too," Pappy said. "As soon as I saw their lantern light, I opened the door wanting to know if you were alright. Your Mother scrambled into the house as quickly as she could and the boys gathered around you wanting to help. They soon had you settled back in your special place in the dresser drawer again and sleeping peacefully."

"I still remember how it felt to get my hands warm again after being so cold. They began to burn as they warmed up. When I was better myself, I put on my outing gown and crawled into bed with your Pappy. "Did you pray, Mother?" I said quietly, as Pappy left to light his pipe by the fireplace.

"Oh yes, Emily," Mother said. "I whispered another prayer as I lay there, thinking of you, and also praying that someday your Pappy would come to the Lord. We made a good team, but I needed help to bring you children up in the right way. I understood at the end of that night that even though you were a fighter enough to make your Pappy proud, you would need the grace of God just to survive in this mountain country."

The only picture of Dallas and a rare one of Murphy – two loving, gentle brothers. Murphy would later leave the mountains only to find his fate in the horrible accident which almost cost him his life in Chicago. Dallas stayed behind and would meet his fate in the coal mines.

CHAPTER 7: A Bitter Season

But as the months passed, the memory of that harsh winter faded. Fear isn't something you can dwell on when you're held to this world by such a fragile thread. The family had the chance to be happy and they took it. Soon they were all doing pretty good. The older boys found odd jobs working for people doing whatever they could do to help out with the family. You went to work young in a mountain family, because you needed all the hands you could get. More often, boys would choose to leave home and work doing something that paid, rather than just hunting, fishing or trading to help the family along. Meanwhile Pappy continued to sell shoes and sometimes he went to Mount Vernon to sit on jury duty. Mother tried as best she could to put weight on me after my bout with pneumonia. I was healthy enough, but stayed small. Mother was a born again Christian and relied heavily on her faith in those months, praying for God not to take me. She never missed a Sunday church meeting. Tent revivals were popular in those days and sprang up throughout the hills. If you were a mountain family, you can pretty much guarantee that you're also Pentecostal Holiness. Holiness folk believe strongly in the working of the Holy Ghost, first witnessed as tongues of fire resting on the disciples on Pentecost Sunday. Many times you'll see speaking in tongues at a tent revival, or miracles being done, or demons being cast out. Sometimes the tent revivals handle snakes, but she never did come to believe in the ways of the snake handlers. But she enjoyed gathering with her friends for meetings under the clear star-filled sky. Mother enjoyed praying at the meetings. She would kneel in the sawdust, spread on the dirt in the tent, praying and rejoicing in the spirit of God's love.

During that time, Johnnie married and moved back to Harlan. He had a sweet little wife named Bessie, and Mother just loved her completely.

"I still miss Bessie," Mother says whenever I ask about her. "They were the perfect couple. Some months after they moved to Harlan, she wrote and told me the next time they came to see us she'd be bringing me something really pretty. I knew I was going to be a grandmother. Amazing thing was that I was also expecting again."

"I was sick with the pregnancy when we received word Johnnie's wife and baby died during childbirth. Uncle John and Aunt Susan went to be with him. It was such a terrible shock. They laid Bessie and the baby out together in the same casket. She was such a pretty girl, lying there sweetly holding her precious baby in her arms."

Death during pregnancy was so common during those days. No one was close to a hospital, and no one owned a car that would you there quickly if there was an emergency. Having a baby during harsh weather risked the chance that there wasn't enough for the mother to eat while she was expecting. Many times she was just worn out before her labor pains even started. The midwife did what she could to save them both, but with Bessie it had been a hopeless case.

People came from everywhere to pay their respects. Bessie was carried to the top of the mountain just like my sister Sudie, and gently lowered into the ground with her baby. The crowd sang their good-byes softly.

There's a land that is fairer indeed

And by faith we can see it afar

For the Father waits over the way,

To prepare us a dwelling place there.

In the sweet bye and bye

We shall meet on that beautiful shore.

In the sweet bye and bye

We shall meet on that beautiful shore.

"Johnnie knew the words well," Mother said. "We all did. I watched my son as he stared at the dirt, his body trembling, his face showing his sorrow. He had gone to a place in his grief where he was lost to us, but I could feel his pain without speaking to him at all. When he allowed it, I held him to my breast like I did when he was a baby and your Pappy's tears dropped off his face to the freshly dug ground."

The only picture of Johnny and Bessie. Bessie was pregnant when this picture was taken. She delivered soon after. The picture was to be a gift to her mother-in-law, Martha.

"The young girls in the area, many of them as young as Bessie and friends of hers, handmade simple flowers and dipped them in wax and placed on top of the earth that now covered Bessie and her child. It was such a strange custom, one I had done myself when I was young, but what a miserable task for a child. Thinking about it made me shiver like a ghost had walked over my own grave."

As she told the story, I could imagine the day. Often I had walked in Kitt's Cemetery, reliving the sad good-byes said by family and friends of mine. I walked with the ghosts and imagined the bleak day, sorrows hanging like a vale. The wind whipped through the trees to take Bessie's soul up to heaven, and it tugged at dresses and played in everyone's hair. Quiet sobs rose up to heaven. Living in mountains as they did, they'd sing songs that had meaning to them.

The saddest day of his life was the day Johnny buried his precious wife, Bessie and child. He would never be the same. His smile was gone forever that day.

Nothing in my hand I bring,
Simply to the cross I cling;
Naked, come to Thee for dress;
Helpless look to Thee for grace;
Foul, I to the fountain fly;
Wash me, Savior, or I die.

Rock of Ages, cleft for me,
Let me hide myself in Thee.

God was a rock to these people, as harsh and as steady as the rock of the mountain they loved. They turned to it for survival, but its ways were hard, and sometimes it would break your heart. I could see them standing around the freshly dug grave, with nothing left to them but to sing and pray.

And the singing would build from the bottom of their feet, and everyone found their full voice in it. It was soothing to the soul as nothing else was.

Oh they tell me that He smiles on his children there
And His smile drives their sorrows all away
And they tell me that no tears ever come again
In that lovely land of unclouded sky

Oh the land of the cloudless day
Oh the land of an unclouded sky
Oh they tell me of a home where no storm clouds rise
Oh they tell me of an unclouded day

In my mind's eye I drifted down the hill with them, as the sound of the singing seemed to push them home to the comfort of their families. I fought back tears of my own, realizing that a day that should have been a celebration ended on the bone-chilling note of death.

In the months that followed, Johnnie almost grieved himself to death. He wasn't satisfied anyplace. He was working in the mines throwing himself into his work, but still his grief was more than he could stand.

Again Mother prayed. And again the mountain rescued the family from despair. Again the changing seasons soaked into the air around them to draw the fear out of their bodies and carry it into the air like smoke. Spring came. Mother and the rest of the family began getting ready for her garden. It was the best thing that could happen, because she was at her happiest there.

By this time I was old enough to be moving around on my own, and I was trail after her, fascinated by the butterflies and hummingbirds that would dance in the yard around the garden. One evening, after watching the same little hummingbird dart in and out of the flowers for days, I decided I would catch it. "Woodrow, I am going to catch that little bird," I shouted in my childish confidence. "It is pretty and I want to hold it."

"You could never catch a hummingbird, Emily, they are too fast." He could tell me no different. It danced like a little lady, in and out of the flowers, sipping from them like cups. First she'd hover just next to it, then stick her head far down inside. When she'd had her fill, she'd stand back from the flower before zipping away to another flower along the row.

I felt myself getting drowsy as I watched her glide along the air. Finally after what seemed like hours of waiting, the little hummingbird flew right into the flower close by me. I quickly darted my hand out and grabbed the flower and the bird both. I had it!

No sooner had I closed my hand on the bird then I felt its pointed beak boring into my palm. Terror raced through me, and I expected to see her sharp little beak poke through the skin on the outside of my hand! I let it go instantly.

"That sure was one of the funniest things I think I ever saw you do," Woodrow said with a laugh. "But no one minded. You were the family's precious jewel that spring. Everyone thought you were so great, and you kept us from thinking about Johnnie's troubles, and the dead baby. You were the cause of some of our sweetest moments."

As time passed, I remember more and more about living in the mountains. I was interested in everything. "Oh you were interested in everything all right," Woodrow countered. "You were directing us boys around like you were a princess and we were your willing subjects. But we were weakened by the spring air, you know." I poked him with my elbow and he poked me back. "You know better, silly, we always did what you asked in those days, now you're just getting it back. Everyone did what you wanted them to do back then. Pap wouldn't punish you either."

I smiled, because I didn't want to tell him about what Pappy did that spring. One day he up and asked me to take a walk with him through the orchard. He talked to me separately because he didn't want to hurt the other children's feelings.

"Emily, I want you to do something for me," he began.

"What's that, Pap?" I asked. I loved him fiercely and would have hung the moon for him if he'd asked.

"Well, the others in the house call me Pap, but I want you to call me Pappy instead."

"Why's that?" He hesitated, then said, "Well Emily, you're the girl of the family, and I just think that my daughter should have a different name for me than my sons." I thought about it later, because it seemed like an odd request, but then I just settled on the idea that it was his way of giving me a different place in the family, a place that was set aside from the rest. I called him Pappy from that day on.

Truth is, everyone treated me differently. Aunt Susan kept busy sewing pretty things for me. Where the rest were happy to have clean clothes in good repair, they gave me the best they could offer.

Like when I was real young, I realized that I was tender headed. When Mother used the brush on my hair I thought she was pulling it all out it felt so sharp. Not meaning to, I would let out a scream that would bring several people in the house running, thinking I'd stepped on a snake or something. Because of that, Aunt Susan made me a yellow bonnet. It did the trick. I loved that thing so much I refused to take it off, and both Aunt Susan and Mother would have to hold me down to untie the bonnet when they needed to wash or comb my hair.

About that time was when I also discovered that I hated to have dresses that pulled over my head because I felt like I was being smothered. It started off slow, but finally one day got to be too much. Mother was helping me into a dress that she'd bought it from someone down in camp for a nickel. The neck got caught going over my head, and I was sure that I was being smothered. I fought as hard as I could to get that thing over my head. The minute I was sure I was destined for Kitt's Cemetery, my head popped through.

"Lots of people are smothered to death like that," I said loudly. Because of that I really fell in love with any dress that buttoned down the front. And soon after that, the only thing Aunt Susan would sew for me was dresses that buttoned down the front.

"You all spoiled me, I guess, Mother," I said.

"I guess some might see it that way, Emily, but we didn't. You were careful with your looks and took special care of things. I think treating you different made us feel different about things too."

"As a matter of fact, I remember once when you were really young. You were out in the orchard with your Pappy looking for apples. Now his crutch went down into a hole. It threw him off balance and while leaning over on one crutch a snake crawled out of the hole and began striking at his face. He hit at it with his fist. Oh, you were terrified! You'd think you were worried for your old Pappy, but oh no. You jumped up and down crying for him not to hurt the poor little snake! You should have seen your face when he regained his balance and killed the snake. For years he'd tell the story that you felt sorrier for the snake and wanted it to get away. But that's the way you were, you saw things differently, and it was fun to be around you because no one knew what you'd come up with, or what you'd say."

"And your Pappy loved to have you with him. He'd take you robbing the bees of their honey, or just about anything that didn't involve hunting. And you were really good at helping him when he went out for that honey. You'd help him tie string around the long arms of his shirt and pants so bees wouldn't get to him and sting him. You'd hold the smoker he made to calm the bees down, and then you'd just sit quietly by while he collected the honey."

"And he was thinking about you all the time too. When he was away, say in Mount Vernon selling shoes, he'd always bring a little something back for you, like sweets or apples that he'd hide in his coat pocket for you to find. I thought at first that the boys would hate that and take it out on you that you got special treatment, but they just accepted it as the way things should be with a little girl in the house. It was nice."

And so that's the way my early years passed. I was part of a big and loving family. They all treated me like I was the finest thing alive, and I never had any reason to think that I wasn't loved and cherished. I grew up much like my own Pappy did, taken care of by my mother and by Aunt Susan. I'd listen to the boys talk about what they'd done hunting and fishing, and I learned how to take care of the animals and the home. In the evening, after mom had fixed us something wonderful to fill our stomachs, we'd sit around listening to the sound of Pappy's banjo. We'd tell stories to keep each other company and we'd make toys out of old rags and play with them, tossing them through the air and trying not to get into too much trouble. Woodrow was the closest to me in age and I loved to be around him as much as I could. We'd make up the greatest games and keep the others in stitches acting them out. I loved being the youngest sister in a family of boys. It was the best possible thing in the world.

And of course even if the boys had been jealous of me, after a few years passed the boys were too busy to worry about the treatment I got. It came time for the ones just a bit older than me to finally go to school.

CHAPTER 8: Favorite Things

School conditions were the best we could manage in a mountain community. In our case, that meant a one-room building that was in town, not a far walk from our home. We reached it by taking the swinging bridge into town, and it sat at the edge of a hollow. Before I was even born, a few men in the area gathered to raise the building, and the rest had seen it as the chance to have a barn dance. So everyone had come together to play music and raise this building, and before they knew it, they'd finished, and not a single law had to be passed and not a single tax had to be collected. They just decided to do it and so it was done. That was the mountain way.

It's strange for me to think of women going into teaching now, because teaching back then was a man's job. Lots of the boys and girls in school were very rough. Boys would often bring guns, maybe having even shot a squirrel or something for dinner on the way, wanting to leave the animal hanging from a limb or skin it real quick before going into the building for lessons. It was the teacher who had to be the one to tell them to leave the guns at home or at the door. But that almost never happened. Children grew up fast in those days and were used to being treated like adults in the sense that they earned their own way and on how the family relied on them for food gathering, so they weren't used to minding adults the way kids are now. Sometimes they'd do terrible things, like spit in the teacher's face and jump out of the windows. The teacher would be lucky if the boys didn't try to whip the teacher before they left too.

And if you were a teacher, you didn't get paid more than what the community itself could pay you, which often wasn't much. And you had to conduct yourself with the utmost in character and integrity, like being a preacher or something. People were always looking at you to be a good role model and to never do anything that would give you a bad name. It was like living in a glass house, as they used to say. So who was up to living like that, and having the chance of a student beating you up to top it all? Few people for sure, and especially not a woman.

The boys had a great schoolhouse though, and I was so jealous of them when they went. Going to school was like a vacation for many mountain children, who would go to school when they'd otherwise be working or hunting or helping with keeping the family going. It was hard to complete your education when there were so many people depending on you to help out the family, but I think the children who went to one room schoolhouses really got the benefit of a great education.

We didn't have lots of things that kids nowadays had, but how would we know the difference? And so we did the best that we could, and our imaginations made up the rest. When we gathered, different age groups would sit in different parts of the classroom, but if you were smart, you could learn everything that was going on in the room at once. Many of the young kids were working several grades above their own, and the teacher saw no reason to stop them, because it was likely that the kid would have to drop out early anyway to help take care of the family at home.

The building was pretty big, in our case it was almost as big as our house. It had an ancient old coal stove that wasn't in the best of condition, but we needed it on those cold winter mornings. It was always the teacher's job to get it running in the morning so that it would be at least a little warm by the time the children got there.

We didn't have desks like you see now either. They were wooden benches that someone had made from chopping a big tree trunk in half. They put legs on the rounded side and that was the bottom. We sat on the flat side of the log.

We didn't have books either, most of the time. The teacher had some books that he'd teach from, but our lessons were taken on a piece of slate, and we'd write on it with a piece of chalk. Many of our lessons had to be learned and recited from memory.

You had to be pretty good at your memory lessons to make it in school, and some of the boys had a harder time. Dallas couldn't stand school, but it had less to do with the lessons than with the competition before and after. One girl, named Effie, picked on Dallas until he was miserable. She was much larger than him and every single day she'd meet him before or after school and pinch him or knock him around, scratching him in the face and kicking him. Dallas was more than a little afraid of her and didn't want to fight.

"Dallas, that little girl is gonna get you bad one day," I told him when he came home looking even more miserable than usual. "You have got to stand up for yourself." He agreed with me, but just couldn't make it happen. I worried that he'd quit school altogether, which meant lying to Mother because she wanted him to go so bad.

Finally, Dallas decided to handle it his own way. Finding Pappy's sharp pocketknife, he had to figure out a time when Pappy wouldn't be looking for it himself. Then he took it to school with him. When Effie cornered him after school that say, she came away with a large gash in the side of her arm. Pappy did find out about it, and Dallas got a good hot seat licking, but Effie never bothered Dallas again and he decided it was worth it.

I was so proud of him that day I could barely sit down myself. "If ever anyone bothers me," I whispered to him quietly that evening, "I will stand up for myself."

But it was really up to the teacher in those days to keep the order and teach the kids manners and behavior, as many of them had parents who just didn't know any better themselves. Eventually, just such a man was hired. Mr.

Hodge carried a stick and after a few bouts with some of the toughest children, they found he was just a bit tougher than they were. For the first time, there was order in the little schoolhouse on the mountain.

Not that this ended the mischief. Dallas and Murphy were close when they were young and were always getting into some kind of mischief at school and home. One day Murphy came running in yelling for me to come quickly. "Dallas is hurt," he screamed. Mother took off running like the devil was after her around the hill where Dallas was hiding. When she came back with him and I saw him, I started screaming too. His face was covered with blood, and his arms were bleeding. He was white with fright and didn't want me to see him.

When the story came out, it turned out that he and Murphy had found dynamite caps, probably something tossed away from blasting through the rocks in the mine. Dallas had beat on one with a rock and it exploded. He wasn't seriously injured but it had scared him enough to know never to try it again.

Another time, Pappy missed his glasses, which he only wore for reading. He asked Mother about them, then began with the children one by one, determined to find out which kid had done it. With so many of us, we'd learned that we could blame some things on others, because they were more likely to be suspected anyway. Knowing that it would keep him out of trouble when it was his turn, Sam told it that Murphy and Dallas knew where the glasses were.

Come to find out, the boys had beat the lenses out and hid the gold rims under a rock. They had done this because one of the big boys at school told them that gold was worth a lot of money, so they had decided to sell the gold rims for whatever treasure they could get.

"Your pappy was furious," Mother said seriously. "We had no extra money to buy another pair of glasses. The boys didn't understand this of course, because they thought we had all the money in the world if we could afford golden glasses anyway. But, he was settled about it, and made me agree to punish them both."

"We had an unused empty room we stored things in. When the boys needed punishing they were taken to the empty room. On the wall I hung an old raincoat and when I felt the boys did not need to be punished, I whipped the old raincoat making lots of noise. They'd jump and yell, promising not to do it again. They'd cry. They'd carry on. Your Pappy thought they were getting a good hot seat-licking. Both boys made a show of limping back into the kitchen to make sure Pappy thought that I'd been strict with them."

"Took me a long time to catch on to that little game," Pappy said with a laugh. "But at least Dallas didn't get through that night without a little pain."

"That's right, I almost forgot," Mother said. But I hadn't forgotten. Later that same night Sam and Dallas sat on the bed and Woodrow sat across the room at the old plank table eating a steaming hot baked potato. Dallas said, "Give me a bite." Woodrow looked up and without warning or batting an eye whizzed the potato right at him. The potato was red hot and it stuck to his ear. Dallas screamed and jumped around. Mother ran to him and had to hold him down to dig it out of his ear. Everyone was hysterical with laughter, watching poor Dallas jump around like a kangaroo. Mother decided to let it pass without another pretend whipping.

"Boys will be boys," she told Pappy. He read his paper like he didn't care, but he was smiling behind the page, I saw him.

My family was always high-spirited like that, with the house full of boys. I think Mother sometimes felt closer to us than she did to Pappy, like we were all her younger brothers and sisters. We could make fun from the smallest things. Everyday just about we managed a game of hiding-go-seek. I loved being the baby in those days. All day I would wait for the boys to come back from school so that we could spend the evenings together. But the good thing was that I had Mother all to myself, and as I grew I learned how to take care of the house, doing everything that she could before I was even ready to go to school myself.

Just one evening I remember like it was yesterday. The boys came home and we all got heavily involved in a game of hiding-go-seek. They didn't always let me play out there after dark, but this time I was determined to get lost so that no one would find me. To make sure of it, I ran away from the others around the crest of our mountain and over to my favorite rock.

I was just like Mother in that I had chosen the rock in the woods that was my favorite place on the mountain. This was the place where I wanted to be laid out like a highland princess when I died. It was perfect. The rock laid flat, jutting out from the slope of the mountain like a large table used by the wild animals, where they would stand and hold their forest council meetings. I could just see a large panther standing there above all the other animals, discussing the humans and who had eaten them and how many. They would bring in all the bones of quiet little mountain men who'd mysteriously disappeared. They'd just want to show them off, but then they'd complain that the mountain men were so solitary that they weren't even missed. That was bad, because if no one knew about their wild exploits, then no one would be afraid of them, and humans didn't taste all that good anyway, so they weren't really worth the trouble.

And when I died, the community would all show up to bury the little girl who had been so small when she was born that her head fit in a teacup. And they would lay me out on this rock, and all the forest animals would join them, bringing wild flowers and wild blueberries to lie all around me. My hair would be brushed until it glowed. The hummingbirds would weave flowers in my hair with their little beaks. Everyone would cry.

The problem at the moment though was that I was alone, it was getting very dark, and no one knew where to find me. There I hid, trying to stay still and quiet, hardly breathing at all. But as I squatted there, a fox passed close by with a chicken in its mouth and it scared me to death. I honestly thought I was going to pee my pants. Trying to stay brave, I waited until it had gone a way around the hill, then I stood up and yelled, "You can't get me."

With that I ran home as fast as my baby legs would carry me. They didn't catch me, actually. But I couldn't stay another minute in the dark, even at my favorite rock.

Some people could look at stuff like that and think we were in real danger living so close to wildlife and the open land that could swallow a little kid like me up. But I always felt loved and safe. Sometimes I even felt too close to my parents, like they never wanted me to grow up.

Now I was my daddy's heart. Sometimes this got us into a pickle. There was the time that I came upon Milty and Woodrow sitting on the porch whittling. I'd been with the others playing, but when I saw what they were doing, I decided that all I had ever been meant to do was whittle. I sat down next to Pappy on the stairs and he couldn't say it. Instead, he showed me how to hold the knife. In quick order I had all the steps down and I was just starting to feel really grown up. But then I left the knife slip and it cut deeply into two of my fingers.

Pappy never let me whittle again. He bandaged my small fingers softly telling me that he was sorry he ever allowed me to whittle. It had hurt, but I was still disappointed that he took the knife away when I was still just learning.

But Pappy loved me, and we did love in great measure in our house. But other things were really hard to come by. We survived on what we could grow or hunt or bargain for.

One winter in fact I remember how Mother was getting ready to go through the worst of winter without a winter coat, because there was just no money for one. But that year proved to be one of the best instead of the worst. One afternoon we heard the motor of a car traveling along the road. We watched it come into view. It was a nice looking car passing in front of the house. As it went by a large box flew off the top. Milty said, "Sam run and get the box." Sam ran down to the highway and picked it up.

We waited nervously, afraid to open that box in case the strangers came back in their car. We had no way to return it to them, but still we waited. Finally, after several hours had passed and night had fallen, we decided that they weren't coming back. Carefully it was opened and blessings of all blessings, we could not believe what we saw.

I know it was the most beautiful coat I had ever seen, tailored-made and very expensive looking with a mink collar. The coat fit Mother like it had been made specifically for her. She smiled from ear to ear and I knew she was praising God's great and glorious name for providing in such a remarkable way.

So not only would Mother not freeze this winter, but she looked like a queen. Everyone jumped with delight watching it. I looked up to the sky and breathed a quiet, "Thank you dear Lord."

Miracles like that didn't happen every day though and other times our parents really struggled just to get by and keep us from feeling too poor. I think our saving grace is that we had our family near us. I can't imagine what it would be like in the mountains without family like Aunt Susan and Uncle John. Of course, many men had the mines to work for and could make a pretty good living if he was willing to work hard. But in the end the hard conditions in those mines would break down his health, and all he'd have to show for all that work was a body that was always tired and always shaken by the terrible cough that came with the Black Lung. I was glad that Pappy was spared from this, and I was so very glad that Uncle John and Aunt Susan loved us like we were their own children.

The best thing about them was how they treated us at Christmas time. Of course when I was younger, I didn't realize that they were the ones who gave us Christmas. I just knew all that was Santa Claus. But I do remember one special Christmas that I spent with my favorite brother Woodrow and my favorite relatives.

Aunt Susan and Uncle John asked Mother if we could spend Christmas with them. At the time, even though Mother hated being away from us, she decided it was the best thing to do. Mother was pregnant at the time, and sending us over there for Christmas week would help her out a lot, give her two less kids to watch out after when she was sick most of the time and not a lot of fun to be around.

Oh and it was the greatest adventure. We ate like pigs the whole week, since Aunt Susan was just about the best cook ever. Each morning we'd wake up to biscuits with honey and butter, fried sausage and eggs, and just about anything Aunt Susan could think up and we could ask for. We'd spend the time in the house, or helping Uncle John with the chores, and then the evenings we'd listen to Uncle John play his banjo and we'd sing songs until we couldn't hold our eyes open anymore.

Then Christmas day came. I was up earlier than everyone just to see what Santa Claus had brought. I snuck out of the bedroom real quiet, and found treats under the tree for all of us. Sure enough, Santa had left a bit of peppermint candy for each of us, broken into four pieces, each with a tag on it for each person. "Miss Aunt Susan." That was a tiny piece. "Mr. Uncle John." That was an even smaller piece. "Miss Emily." Mine was a pretty nice size really. But then I saw the last tag and I felt like throwing up. The piece with the tag that said "Mr. Woodrow" was the biggest of the group. Realization struck me. Santa hated me and loved Woodrow best. That's when I began to cry.

My crying woke everyone up. Woodrow crawled out of bed and stumbled into the room, wiping sleep out of his eyes. "What's wrong, Emily?" he said when he got to my side.

"Oh Woodrow, I must be rotten. Santa loves you the best. Look at that big old piece of candy you got, and look how small mine is?"

"Oh Emily, the size of the candy has nothing to do with how Santa feels about you," Woodrow said patiently, patting me on the arm.

"He's right, Emily," Uncle John picked me up then and nuzzled my cheek with his bristled, unshaven face and I giggled. "He got the bigger piece because he's bigger than you. It makes perfect sense." This logic seemed to meet with everyone's approval. They had to be kidding. They were just trying to make me feel better. I cried more. Santa hated me.

I guess it's strange to think of a kid getting so worked up over a piece of candy. Now days kids get all kinds of gifts and still want more. But the candy was all we were going to get from Santa that year, and so it made a big impression on me that my piece had been smaller. To prove to them that Santa really did love me, I slipped into the kitchen and poured a small glass of water on the floor. Then I quietly slipped back out and pretended like nothing had happened. Later, Aunt Susan went to the kitchen to start breakfast and noticed the water.

"How did that water get in the floor?" she asked.

I said, "I think Santa peed in the floor because he felt bad about leaving me only a small piece of candy cane." Only now do I understand why she laughed so hard.

But our time with them came to an end soon and we had to return home. Mother was heavy with child and needed our help. By this time Murphy and Dallas were old enough to work in the mines to help out. What this did was give us the ability to shop in the nearby company store on credit.

Mining towns all had certain things in common. When a town built up around a mine, the mine bosses controlled the whole place. Company stores were opened that would charge you more than the local stores. The problem is that the boys weren't paid with real money, they were paid with mine money, only good at the company store. So the company store could charge whatever they wanted to, because the miners had no choice but to shop there.

Now of course we didn't understand this at the time. The extra made it a little easier on the family, and it gave me and Woodrow the chance to get into a little more mischief.

Right after we returned from our visit, Mother sent us to the commissary and told us to draw a dollar each on Murphy and Dallas. As a treat, she told us to each keep a nickel for ourselves.

But when we got there, the devil got hold of us as we got in the door, and we decided it would be a good idea to draw one more dollar than Mother had said.

And we took advantage of it, and a dollar bought a lot of candy in those days. We bought a dollar's worth of Milky Way candy, took off up the hill and found a log under some trees, giggling and carrying on like it was Christmas again.

We both ate the candy until we were sick.

"I don't feel too good, Emily," Woodrow told me. I couldn't disagree. My own stomach felt terrible. We still had a pile of candy between us, and I couldn't eat another bite. It didn't even look good anymore.

"What are we going to do with the rest? We can't take it home or everyone will know what we did and we'll get in trouble." We clinched our swollen tummies and thought hard about our problem. Finally we decided to bury it under a log. When we were sent to the commissary again we'd just come back to the spot and collect more candy bars to eat. It was a good plan and we buried our candy treasure and went home.

A few days later, Mother sent us to commissary again. By that time our mouths started watering right away, thinking about all that candy. We raced down the mountain to the store, conducted our business swiftly and hurried back up the road to our hiding place. I watched over his shoulder as Woodrow dug into the hole that contained our treasure.

Ants poured out of the hole. They had eaten every smidgen.

In January 19, 1922, another cold sleeting winter morning brought another baby boy to our lives. Murphy was thirteen when Elmer Ray came into the world, and Mother decided that he was old enough to stay out of school and help with most of the work while she recovered. So he stayed home and cooked and helped with all of us.

Truth was though that Mother would have her hands full for a while with Ray, who was pale and weak and didn't seem to grow strong. He was weak and his skin looked bad and he had terrible diarrhea that made him smell. I didn't like even being around him all that much, because he smelled and cried all the time. Even at my age I could tell that Mother was scared that he would die.

But that's when we got our miracle. I will remember it because I was sitting with Mother on the porch stringing green beans. Shucky beans were sewed on threads and hung to dry in the sun, then used for pinto or soup beans. Mother had Ray tied in a chair beside us because he was too weak to sit up by himself.

And on that day a colored man passed by the house. He looked at the baby then at Mother and asked, "Your child has diarrhea?" She said, "Yes he does, but how did you know?"

"Well," he said, "I jest know he does and if you will, I ken cure yo child."

"We've tried everything," I heard her say softly. I think that's the first time I ever realized that my Mother was scared; I could hear it in the wavering of her voice. But the old man's voice was soft and affectionate, and it seemed to soothe her immediately. He explained what he would do, but Mother protested. She had no way to pay him.

"I live alone and have no one to do mah wash and if you will wash mah clothes, I will cure your boy."

"I'll be more than happy to wash your clothes for me, if you can do what you say you can." He smiled and tipped his hat, and then he was gone. But later that night he returned with some tea in a jar. He said it was blackberry root tea. He told Mother to give it to Ray along and along. She followed his instructions and just as the old man said, Ray started to get a lot better. Soon he was gaining weight, sitting up and playing with the other children. His color returned to him, and that terrible smell that lingered over him disappeared completely. It had been the smell of death I think, and now it was gone.

Mother was so grateful to that old colored man that not only did she wash his clothes, she gave him dishes of food whenever she could manage it, until many years later when she'd learned that he'd passed away. It was just a miracle, plain and simple, and Mother knew better than to question it. From early on she had known that we'd need the grace of God to live. That was one of those times when we'd received it. There would be other times in the future when we wouldn't be so sure.

CHAPTER 9: It was named "The Howard Spring"

Our family had lived through some hard times, and one of the hardest times began with one of the coldest winters I can ever remember.

The temperature stayed below zero many nights, killing hogs in their beds and much of the wildlife in the forest. We knew that come spring we had to plan for a larger garden than usual, because we weren't going to be able to rely on the forest to feed us at it had in years past. The cold had driven the wildlife further up the mountain, further away from people, which made hunting a lot harder, even for the boys who were young and strong. For Pappy it was even worse.

It was one of those cold nights with little to eat in the house. Mother had just enough to bake a thin pone of corn bread and sliced the last onion in the house. I watched as she divided the bread evenly among the children, gave each a slice of onion and explained that that was all we had. She then prayed and thank God for our food, told us to eat our supper and then go to bed.

As she started to the bedroom I called out, "Where's yours Mom?"

"Oh, she said as she dropped her head, I'm not hungry." She smiled and went off for bed. I could hardly eat knowing Mother had gone to bed hungry. Those were during the times I often cried myself to sleep because I was still hungry.

"Dear God, please help provide our family with enough food to eat. Bless our family. Amen."

Finally the winter passed us. We'd all survived, which couldn't be said of all the mountain families. Many had died that winter, and it had been so cold that the ground had frozen. Many were closed up in their pine box coffin, but had to wait for the ground to thaw before they could be buried. At night I would think of this and it would keep me up nights along with the grinding of hunger in my tummy.

But Mother always loved the spring and the chance to garden, and this year I caught the bug right along with her. I wanted to get in there and plant things so that they would grow bigger and better and bring in a better crop than we'd ever brought in before. I never wanted to see another year like we'd had. Already we were able to pick poke sallet wild and Mother was ready to put some of her own vegetables in the ground.

A problem confronted us though, because that was the year of the gypsies, and they made gardening frightening. A ways out from the house there were large oak trees and a spring. They set up camp there for the spring and summer months. With food so scarce it boiled me up inside to watch them tromp into my Mother's house uninvited to sit at our table and eat what should have fed our family.

But they had evil ways and could put a curse on our family and our land. Mother raised us with so many stories of their ways, and after the terrible winter we'd just lived through, I knew she just couldn't make herself stand up to them. So we shared what we had with no complaints. Even with that they weren't satisfied, and took such a shine to me that Mother wouldn't let me out of her sight, being afraid that they'd run off with me. Near the end of the summer, they tried just that, and she only kept me safe by bribing them with a huge lunch, holding me by the hand the entire time. I helped her and between the two of us, we gave them much of our food.

I still wonder if those gypsies didn't put a curse on us anyway, given what befell us later. The season started with such promise. Uncle John and Aunt Susan, always a blessing to us, bought seed for us that year, and helped us until the harvest came in.

But then Woodrow began to drag around like he was ill. One morning everyone was up bright and early except for Woodrow. When I looked for him, he was still in bed. I dragged him up, and reluctantly he obeyed me, but wasn't his usual self. He dragged around for the next couple of days like he was coming down with a cold.

But something just wasn't right. Finally Mother and Aunt Susan called for the doctor. That's when we found out that Woodrow had typhoid fever.

That was a mighty blow for us. Typhoid Fever killed many mountain people each year, and we knew just how serious it was. Uncle John wrote Pappy, who was doing sales work in another city, and told him to come home immediately. Mother and Aunt Susan hovered over him minute by minute, giving him the very best care they could manage. And I became his shadow as his pain got worse and his fever went higher and higher until I thought he couldn't stand it anymore.

Pappy came just as soon as he received the letter. He was very uneasy about Woodrow and said he was staying until he was out of danger. Beginning that night, Pappy would sleep holding Woodrow in his arms, trying to give him some relief from his pain. And I would crawl up with them both and sleep at Pappy's feet. I just couldn't stand to be away from them for any length of time at all. I didn't want Woodrow to die during the night and not know that I loved him.

The days and nights passed in a blur for me, but slowly it seemed that Woodrow began to improve. One day while Mother was working in the kitchen and I was playing with a rag doll at the foot of his bed, he woke up enough to speak to me.

"Emily, I am starving to death. Please go get me something to eat," he whispered. I was so happy to hear this. I snuck into the kitchen and saw a plate of biscuits on top of the stove, left over from breakfast. I quickly took one of them and returned to Woodrow, who ate it like a wild animal, he was so hungry. For the next few days I would sneak biscuits a couple times a day, sometimes with butter and sometimes with sugar in them.

A few days later, Mother grinned at me as I was helping her prepare breakfast. "Emily, why don't you stop feeding Woodrow and tell him to take breakfast with us at the table?"

She had known the whole time. I laughed. I took a biscuit anyway and tossed it into him. He laughed, and as soon as he finished the one I had thrown, he walked sheepishly into the kitchen to finish breakfast with us.

Not long and he was up and around. But there was more trouble to come to our house, and the gypsies weren't long out of my memory before another curse darkened our door.

My brother, Geoffrey, worked for a lady who lived in town. She paid him to do odd jobs for her. Geoffrey was the kind of boy who was well liked and never met a stranger. Everyone called him Goff. Johnnie, who had decided to move back with us when Bessie died, was now helping out with the family, as was Goff.

I'll never forget how good Goff was to the family. He never really cared a bit about himself; he just wanted us to be happy. I remember one Friday, Goff got his pay and bought himself a blue shirt, which he badly needed, but gave Mother the rest. Mother said, "Honey, you keep this and buy yourself some pants."

But he said, "No, Mother I can make out, you use it for food for the family or whatever you need the most." It made me cry looking at my sweet brother in his pants that had been mended too many times. He loved to go to church and went every chance he got. He worked very hard and picked blackberries when he got home early enough, so that Mother could make jelly. More than anything I wished that he would have a pair of new pants so that he could walk into church looking as good on the outside as he was on the inside.

Now my brothers weren't all about work. They had many friends on the mountain, and they ran around with a bunch of their friends all their life. They were all getting older too, almost grown men. Will Parrott lived a ways up the road from the school toward Pine Hill. He and his brother Link became good friends with Johnnie and Goff. They were around the house a lot.

These were typical rough mountain boys taunting their teacher and always in trouble. My brothers were a lot better than most, because Mother had always taught them right from wrong, but they were also taught to be strong so that no one would take advantage of them. They were hard boys like the others, but they knew the Lord.

I will always remember the day Goff died. I had been making jelly all day with Mother and was just finishing supper when Goff came in all sweaty and tired. He and Will Parrott and Will's brother Link had been picking blackberries all day together. Goff told me that Will and Link had tried to wreck a train by tying some large metal bolts and other stuff on the rails and that he took them off. I asked, "Did they get angry at you for doing that?"

He said, "No, they didn't act like they did." He paused, then grinned at Mother and added, "I sure am hungry. Is supper about ready?"

"Yes, honey, but would you run out to the schoolhouse and fetch me a bucket of water and by the time you get back, I will have supper on the table. By the time you finish your supper I can have the dishes done."

He hugged her, and then said, "Yes, mother, but I sure am starved. I will hurry so I can get back and eat."

We put supper on the table quickly, so that we'd be ready to eat as soon as Goff returned with the water. We waited supper on him, but he didn't return quickly like he'd promised. Finally I sent Woodrow after him into the darkness lit only by the stars and a full moon.

Woodrow came back quickly, calling for Pappy. Even from that distance I could hear the panic in Woodrow's voice. We all took off running. Pappy got to the clearing just before me, and I could see Goff laying on the ground, but nothing else. Pappy bent down to hide him, and to put his ear to Goff's mouth. The silence of the mountain closed around me, as all I could hear was the struggle Goff had just to breathe. He whispered something to his father. The boys got him to the house and suddenly the place was swimming with people.

It was impossible, but all the same, it was true. Goff was dead.

I don't remember much clearly after that, I had to sink away in my mind where none of this was true. I can still remember the screams and crying. The boys talked about what to do and the people were crowding in asking what had happened. The Sheriff spoke to Mother, but she couldn't tell him a thing. I heard one of the boys telling him that Pappy had put his shoulder holster on and a handgun in his pocket and had gone up the road saying he would kill the ones who had killed his boy before the night was over.

I didn't worry too much about the Sheriff, even after he took off. He was a friend of Pappy's and he would find him before he did something. Later I found out that he'd driven up toward Pine Mountain, and had found Pappy before he even made it to Will Parrott's house. Somehow he persuaded Pappy to get into the car. Will and Link were arrested and put in jail.

We learned from the Sheriff that while Goff was bent over pumping his water the Parrott boys slipped up behind him. They used a hoe handle with the hoe broken off and the metal shank still left on to beat poor Goff to death. They took turns pounding his head. He lived for only a few minutes. His water bucket was left hanging on the pump, half full of water.

It was a horrible funeral. The house was full of people. There were so many people on the porch that one end of it collapsed. Someone grabbed up me and Woodrow and put us in the middle of the bed so we wouldn't be squashed. One of the neighbors took Ray home with them. People brought lots of food and sat with us throughout the night.

All I could do was stare at Mother. I am not sure I understood much about God at that age, but I think I prayed. I wanted so much that she would cry, that she would take comfort from these people who knew her, people who had lived here as long as she had and had been through troubled times as well. Some of the people in the room that night were people who'd been with her the night of the first barn dance where she'd met Pappy.

Pacing seemed the only way she had to keep from breaking down. Years later she could still barely speak about that night, but she did say, "I couldn't be quiet that night. I kept hearing my boy tell me how hungry he was. How could I let my boy die hungry?"

I stared at my hands. They were red, and I realized vaguely that I had been rubbing them as if I could rub the skin right off the bones. I reached out to Goff, but he was not there to make things all right. He would never hug me again or play with me. There was a pain in me, such heartbreaking pain that I could not speak it.

My brother died hungry, beaten in the face by friends.

People were kind and tried to help. Because of the distance, almost no one from the family could attend the funeral, but many strangers came when they'd heard about the way my brother had died.

Mother lost the joy of living when Goff died. She never laughed. She did only the things she had to do. I think she was just barely aware of any of us. Truth to tell though, we also spent a lot of time staring out at nothing.

The worst part of it was that Goff had to be buried in Rockcastle, because we didn't have enough money to take him to the Kitts Mountain cemetery near Harlan. He would not rest in family soil, and family would not be able to tend to his grave.

Rockcastle became the family's poison. Soon after the death, Pappy started talking of selling out and going back to Harlan. Uncle John and Aunt Susan had already gone. We waited on the trial, only to see them get a few years at the penitentiary. I remember the last time I saw those boys when they were free, before they'd taken a rusty metal hoe to my brother's face. They'd been standing in front of the old school house with many of my brothers, in tattered clothes and carefree smiles. I wanted so much to live in that memory. The teachers who stood on the porch looking out over all those children would be able to say just the right word that would have turned the path of those Parrott boys.

Back row, right to left, second from left is Goff standing between Will and Link Parrott who would later beat him to death. Front row, left to right third from left is little Woodrow in hat, eighth is Murphy,

Johnny and Dallas, holding sign. Second row right to left, second from right is Sam. Six Howard brothers are in this rare photo. The only known photo of the boys as children. 1922 (photo compliments of Jean Snow, Rockcastle County, Kentucky)

But the words were never spoken. Will and Link would lose a pitiful few years for their murder and my brother with his slender face and his charming ways would never grow old and never eat another meal at home. Our grief was more than we could stand. I could never live around Rockcastle County again.

But Pappy had no luck trying to sell out. As the days passed it seemed that living there made it hard for Mother to even breathe. Finally Pappy told her to take us children back to Harlan until he could sell the house. Uncle John and Aunt Susan let us stay with them until he could join us. There was just no joy in the family. Woodrow and I would leave friends, and Mother would have to leave Pappy again. She cried every day as she packed for the long trip, cried as Pappy took us to meet the train.

As the other children boarded the train to go, I lingered so that I could see them say goodbye to each other. For some reason it felt so different this time, like there was a new and painful strain between the two of them. My Pappy's face was lined with pain and a weariness that was so unlike him. He was giving us up, so that Mother could be away from here. He was going to stick it out with his own demons to keep him company, so that Mother could be away from here. His hand reached out slowly to touch hers, and they barely moved. But suddenly all the years fell away between them, and I saw them as they must have been when he was courting her at the tender age of thirteen.

YOU ARE THE ONLY GIRL IN ALL THIS WIDE, WIDE, WORLD THAT SUITS ME. WILL YOU BE MY SWEET HEART? LAST NIGHT I HAD A BEAUTIFUL DREAM, AND IN IT YOU

WERE THERE, BUT MORNING CAME AND I AWOKE TO FIND MY DREAM WAS BARE. ALL MY HOPES WERE SHATTERED. NO MORE LOVE I'LL SHARE. UNTIL I HAVE THIS DREAM AGAIN, AND MAYBE <u>YOU'LL BE THERE</u>?

She touched his face until he looked at her. "You are the only one in all this wide wide world that suits me," she whispered. "Will you be my sweetheart?" His hand tightened around her fingers. "For better or worse," he said with tears shining in his eyes. Healing tears. She kissed him on the cheek and I boarded the train before they saw me. It was their time alone, and it would be the last time that they'd see each other for some time.

She cried all the way to Harlan. For the first time in weeks though, I imagined that she was crying for Pappy instead of just crying for Goff. I never went back to Rockcastle, but yearned to know about my brother. It would be many years later through my daughter, Joyce, and her curious search for her roots, that she learned about my brother. She went back to Rockcastle and met Jean Snow, the director for the local genealogy center. Jean knew all about my brother's tragic death and revealed the spring where Goff died had been named "The Howard Spring." Jean was kind enough to take Joyce back to the spring, the school and helped her find the house where I was born. She also sent a picture with six of my precious brothers standing in front of that school. It was the most precious Christmas gift I could have ever imagined receiving and will always be grateful to her. Just to see them standing there, but tragically also seeing the Parrot brothers standing in the pictures. When I looked closely at the date on the picture, I realized it had been taken two years before they killed Goff. The school has since been torn down. The big tree is still there overlooking the spring and the house is still sitting on the side of the hill.

The only formal picture of Johnny

When my mother took us back to Harlan, I was surrounded by family, which was really fun. The Howard clan almost smothered us in love, and took to me especially like I was a China doll, playing with me and always telling me how pretty I was. They couldn't believe that I was so small and delicate.

But Pappy was separated from us, because no one would buy our house. Mama stayed busy with so many people to look after, and I tried to help her as much as I could to keep her from brooding. All of a sudden though, a few weeks after we moved, mama got sick and I heard later that she lost another baby.

She had been scrubbing the floor when she felt a sharp pain in her stomach and dropped to the ground. The little boy was stillborn. And that is when she took sick with the childbed fever, and everyone thought we would lose her too. Uncle John wrote Pappy to come help, and when he got the news he lost no time in returning to Harlan.

I spent a lot of energy caring for Mama, and I wasn't the only one. Everyone prayed, because there was so little we could do, and in the small hours or the morning I would hear the other women whisper how Mama didn't want to get better, and how she wanted to go to heaven to be with her boys.

But then Pappy was able to return to Rockcastle. I think it was really only the care that Pappy gave her that kept her from joining her boys, and slowly she started to get better. At first I was sore that Pappy didn't want to be with me, and I cried something terrible until Woodward told me that I was being a baby. That shut me up real quick.

And while Mother was getting better, you couldn't ask for better, being with Uncle John and Aunt Susan. Everyone knew there was plenty to eat on their table. They had good milk and butter with fresh hot cornbread made from Uncle John's corn mill. Aunt Susan often made her famous banana pudding. I think Pappy was feeling left out of the family, and I missed him terrible when he had to go back on the road. I think he felt good that he was leaving his family in good hands though, and it made the going a little easier. We missed Pappy all the time, but as a traveling salesman he tried to visit as much as he could. I tried to turn it into a game, wondering when he'd come walking up with his crutch, carrying his saddlebag filled with shoes or books or whatever he happened to be selling on this route. I am sure that being surrounded by our family kept us all from missing him too much. We were the happiest when he came home and we were all together.

A few years flew by just like that. Often my brothers would stay out of school when they were needed to keep the house going by hunting or collecting firewood. Squirrels were plentiful and Pappy often took Woodrow hunting when he was home, letting him carry his gun. Whenever Woodrow went, I got to go too, carrying the squirrels and feeling proud to help to bring home food. Sometimes even Mother killed squirrels by throwing rocks at them. Everyone played a part in helping the family eat and keeping the house warm enough not to freeze.

But life was hard for Mama, for she was always pregnant. I remember when the third girl was born to our family in July 18, 1924. We let Johnnie name her. "I will name her after my wife," he said. He named her Bessie Mae, for his sweet wife who died in childbirth along with her baby. Pappy said that he'd like to name her after his sister Aurelia, and she was also named after her Great Grandmother, Marie Aurelia Bonaparte Mills Howard. It was settled that her name would be Bessie Mae Aurelia Howard. I kept giggling when they said it, because I couldn't imagine such a long name for such a little girl.

Bessie had light brown hair and blue eyes like Pappy. She was a pretty baby, weighed around seven pounds and laughed a lot. But she didn't seem to be real strong. Mama had her and Ray to the doctor often, but it did little good. Bessie had trouble with her ears. She began to grow into a short, plump, pretty little girl with a big smile. Little Ray was the same way, and both of them took a lot of Mama's time. She found it hard trying to care for two sick children, and harvest the garden that was planted in the spring. She carried Bessie as she pulled corn from the stalks and kept Ray to her side as she sat on the porch stringing her beans to dry for making shuck beans. I remember how they cried even after eating.

That's when I started helping her out more than I ever had. There was canning to do, to put up her vegetables for the winters' supply. There was all the laundry for the family to be washed on the scrub board, sometimes scrubbing until your hands bled. We kept two cast irons on the stove to use while ironing.

The boys were busy too at least. They had to carry most of the water to the house for baths and cooking. They were outside all the time hunting and looking for wood and working in the garden right next to us. They all got really strong and seemed like big men to be before I was even old enough to go to school.

When Sam was thirteen, he began to skip school to ride around with a man named Bill Floyd on a produce truck. He soon quit school and stayed with Floyd. He paid for his room and board and bought his own clothes. He seemed happy that Mother and Pappy agreed to allow him to stay. I don't think they liked it much, but I overheard Pappy tell mother, "Martha, if we made him come home he would just run away and get into bad trouble. At least we know where he is." It was also one less mouth to feed, and I think that helped us out a little.

Woodrow and I helped out by taking care of Ray. He was like our pet, and we kept him so busy, playing with him, chasing each other, laughing and yelling. We played out from the house near the road going around the mountain. One day as we were having fun a strange man came by and asked if he could take our picture. We had never had our picture taken before. The man sat us down on the hillside and we waited, our hearts beating with excitement, as he placed a dark cloth over his head. The he stood in front of this big box and there was a big light and a huge pop that scared us to death. He told us he would bring a picture back later for us to see. He kept his word and later returned with pictures, giving one of them to Pappy. Woodrow and I felt important and talked into the night about the strange man.

With Pappy still living in Rockcastle, Johnnie stopped by often on his way home to check on us. I think he also liked spending time playing with Bessie, which helped out Mama alot. Bessie was Johnnie's favorite because she was named after his wife and he still missed her so much. I remember one Saturday evening he stopped by on his way home. It was snowing and he had been to town. He handed Bessie a paper bag. She opened it and pulled out the most beautiful hat. It was a lovely red with a large pompom on top and the ties had large pompoms on the end of each of them. It was edged in something white that sparkled. There were little sparkles all through the rim. I had such envy in my heart over that hat. I thought if only I had a hat like that I would be a princess. I don't think I ever wanted anything as bad.

No one ever knew how I felt about that hat, and I never let onto Bessie how much I wanted it. I never got to wear the pretty hat out with the group, but when no one was around, I'd slip in and hold it and try it on. I wondered if a fairy must have made it for it to be so pretty. It was made like a tam and could easily be put on and off the head. I felt guilty, but I also wanted to see what I looked like wearing it, so that I got the piece of a broken mirror I hid under my mattress. Each time I stood in the sun and held the mirror so I could look at myself in the pompom hat, I decided that it would be the last time I would wear it. Gently I would put it back in place and never tell my secret to anyone.

But that hat is what first gave me the idea that I wanted to wear pretty things like that. I just knew that when I got older I would find a way to wear beautiful things like that. That hat is what set me to thinking how I could come up with the money for such things. That's where berry season came in, and became my very best friend.

Berry season was always something we looked forward to. During berry season the older boys often spent the entire day picking berries for mother to use. They brought in buckets of blackberries for making jam and jelly. Apples came from Uncle John and Aunt Susan's orchard for making apple butter and drying. When they were in season, the apples were made into fried apple pies by rolling out dough and filling it with apples, cinnamon, sugar and butter. Then they were fried to a golden brown on both sides and rolled in sugar while they were still hot. Apples also gave us variety for breakfast, when they could be sliced with butter and sugar and served with hot biscuits. Even after the picking season was over, we kept apples through the winter by wrapping them in straw and storing them in deep holes near the cabin.

I remember that berry-picking season because it was the summer Kenneth Mullins became our friend. He started as Woodrow's new friend, and he came to play most every day. One day he stopped me as we were headed into the woods for a game of tag.

"Emily, I claim you for my sweetheart." I stared at him for a minute, because I thought he meant that he'd tagged me. "You can't do that, we haven't even started playing yet."

"No Emily, this isn't a game. You are now my sweetheart and I promise to love you always." I liked the sound of that, so I started to skip away, then tossed over my shoulder, "Okay Kenneth Mullins, I agree to be your sweetheart." And just as simple as that, it was all settled.

I tagged after Woodrow and Kenneth like the finest lady, playing in the field while they tried to shoot birds with their slingshots. I always thought they were really good shots, but I realize now that they never shot any birds. But Woodrow made a slingshot for me too and we all talked about how good we were shooting.

One day they were going to hunt for rabbits and maybe bears, they told me. They took turns carrying me over the briers putting their arms around me and lifting me over with their knees. I felt like a princess, being carried around by my brother and my sweetheart. The day was wonderful though we never found any bears and chased the rabbits until we nearly dropped from exhaustion. And there were more adventures, as another time we found an old quilt half buried in the dirt. That meant money, because we could give it to the ragman who came once a week collecting. We pulled and tugged and finally dug it out, stuffed it into an old sack with some more old rags that Mother had given us and it filled the sack. When the ragman came by he bought the sack for fifty cents. We jumped up and down screaming, "We're rich, we're rich!"

We danced and screamed and hugged. We had never earned that much money and we kept it a hushed secret. Off to the store we went and got lots of candy. We ate until we were sick and saved the rest of the money for another day, hiding it under a rock up on the hill next to an old oak tree. That night at supper Woodrow and I looked at each other giggled and laughed until our sides ached. We weren't hungry at suppertime. I could tell that Mother thought we were hiding something and the others thought we were crazy.

Oh, Woodrow and Kenneth and I were the best of buddies.

I trailed after the boys every day. We often hunted in late afternoon when the sun was almost down. One time we decided to hunt birds in the evening. Off we went with our slingshots. I had never shot a bird and Kenneth and Woodrow said, "Emily, I bet you can't hit that fat little bird sitting up there on the limb."

I took aim and pulled back my sling. The bird fell off the limb and landed on the ground. We ran over to it but it got up and flew away. Woodrow asked, "How did you do that?" I didn't know. It was the first and only bird I ever shot. I never took aim again.

But my brother was off to other things already. "Let's go rabbit hunting instead." Our attention turned from the birds to skipping off down into the field to hunt rabbits. There was a creek that ran through the field. We walked next to it and Woodrow told me to yell if I saw a rabbit. It was a hot day and I was tired and sleepy. All at once a rabbit jumped up right at my feet. I was so frightened I screamed. Woodrow ran to me, but I was crying so hard that I couldn't tell him what I had seen. He put his arms around me and took me home. I went to bed and he went back to look for the rabbit. About an hour later he came yelling for Mother to see what he had. I jumped out of bed. We both ran to Woodrow to see what he was yelling about.

He had caught a rabbit. The poor thing was naked of fur. In his excitement he told us that it ran into a hole and he used a forked stick to twist it out. He held it out to us and the smile he wore made him look like a king.

Mama and I helped clean the rabbit and cook the scrawny thing trying to stretch one rabbit with a pan of gravy and hot biscuits. She kept bragging how proud she was of Woodrow for supplying the food.

Soon though, summer was over. The wind blew colder and the days outside got fewer and shorter. We saw Kenneth less often and started preparing heavily for the cold winter to come. It was fall and time to fatten the hog for killing and store all the food we could. The fall always was a little sad to me, as times always seemed to get a little harder. Pappy couldn't sell books or shoes this year either. He said he would walk for miles carrying his saddlebags stuffed with shoes and books, but hardly ever sold any. As Christmas got closer and closer, I knew that he and Mother were worried that there was little money for food, much less for toys. We didn't spend much time being disappointed about it in those days. People just didn't carry on about toys at Christmas the way they do now.

I know though that a few days before Christmas Pappy told Mother there was a man who wanted his saddlebags real bad and it looked like selling them was the only way for them to have any Christmas for us. I cried then, because I knew how Pappy felt about those bags. Mother told him there must be another way, but nothing turned up and he sold his beloved saddlebags.

Christmas morning everyone was up bright and early. We had always gotten an apple, orange, a bit of candy and three or four nuts before, but this time we got something extra. Woodrow got a pocketknife. Bessie got a tiny doll and Ray got a tiny truck. I got a little red handled pair of scissors. I think we were the happiest children in the whole wide world. Woodrow and I talked and talked of how good old Santa was and that he sure must love us a whole big lot to bring us such a good Christmas.

And in much the same way each year, the years just melted away. Mama had a child almost every other year. Pappy still had to sell the house in Rockcastle to settle his clan and be back with them. His luck seemed bad, but I knew he wouldn't give up. We depended on him and Mother gave him her support knowing everything would work out for the best. Patience and time would prevail.

CHAPTER 11: Johnnie's Troubles

Harlan was a mining town, and because of that, it was a company town. The rush for coal was much like the rush for gold. The company bought huge tracts of land surrounding the mines and so they provided the doctor's office, the school, the commissary and a group of houses to fill the needs of miners flocking to the area. Company men controlled these shoddy houses. They were all pretty much alike, with two or three rooms and a toilet. A drilled well met the water needs, roofs were covered with thin tarpaper and rents were mostly ten dollars a month. The toilets emptied into the rivers. When I knew them, the waters of the Cumberland River were full of muddy sump water.

After many years of traveling, Pappy at last found a buyer for the place in Rockcastle. We were still living with Uncle John and Aunt Susan, but Sam had already moved out and Johnnie remarried.

After selling the house in Rockcastle, Pappy couldn't find a place in Harlan. Our family had really grown and it seemed there was no house large enough to fit. Johnnie told Pappy we could come and stay with him and his wife until he could find a place. His second wife's name was Hettie. He was trying to find peace of mind and thought he had found the solution, but found out later it was not so. Hettie was a real piece of work. Pappy knew Johnnie was not happy with Hettie and that it would create more problems, so he said no. But Pappy finally bought near the outskirts of the mining camps, high on the mountains to escape the turbulent waters during flash flood season. It was around the hill from Johnnie's. It was cheap property, but he could get the family back together.

Now there was room for everyone to be together again. And it was getting to be school time for Woodrow and me. Pappy wanted us to go to the Harlan School with lots of rooms rather than the one room school in Kitts Holler.

"It's a better school and they will get better book learning," he said to Mother.

We were happier than ever, but for one thorn. Johnnie's wife was spending her days off somewhere while Johnnie was in the mines working. Sometimes when she got back late, almost time for Johnnie to be home, she stopped by the house and got Mama to send me home with her. What she wanted was for me to peel potatoes or set the table or whatever to hurry up supper. She couldn't cook for nothing, and fried the potatoes so fast they were most always burned. It just wasn't right for a miner's wife to feed him bad food after he'd worked so hard that day. She was a sorry wife. Most wives had cornbread, onions, fried potatoes and beans waiting, but poor Johnnie, most times, came home to an empty house. I could fry up potatoes perfect, had known how to do it for a while now. I couldn't understand why she couldn't figure it out, except she was always in a hurry to show she'd been doing more all day than just wandering around looking for other trouble.

That's when she realized she could have the house cleaned and supper ready by the time Johnnie got home if I helped. Johnnie hardly ever got a good supper without me helping.

Johnnie was happy when Hettie told him she was with child. He told Mama that maybe a baby would keep her home more. Sometime later mother told us that Hettie had a little baby girl, but it died at birth. They named the baby Mary Elizabeth, and buried it on Kitt's Hill down the hill from Johnnie's first wife and baby.

Poor Johnnie, he had looked forward to this baby. It seemed that nothing was going right for him. He worked hard in the coal mines, coming home covered with the Black Diamond Dust, wearing his carbide light attached to his miner's helmet, hungry as a hog, but could never draw much of a payday. Hettie stayed gone all day long, often going to the commissary drawing "scrip" on Johnnie's paycheck and just barely getting home before Johnnie got in from work.

And Mama was expecting again and feeling very poorly most of the time. She was doing all of the cooking and work around the house. Johnnie thought his wife was doing it and Mama let her take credit for it to keep from them having any trouble. She had her hands full with all my brothers and sister and now pretty much taking care of Johnnie, now 23, and trying to keep up with Hettie. I remember one time when Johnnie's work clothes were all dirty and he had nothing left to wear to the mines, he told Hettie to please wash clothes. Work clothes miners wore were called bank clothes. Hettie told Mama she didn't have time to wash them. "I am going down to the camp to visit my sister. You can wash his clothes for he is your son and I don't have the time," she said.

So mama scrubbed them on the scrub board and had them all ready when Johnnie came from work. He told Hettie how sweet it was of her to fix them up for him. I watched her stare at Hettie but she never said a thing. I wouldn't have done that. That phony, lazy woman did not deserve to be Johnnie's wife. I wanted badly to tell on Hettie, but I knew to keep my mouth shut for fear of getting in trouble with Mother.

But she did get caught in lying. A few days later Johnnie got home a little early finding Hettie gone. He cleaned up and went to look for her. She was coming up the hill. He had missed his two beautiful .45 guns, with long barrels and walnut handles and the set of holsters for them. When he met her he asked what she had done with them. She told him several stories about them. He flew angry and finally she said she left them lying under an oak tree. He knew she was lying. He also knew she had given them away to some man.

He had suspected her cheating on him, but had no proof. He held her trying to force her to tell where they were, but when she broke loose from his grasp she ran to Mama screaming, "Johnnie is really going to kill me this time." Mama hid her behind the couch and when Johnnie came in he said, "Mother, where is she? I mean to make her tell me what she did with my guns."

"Now Johnnie, if you will promise not to harm her I'll tell you where she is." She put her hand on his arm and talked calmly until he quieted down and he agreed he wouldn't hurt her. Hettie jumped up from behind the couch and said with a smirk, "Here I am." She never did admit what she did with his guns, but later he found out she gave them to a taxi driver. They were his prize guns and he never got them back. He was heart-broken.

But Johnnie let it go at that. He didn't do anything about Hettie and her ways. That made me about as mad as anything. I would have stood up to her and tossed her out of the house. She came from nothing, and we came from nothing, but my brothers and sisters had been taught right from wrong, and they lived in the Lord. This woman had obviously been raised without the Lord, just looking out for herself. After a while of thinking all this out, I was just too undone with it all and I tried to stay away from her unless I was made to cook. One day Johnnie came rushing in all excited. He announced, "Guess what, I have a big baby girl at my house. She was born last night and is doing just fine."

Mama said, "Oh, I am so happy for you. How is Hettie?" He replied that she was doing just fine. Mama said with a twinkle in her eyes, "Milty, we have a grandchild to go see."

The baby was born at home. Woodrow and I couldn't go. Mother depended on me now that I could care for the children, cook and clean house. So we stayed with Bessie and Ray. When they returned they were laughing and seemed delighted and happy. They said, "It was a very pretty baby and we shall all go for a visit soon.

132

They named her Gladys after one of Hettie's friends down in the coal camp. I loved when they brought Gladys down and everyone played with her. Mother would hold her lovingly and tenderly in her arms, sometimes with tears in her eyes remembering the children she had lost.

Having a baby seemed to make Johnnie think about his future. One day not long after Gladys was born, Johnnie told Mother he felt he ought to get out of the mines. "Mom, I feel that I am going to be killed if I don't get out of them. It is on my mind all the time. There seems to be more and more accidents and the dust is so thick that I cough and spit up only black dust. My lungs sometimes feel on fire."

She said, "If you feel that strongly about it son find work elsewhere." And when he made up his mind, there was no changing it. Soon he was able to find a job driving a truck for a prison, hauling prisoners for the road crew.

Things didn't go smoothly for long though. One of the trucks had something wrong with the steering gear and was in for repairs. Johnnie's first day on his new job he was given the wrong truck to drive. He was on his way to pick up prisoners when the steering gear locked. The truck turned over, pinning him. He was hurt bad.

I was scared when I found out. Johnnie was one of my favorite brothers. He stood straight and tall, his hair was thick and black, his eyes were deep blue like Pappy's and he was exceptionally good looking. I just knew something dreadful was wrong. I prayed out loud for my brother, but felt a deep worry.

The first night was hard for everyone. Hardly anyone spoke. Johnnie was not responding and by the third day his condition worsened. He lived three painful days with Mama by his side. They would not allow Woodrow or me in the hospital, so we waited at home. Finally, Mama came to us and said, "Now children, Johnnie has had a rough hard life, but he told me before he went to be with our Lord he had made things all right and was ready to go." She cupped her face in her hands and cried.

My parents didn't talk. I fixed supper but Mama didn't eat. Poor Johnnie, he hadn't had much of a life on earth, but he would have a beautiful life in heaven.

Mother and Aunt Susan's grief seemed too great for them. I was becoming accustomed to the ways of death. I watched again as mother rubbed her hands, heard the chilling wail that came from her small frame. The sorrow on her face would be planted in my mind forever as she stood on the wobbly porch as crowds of people came to pay their respects.

Johnnie was set up in the front room lit with candles and kerosene lanterns. A musty strange odor came from the room arising from the blend of waxed flowers and the smell of death. It was the mountain custom to sit with the corpse throughout the night and up to the burial. Turns were taken sitting round the clock. During the night you could hear mumbled small talk as you slept, talking in hushed tones throughout the night. The whole house would be warm from all the bodies, and the smell of food would keep you awake, as it sat in all kinds of borrowed dishes on the rustic table near the stove.

The country preacher read a few scriptures then told what a good person Johnnie had been and how he worked hard and helped with his family. I listened to the crowd sing the familiar "In the Sweet Bye and Bye." Then they sang a favorite of Johnnie's to remember him.

Precious memories, unseen angels
Sent from somewhere to my soul
How they linger, ever near me
And the sacred scenes unfold.

Precious memories, how they linger

How they ever flood my soul.

In the stillness of the midnight

Precious, sacred scenes unfold.

I had one less brother. Who would be next? "I could never lose Woodrow," I said to myself. "I loved Johnnie, but Woodrow is my buddy." Woodrow and I were sent to Aunt Susan's until the burial was over, but we watched as Johnnie was loaded onto the flat bed to be carried to the graveyard. The crowd slowly followed behind going the long distance to the graveyard on the mountain singing "In the Sweet By and By."

I remember how Mother got pale and could not make herself work. Friends dropped in trying to cheer her, but she couldn't get over her grief. Lots of times I saw her standing with her hands clasped looking up to the sky as if she was asking, "God why?"

But life had to keep you moving in one direction, and always has a way of dragging you along whether you like it or not. Without warning it was time for Woodrow to enter school. It was near my sixth birthday and I wanted to go too. I looked forward to going to school and could hardly wait for the day to arrive. Aunt Susan spent long hours working on school dresses for the big day. I chose a striped long sleeve dress with a wide border around the hem and sleeves. The border and neckline of the sleeves had all been brier stitched. I laughed whenever I saw it, because it looked like the foot of a little bird had walked all the way around the edge of my sleeves. These weren't just stitches to keep the dress together, they were stitches to make it look pretty, and I knew they were just for me. She also made a hat to match. I busied myself for bed and could hardly sleep thinking about learning to read. Pappy had always brought the Harlan Daily Enterprise home and read by the old oil lamp every evening and I had often looked at the paper and wondered what the words said. "Now I will read every inch of that paper like Pappy," I thought I stared at the ceiling. Dosing off I dreamed of my first day at school. Kids would be laughing, running and playing on the large swings on the playground. I would be a part of it.

Morning sun streamed through the hole in the curtain hitting me in the face. I jumped out of bed and grabbed my beautiful dress. I felt like a million dollars in the new outfit. Then I brushed and brushed my hair until it shone and put on my hat. I could hardly eat breakfast. There was no sadness to life that day. I thought, "I will learn to read real fast so I can read stories."

Aunt Susan packed a lunch and off we went. I skipped along, singing and whistling. I felt proud and knew no girl could be prettier. Aunt Susan held my hand, walked up the steps to the big school, went over to the big desk sitting in the middle of the schoolroom and tried to enroll me. The teacher looked asked her how old I was and Aunt Susan replied, "Why Emily is six years old." The teacher asked for my birth certificate. Aunt Susan told her that they didn't have one, but insisted again that I was six years old.

It was no use. The teacher replied, "She is too small to be six years old and we just cannot enter her in school. We can't be responsible for such a small child."

I felt like a friend had slapped me. For a second I just stood there, stunned. Then I cried. Finally we left, a sad pair indeed. I think we were all feeling hurt and disappointed, but I was the worst of all, because it was me who'd been kicked out of the line at school.

"I'm so sorry, Emily," Aunt Susan said. "I wish we could have gotten you in, but she just didn't believe that you could be such a tough smart little girl and be so small. She just didn't know any better. Here baby, have a nickel and we'll go to the store."

"I don't want to go to the store. I can't imagine anything worse than this. Did you see Penny in line? She got in."

You mean Anna Ruth?"

"Yes ma'am, I call her Penny. She's bigger than me, and she got in just fine."

"Well that's it, sweetheart, she's bigger. I'm sorry. We'll go to the store anyway, I have to get a few things and maybe you'll change your mind."

"Penny will laugh because she is going to school and I can't go," I repeated. A piece of chocolate barely cut through my misery. When Penny returned from school I poured out the story. A true friend though, she didn't laugh at all. We cried together. She felt bad that I could not go to school. Penny put her arms around me and said, "Oh, I wish you could go for I miss you, but maybe it won't be too long until you can go." I felt a little better as we began playing. Soon it was time to go home so I slipped through the hole in the fence separating our houses.

But my good mood didn't last. That evening Aunt Susan told Woodrow and me to feed the chickens. It was almost dark and time for the chickens to roost, so she told us not to throw out much. Out of boredom and feeling sorry for myself, I threw out all the corn over the back lot. When she came to the door later and saw the mess she became angry. "Now you both just get out there and pick up every grain and do not come in until you are finished." We knew she meant what she said. By the time we finished it was well after dark. We were tired and hungry and told Aunt Susan we were sorry and would never do such a thing again. I learned my lesson and tried from then on not to feel sorry over the school because feeling sorry for myself just got me into trouble.

The next morning we went home with all the stuff Aunt Susan packed for us in the way of food. Everyone was excited when we arrived. We all knew Pappy hunted ginseng in the mountains to sell bringing in enough money to supply some but she made things easier when she sent bags of food home to feed all the hungry mouths. So all was not lost. I couldn't go to school yet, but at least on this day I brought home food for the family.

The only picture of Emily as a child – center – Ray on her left, Woodrow on her right.

CHAPTER 12: Uncle John

Coal mining like what Johnnie did was the way most men in Harlan made a living. Logging was one of the others. Our mountain held good wood of all kinds, and logging was in demand with huge sawmills creeping up through the mountains. This brought down acre after acre of quality timber, cutting the beautifully carved mountains into muddy roads using mule teams and logging trucks carrying the logs to the sawmills.

The forests were being stripped of their beauty by both logging and mining. Piles of sawdust from the sawmills were stacked nearby and large hideous slate dumps rose high near the mines. These unsightly stacks also posed potential dangers to children playing near them. Sometimes the slate would catch fire and burn for weeks. It ruined people's lungs, especially the miners who worked without protection.

Pappy would never work in the mines because of his leg. He cautioned us never to play near the sawdust piles or slate dumps or go near the mines. "You could burn to death if you fell in the burning slate dumps. They burn underneath where you can't see what's happening. You are to never go near them."

I was almost eight years old around that time. I was still small for my age. Each and every year, both Mama and Aunt Susan tried to convince the teachers that I was old enough to go to school, but each time they were told I was too small or not old enough and the school would not be responsible for me.

This year was different. Again, school clothes were made ready. It was 1927, the year of the big flood. If it hadn't been for the joy of finally getting into school, I probably would remember it only for the bad that happened.

Floods were always a threat in our area of the country, which is why it was always a good thing to find a place to live in highland, above the flood plain. But that year we were hit hard, and I can still remember Pappy reading the paper to us of what people outside the area reported.

"The death list of this terrific storm has reached sixteen people, and may soon reach as high as twenty. Twenty nothing," he paused. It will be much bigger than that." Pappy was right, it killed nearly a hundred mountaineers. He read on. "Property damage cannot be estimated. Homes are destroyed; livestock and poultry drowned, and whole farms practically ruined. The fury of this flood has far exceeded anything in this reporter's memory. Numbers of the dead have been found, but searchers still face the gruesome task of tearing into the banks of the streams in hopes of finding bodies."

Then Pappy read of the stories of the brave men who endured the flood conditions to help others. "Several businesses along the river's path were hit hard. One manager had to drag a number of cars out of the water. The storm flood cut off all power. People wandered about the streets, laughing and joking and making the best of a bad situation, albeit a tone of the hysterical could be detected in the laugh of many. Men everywhere discussed the storm and its effects. Practically all the coal mines in the county suffered great losses. The superintendent reports that the city is greatly damaged as well. And many natural phenomena can be spotted as well during this time. A colored boy on Train Number One declared that his brain was absolutely clear when he counted 24 snakes in one herd on the river near here Monday morning."

"Incredible," I breathed.

And Pappy read on, of husbands being torn from their wives and hurtled down the river. Of people working together to save bridges and hack open the roofs of homes and businesses to pull people to safety. Then he read the list of the known dead, and he and Mother talked about who among them were known to us.

The mountain felt ruined. But still, my memory of my first day of school still overshadows the flood. Tragedy was a part of life, to be accepted and survived. School was a great event.

I had been planning my first day for years now, and my friend Hettie was still around to help me carry out my plan and get me ready for the big day. Woodrow had taught me to spell some words and count. I stretched my body trying to look taller and walked up those familiar steep steps into the big schoolhouse. Oh, would I be accepted this time?

By this time I was thinking almost out loud. "When you go to school it makes you important and responsible," I thought. I will now take Mom's place in the family and help when I come in from school for now I am grown." This year she was again with child, and I knew I would be needed to help out. Going to school meant to me that I was responsible enough to be treated like I was older.

And this year was my year. At last I was accepted. I had waited patiently for two years and now my time had come. I was given a desk.

When the teacher called "Emily Nancy Howard," I smiled.

"I am here."

After school and on weekends I cooked and cleaned while my parents went to the mountains to hunt ginseng. Woodrow and I drove the cows in from the mountains in the evenings. The other children had chores, bringing in firewood, water from the spring, but Woodrow and I were a team and were given many responsibilities together. One day we came in from school and we had a brand new little baby brother. Mother said, "We will name him Damon."

He was a sickly child from the start. One night soon after I overheard my parents talking. "I don't think we will be able to raise little Damon," Pappy said. "He is getting weaker and weaker all the time. Doctor Bailey said he was doing everything he could, but nothing seems to be helping him. He is said to be good with children. Damon is almost three months old, but something is dreadfully wrong."

Mother took him the next day to Doctor Bailey. He gave her some red liquid medicine for Damon. He said, "Martha, give this to him right away. That's all I know to do for him." She did as she was told and Damon died the next day.

It was sad looking at this cute little fellow lying still and cold. He'd been with us just a very short time, but I had loved making him laugh watching him kick his feet and coo. I cried knowing I would never hold him again. Death was no longer a new word or a new feeling but it was a bitter emotion that welled up inside me. I scared myself sometimes with the strength of a feeling that I couldn't understand. It was even worse when I overhead Aunt Susan. "Martha has had too many children and had to work too hard. She didn't have the right kind of food while carrying this baby."

So it was another funeral and days of mourning and months of depression to follow. I know my parents talked about not having any more children. They consoled each other and tried to spend more time together. They loved those mountains, the trees, and the change of seasons. They enjoyed walking for hours through the scented silence of the woods. They breathed in the smell of honeysuckle and mountain laurel graced their trail. Red robins flew from tree to tree, ground squirrels scampered across the trail and at rare times a lonely green snake lay in grassy areas. Soft rays of sunlight warmed them.

They chose a special log under an oak tree to provide a seat for their picnic lunches of biscuit and jelly. They watched the squirrels scampering from tree to tree while they ate, slipping them morsels of their biscuits. It was a large part of how Mother healed from the strain of losing her babies.

But the babies didn't stop coming. Before too long, Mother was pregnant again. It seemed though that Pappy spent more time with her this time and took special care to see that she had what she wanted.

"Oh I remember one day in particular about that time," Mother told me with a smile in her eyes. "I had a fierce craving for sarvest. This is a tart berry that she loved when she was pregnant. "Your Pappy knew where a big tree of it grew, and he wanted to take me there, saying we could look for ginseng on the way. So that's what we did, we set out."

"Finally we found the sarvest tree and as he had said it was full of nice ripe sarvest. I ate and ate until Pappy broke off a limb just hanging full and handed the limb to me. He had the best chuckle watching me eat those berries while we walked along the trail. The sun was fading, it was beginning to get dark when suddenly we heard a scream sounding much like a woman. I said, "Milty, do you think there's a woman lost?"

"Could be, Martha, it certainly sounds like it." So he answered back. We heard it again. We were standing under a tree half-fallen over; the leaves were dry making a rustling sound under our feet. As Milty kept hollering, the screams came closer and closer, then we heard the leaves in the fallen tree rustle, turned looked up and there stood a panther on a branch of the fallen tree.

I started to run, but your Pappy quickly grabbed me by the arm, and whispered, "Don't make any sudden moves or we will be goners."

The panther followed us closely as we walked. After a little while, your Pappy says, "Martha, if we can make it to the fence it won't cross over."

Moving carefully we made their way to the fence and quickly crossed. As we approached the house we both looked back, watched the panther rear upon the old split rail fence and stare at us. My heart was up in my throat I can tell you. When we got in the cabin, we shut the door behind us and bolted it. I don't think I've ever been quite that scared of anything in my life."

Well of course the next morning it was almost impossible to get Mother to let us go outside, and it took most of the morning to talk her into letting Woodrow and me visit Aunt Susan and Uncle John to spend the night. Finally, she said we could and off we went. They were always pleased to see us running into the house, and we loved to hug their necks and eat at the big table with lots of people who came for her cooking.

Late in the evening after supper Uncle John got out his fiddle and began to play. He could play that fiddle! Several neighbors dropped by for an evening get together.

"Well hey there, Keeten," Uncle John called to a neighbor who showed up that night. "Now how long has it been since I've seen you darken my door?"

"Oh, about the last time Miz McCreary made those apple dumplings of hers," he said with a laugh. "I could smell them from my front door." Old man Keeten was a widow and Aunt Susan would often make a plate of food and leave it on a chair near is front door. But he loved to visit whenever he was feeling good and dance as Uncle John played his fiddle. He sure could buck dance, clicking his feet and stomping the floor while everyone clapped and laughed. We loved every minute of it and pounded our hands on the top of our legs adding to the rhythm of the fiddle and the sound of Keeten's feet against the bare floor. Uncle John played "Copperhead in a Pine Knot Hole" and "Granny Put the Kettle on" on his fiddle as he tapped the floor with his foot. Then he switched over to "Fire on the Mountain" which was just about my favorite piece ever. He played on, into the evening, until everyone was tired. Then as a last request, to tell everyone that he wouldn't play anymore, he finished with "Fiddler's Drunk and the Fun's All Over." After that Aunt Susan popped popcorn and everyone sat around telling ghost stories.

Uncle John with his fiddle and Aunt Susan (The fiddle was left to Emily Howard and passed on to Joyce.)

"So what will it be?" asked Old Man Keeten. He was a wonderful storyteller and he loved entertaining Woodrow and me.

"Tell the story about the German and his Indian wife," Woodrow barked. I settled back against Woodrow's back, because I loved this one too.

"Oh, well that's a good one, son," he said, tapping his pipe against his shoe. Now there was this Indian woman who lived over near what we call Hoss Hole now, but back then they called it White Owl Valley, because basically it was full of owls. They'd hoot in the daylight there were so many, and they felt safe in all those numbers. It was the hooting of the owls that the Indian woman loved, you see. They kept her company and she'd sing with them when she felt like it. That's how the German found her."

"What was he doing?" Woodrow asked.

"Well son, he was hunting for gold in the mountains, gold he'd heard about from people down in the next county. He'd heard that Indians and Civil War generals had hid gold in the caves all around White Owl Valley, and he was hoping to find himself some of that gold."

"Did he find any?" I asked. I would be interested in finding some of that myself.

"Oh no, Emily darling. He certainly did not. But when he came through White Owl Valley he heard the most beautiful singing he'd ever heard, and when he peeked through the trees, he saw that Indian girl working in her garden. He decided then and there that he was going to marry that girl, and make her his wife."

"And did he?" Woodrow asked.

"Oh yes, and so he did. And they got on well for a few years, you know. The only thing that the German grew to dislike about his little wife is that each and every night before they went to bed, she would tell him that she loved White Owl Valley and would never leave it. Now he loved her very much, but he wanted to find that gold too, and he knew that he'd searched every cave high and low around White Owl Valley and hadn't found a thing, so he was getting an itch to move on."

"And so he ignored her wishes," I said, knowing full well that he did.

"Oh yes, he did, little lady," Keeten chuckled. "He got drunk after a night of dancing and fiddle and banjo playing. He got into a deal with a man there at the party and he signed the sale papers. Later that morning after he'd sobered up, he went to tell his wife."

"Was she waiting for him?" Woodrow asked dramatically.

"Well, in a manner of speaking, yes she was." Keeten paused for dramatic effect and I pressed myself even closer to my brother. "You see, she was dressed up in her white wedding dress, and she was hanging from a tree. She had heard about that deal the German had made with his friend, and she had no intention of leaving. So, she hung herself. Oh, but that's not all," he said after taking a smoke off his pipe. "You see, the man was so upset he tried to cut her body down, but all of a sudden these owls swarmed out of the trees and started attacking him."

"What did he do?" I almost screamed, imagining the claws of those owls digging into my neck and my head.

"He fell out of that tree and he ran as fast as he could! He made it for the cabin and locked the door behind him. And wouldn't you know that those owls pounded the cabin door all night long, mad as hornets about what he'd done to his wife? Why the next morning he had to get neighbors to get her out of the tree to bury her, and he left as quick as he could for Texas, just to get away from the white owls of White Owl Valley." Woodrow and I clapped enthusiastically and the rest of the room broke out into laughter and applause.

Everyone soon left and I slipped into bed with Aunt Susan. I tucked my knees against her and snuggled down into the big feather bed thinking about the haunting figure of that Indian woman in her flowing white dress as she swayed in the wind. Her hair blew all around her like twisting snakes, and the owls swooped around her like bats. I shivered and Aunt Susan patted me reassuringly. "You go to sleep and stop thinking about that story, or you won't have any appetite for breakfast in the morning, baby." Those words were the charm, because my scary visions gave away to dreams of eggs and sausage and hot biscuits smothered in jelly and honey.

Late the next evening we left for home. It was a fall evening, the first chill of the winter winds were upon us. I helped with the dishes Woodrow helped bring in wood for the fire. We were both tired after the visit and Aunt Susan had loaded us down with food for the family. We went to sleep listening to the howling gusts beat against the little cabin door and talking about our panther and telling ghost stories.

The next morning we let the cows out to graze in the mountains. When evening came and it was time to fetch the cows we were still talking about the panther. Woodrow said, "Emily let's ride the cows in and if the panther comes it will get the cows first and not us." I had never ridden a cow. Afraid to climb on, Woodrow pushed me up onto the back of one of the old heifer and away we went. We screamed and laughed as we steered the cows back home. This would become our daily routine.

It was peaceful on the mountain. Everyone seemed settled. We now had three milk cows, Cherry, Jersey and Pretty. When Pappy first brought the cows up the holler he said, "One is for Emily, one is for Woodrow and one is for Bessie. Now, pick the one you want." There was one with a bad burn on her back and some of her tail burned, her color was almost red and she had a real pretty head. I said, "I want her, Pappy and I will doctor her up and she will be real pretty." Bessie wanted the smallest one and Woodrow wanted the biggest and light colored one. So it was, we each had our own cow.

We learned to take care of the cows and chickens and the guineas. To this day I love guineas, with their round bodies and black feathers with round white spots all over them. They were like little watch dogs. When anyone came around they let out a strange sound unlike the chickens, which said you had company, but otherwise they were quiet. They hid their nests making it difficult to find their eggs, often laying them in a stump hole or in a hole in the ground. Mother used a long handle spoon to dip the eggs out of the nest, because just touching the nest made the guineas quit the nest.

Mother taught all of us to milk the cows, but I caught onto it fast and was chosen to do most of the milking. I sat on the stool, grabbing the tits and in rhythm pulled and pumped them, filling the pale with warm, sudsy fresh milk. I loved to churn the butter too, and became very good at it.

Our soap was homemade. A large black cast-iron pot used to boil clothes in was also used for making lye soap. A hot fire was built and the pot was placed over the hot coals. We saved pork grease for the soap. Liquid was strained from a tub of ashes and soaked for days. The alkaline liquor was poured into the hot pot, pork grease was added and was stirred until thick. Small amounts were poured onto a flat board to test the thickness. The blend was poured into molds and cooled then cut into bars of lye soap. It was an all day job, but a means of having enough soap for the whole clan.

I remember those days so clearly and how much work it was. But we had so much fun having Pappy with us and being together as a family. I felt sure that it would all go on forever and we had finally found a routine that we could live with all the rest of our lives. Riding the cow's home, tending the animals and planting the garden to keep us in food. But a shadow passed over our lives in December, when Lloyd Lankford delivered the news. Uncle John passed away. It was a shock to everyone, but especially to Woodrow and me.

He was an old man by this time, being over 70 years old, but no one had expected it. He seemed like the kind of strong man who'd never leave us, and it seemed like it just stunned everyone. "Most likely a heart attack," I heard Lloyd Lankford say. He waited for Mother to get ready. He had a car waiting down the holler, but they had to walk a long ways out of the holler to get to the car.

Mother looked down at Woodrow and me and said, "Now children, I am sorry your Pappy and I have to leave you for your Granddaddy has died and gone to be with Jesus. Don't cry for he is now with our other family already in heaven. Watch out for Ray and Bessie. I will be back as soon as I possibly can. I love you and I will pray for you."

We said little after she left. I thought I would choke to death. We both took turns crying. He was a good man. I could not come to terms with him leaving and never coming back.

Late in the afternoon Mother returned and said Pappy was staying with Aunt Susan and the doctor had to give her something to make her sleep. Dallas would be staying also, but Murphy would be home later.

The day of the funeral was heartbreaking. I looked at poor Uncle John for hours. He looked like he was just asleep. His thick dark hair was partly gray and combed so pretty down a little on his forehead and swept back from the sides just like he wore it. His handlebar mustache was neatly brushed. How I wished that he would open his blue eyes and speak to me and hold me on his lap as he always did. I slipped my hand up to his face and gently touched him, my thoughts of his sweet kindness and fiddle playing.

"One more round of Fire on the Mountain?" I whispered the question to him, but he would not answer. It seemed so wrong that his face would be so cold when it was always so warm and crinkled from smiling. Sweet loveable Uncle John who had kept the family from starving many times was gone forever.

My heart was breaking. The house was full of people; someone put their arms around me. I was blinded by tears and could see no one.

People were crying all over the house. When they moved the casket out, loading it on the wagon for the journey to the cemetery, Aunt Susan held onto the back of the wagon crying and calling his name. Her cries were chilling as she screamed out, "John, please don't leave me." Some of the men had to tear her hands loose. She and Uncle John had never been separated.

Doctor Howard and Doctor Cawood helped her to the house and gave her a sedative. She soon fell into a strange restless sleep. She could not be alone, neighbors took turns watching out for her and Dallas moved in to continue caring for her.

Things began to settle and everyone kept busy trying to overcome the sorrow. We'd been told keeping busy and trying to be a help to someone else was the best way to overcome sorrow. Mother said, "Children, don't ever just live for yourself, always try to be a blessing to someone else as you pass through this life, for life here on earth is far too short to live it selfishly."

She was right. Wasn't Uncle John the most unselfish man in the world, second only to Pappy himself? Like Aunt Susan, I didn't want to think what life would be like without him. And now he had joined the rest of our family up in Kitt's cemetery. Soon the wailing would stop and the people would leave. He would sit with the rest of the family and catch them up on what we were doing down here. He'd tell them about mother and Pappy and all the kids, even me. They would welcome him into their world with open arms. Please keep Uncle John safe. We will miss him so.

Uncle John and Aunt Susan (Aunt Susan always wore the beautiful broach
with gold chain
and matching earrings). A tintype

CHAPTER 13: The Election

That January I remember my parents sitting in front of the fire grate talking. Mother said, "Milt, I hope this will be the last baby. This year has been so hard. I just don't have the strength anymore to do the things I need to be doing."

Pappy agreed with her. He was fifty-one that month and Mama was forty-seven just that May. They were talking about their sixteenth child. "Yes," he said with a smile, "I guess we both do feel a little tired."

And so her birthing time came, and on the evening of January 24, 1929 another girl was born. "We shall call her Ruby Lugene Blanch Howard," said Pappy. "She is going to be tiny like Emily." Mother suffered through the birth barely remembering the midwife saying, "She's pretty, with very fair skin and I believe she will have blue eyes and blond curly hair."

The midwife told Pappy to keep a close watch on Mother and the baby and to keep them warm. Our house had no insulation and the heat from the hearth put out very little warmth. The midwife again checked the new baby before leaving saying she would return. When the midwife returned the following morning with her black bag, she pulled up a chair and sat down beside Martha's bed leaving the black bag on the floor.

Little Bessie kept circling around and around the bag looking strangely at it, finally got in front of the midwife and frowned as she looked up into her face with her hands on her hips. She pointed to the black bag on the floor asked her if she'd brought another baby in the black bag. The midwife laughed heartily and said, "No little one, I don't have another one this time."

Mother was older and each birth was harder than the last. She had scar tissue from having so many babies. The midwife warned Pappy that she should not have more children.

Ruby was an easy child to tend for she was small like me. Our parents often left for the day leaving them in my care. I was now a good cook and had learned to organize work early in life, first cleaning the house and deciding how to entertain brothers and sisters and planning the evening meal. Ruby was growing fast, often running after Bessie or trying to catch butterflies.

Little Bessie was five before her ears quit bothering her. Mother was real pleased with the way she was growing. Ray was seven and still pretty sickly and hardly strong enough to go to school. The doctor said it would be better to wait and start him at eight, then maybe his legs would be stronger. I told Ray not to worry, because I didn't get to go to school until I was eight and it really wasn't so bad to wait. The doctor said that he had rickets, which caused his bones to be soft caused from a lack of vitamin D. There were too many children to properly clothe them much the less feed them. We often went to bed with a slice of cornbread and were glad for it.

Woodrow was now thirteen and I was ten. One day Mother went down into the coal camp to visit friends from church leaving us to care for the house and children. We took Ray, Bessie and Blanch around the hill to play.

We found a large long piece of tin, bent up one end and slid down the side of the mountain onto an old slate dump. Woodrow rode Ray and I rode Bessie. Taking turns we dragged the old piece of tin up high on the mountain for a good start, not realizing how fast it could go. We settled in for a nice ride, Bessie in front, me holding her from behind. The tin picked up speed, giving us the fastest ride of our lives. I leaned way back trying to slow down the tin, but that did not help. When we approached the landing place, the tin hit the landing and continued right on over into a large brier thicket. I thought Bessie was dead. I had torn my fingernails off trying to stop. I said, "Bessie, are you hurt?"

"No," she replied, "I not hurt, less do dats adain." Woodrow helped pull us out of the briers. Again, our guardian angel was with us.

We had lots of adventures that tested the skill of our guardian angels. As the Howard Clan was growing, Woodrow and I were the closest team, going everywhere together and filling our days with climbing trees and playing in the woods. I always went along with Woodrow's ideas because they always seemed so fun.

Once he decided that we should get Pappy's axe and cut a grapevine to swing on.

"Pappy might find out and we'll be in trouble. He won't let anyone have his axe, Woodrow. He uses it for hunting and carries it on the side of his overalls to cut kindling wood or uses it for fishing. He will surely have it with him today."

Woodrow found his storing place and off we went with the axe anyway, soon cutting down a grapevine a long ways back in the woods. It wound up a tall tree on the side of a steep deep holler. Woodrow cut the vine loose at the base of the tree. I was scared, begging him not to swing out over the holler. He grabbed hold and off he leaped going way out over the steep holler. He realized then that he was in danger. I thought I would burst with fear and began to cry. As he swung back I quickly grabbed him before he lost his footing and swung out again. He turned loose of the vine and fell down on the ground looking pale as death.

"Woodrow, don't ever do that again. I know our guardian angel was with us. You could have been killed or drug me off this bluff." We were suddenly tired of poking around the cliffs, climbing trees, watching the ground squirrels and almost getting killed. We hurried back trying to return the axe before Pappy discovered it missing.

We used the axe other times though, slipping it out to cut small bushes to build a cabin, which looked more like a pig pen. We were never caught. We hated for night to come. It was just a big waste of time. Our days were filled with adventures looking for caves and odd rocks, different colored butterflies, frogs, bugs, and birds.

We feared getting caught by Pappy, but he had more important things going on than to get caught up in our adventures. Pappy was being recruited for local political office.

Elections were important in Harlan. I remember the day Pappy's friends stopped by to ask him to run for Justice-of-the-Peace. A Magistrate was the only judge who didn't have to go to Law School. "Milt," they said, "You have a good education and you are well liked by the people of Harlan." Pappy had got the "three R's," reading, writing and arithmetic, which meant he had gone through the lower grades. His friends were sure that he'd win. They said, "We know if you run for the office you will get it. We've been out in the county and most everyone we talked to is for you running for the office." Lloyd Lankford was one of my Pappy's best friends and was one of the main ones pushing him on, telling him that he was the man for the job.

Pappy said, "Lloyd, I've never thought of running for any kind of public office and I don't intend to. I could never be a magistrate." His friends were persistent but so was he and he wouldn't give in.

After they left Mother asked, "Don't you think you could handle the job?"

"I don't know, I've never thought about it, but I know I don't want the job." As Magistrate, Pappy would handle marriages and hear cases in small claims court, which was one step under the circuit court. Election year brought many people out of the mountains to hear the speeches going on at night at the courthouse. Pappy enjoyed the speaking and asked Woodrow and me if we wanted to go. He made us promise not to go to sleep.

At dusk off we went, stopping by the country store for a box of salty crackers and a bag of chocolate cream center candy. We chose a seat close to the speakers and ate. Soon though we were tired and fidgety. Pappy eased his arms around us, pulling us close to his body for warmth. Soon we were fast asleep.

After the speaking we were awakened for the long walk home. Pappy could not carry us with his crutches and us so we had no choice but to wake up completely. Soon we were skipping along beside Pappy singing and laughing.

Well I think that Pappy went that night just to see what he was in for if he decided to run. And what he saw decided him on the idea that he couldn't run. As certain as he was though, his friends never let up on him. They were

 determined to get him in the office and he was just as determined to avoid talking to them. He'd walk into the mountains and hide all day, but they found him everywhere he went. He could not

escape, so he finally gave in and announced his candidacy for the office of Justice-of-the-Peace. When his name and picture came out in the paper announcing his candidacy, you could just tell by the look on his face that he didn't take to it willingly.

He was running in District One. I thought to myself, "Poor Pappy looks like a farmer dressed in bib overalls holding his crutches." Mama was also worried that he looked his best. She'd taken great care to iron both his shirt and his bib overalls, but even the bib didn't hide the missing buttons from his shirt and the frayed collar. I tried to encourage her. "At least he doesn't chew tobacco and sit around the town square hocking and spitting onto the street like the hillbillies do. He does have dignity."

We shouldn't have worried. Pappy was well respected in our area. He had traveled the mountains selling ginseng, books and shoes for years and everyone knew he was an honest man and that his family had never been in trouble.

He was in a race against those who knew all the tricks of a veteran politician, but he wrote out his platform and it was published in the Harlan paper for everyone to read. Pappy had a great sense of humor and he basically told it like it was. Pretty soon it was clear from the talk going around town that no one believed his opponents anyway, because they'd all had dealings with Pappy. They'd also had dealings with his opponents, and the choice became pretty clear. He told the people what he stood for and the fight was on. When Election Day arrived and the votes were all counted he won in the primary in a landslide.

He was in shock when the news was announced.

"That was August 3, 1929, the day your father was as scared as I've ever seen him," Mother said. "He had a fight on to win in the final election in November. People came from everywhere to congratulate him. That at least seemed to give him courage and he seemed surer of himself. His friends had stood by him helping with posters and handouts. He worked hard pleasing the people. He was gone every day talking."

Everyone wanted him to win and our family got in on the excitement, listening to him talk and reading his speeches in the papers. Days were spent working long hard hours traveling around the county, shaking hands and talking to people. The big day grew closer and closer. His friends said, "Milty, we need to be at the polls when they open."

He was nervous, I could tell. We waited anxiously for the news. The next morning we learned he had again won by a landslide. We all cheered, laughed and cried in excitement. Right after he won, all his friends chipped in to buy him a suit, the first one he ever owned.

Everyone was so happy. We talked about how he could now earn steady money and take care of the family and Mama wouldn't have to work as hard. It was strange to think that Pappy had never really had a steady job before in his life, and now in his fifties he would actually be going to work. Mama was very pleased, and seemed to think that this came at just the right time in their lives. "Now the children can have decent clothes to wear," she said. "Yes, it surely will be a great blessing for all of us."

I listened to this and thought, "We can have good food like Aunt Susan and I can get some pretty clothes and I won't be made fun of anymore." I daydreamed about that for hours and I finished up the chores that day. I would be able to go to school with my head held high in store bought clothes and new shoes each year. I kept this up until the aroma from the kitchen brought me around. We celebrated the day with fried chicken, biscuits, gravy, mashed potatoes and a piping hot blackberry cobbler.

Pappy and his friends were pleased with the way the election turned out. He began spending most of his time away from home, up at the courthouse with friends. Soon he was able to take office.

But as time went on, it became clear to us that the election would not improve our lives, either where money was concerned or in our family.

Before Uncle John died, things had been so happy. But the election changed Pappy completely, and I started to really hate that he'd ever even thought of running for office. I started to miss the father that I had known all my life, because someone completely different replaced him.

Even years into his new position, Pappy was foul-tempered and tight with his money. I didn't realize it at first, because it just seemed like a bad mood, but Pappy had taken up drinking. He wasn't used to having so much free time, because before he had to work for everything we had, and work very hard. Now he was expected to be at the courthouse, and he got into bad company up there. He started drinking just a little at first, but it got to be more and more the longer he worked there.

He barely gave mother enough money for seeds and plants for the garden and food. I overheard her tell Aunt Susan," Milty has changed since he went into office. He gets angry every time I ask for anything. He is so tight he seems afraid to turn loose a dime."

Aunt Susan said, "Martha I suppose it's because he has never had much of anything and is afraid to spend it. I think he wants to save it for worse times."

Mother said, "I don't know what to make of it Susan, but I do know that there couldn't be much worse times than now. The children need clothes and we just barely have food enough to go on until my garden comes in."

"Well, all I know to tell you is just bear with him for a while longer. I will try to get a chance to talk to him and see if I can get him to do better." Mother hung her head and I heard her half whispered, "I hope so for he is drinking heavily, he's becoming more like a demon and less like the man I fell in love with on Coxton Mountain."

I know that Mama tried to be a good Christian and pray for Pappy. She prayed for him all the time, and encouraged us to do the same. She took us to church knowing he would not go with her. She wondered if he planned to keep all the money for his drinking now that he was in office.

I especially remember Palm Sunday that year because he was in such a foul mood. He had come in drinking the night before. He yelled at Mother, "Martha, you are not going to church and you are not taking them younguns!"

"Oh yes, I am," she insisted.

He roared, "What are you going to do, make Holy Rollers out of them like you are?" Mother replied, "There is nothing in the world I'd rather they would be." With that she said, "Come on children we will be late for Sunday school." She spoke in gentle tones, direct and strong.

We all knew Pappy was drinking. When he drank he had daggers in his eyes. Mother led us out of the house. As we left we could hear the sound of furniture being thrown and the table turning over.

Woodrow said, "Mom is Pappy tearing the house down?" Mother said, "Don't worry about what he does."

Woodrow insisted. "Mother, we better go back, he's tearing up everything."

She said, "Just let him. There will always be houses and furniture, but there is only one time to serve the Lord." But Pappy would not be ignored. He stumbled out onto the porch with his gun and screamed, "Martha, if you don't come back I will kill your best laying hen." She replied, "And if you do you will surely pay for it."

He walked out into the yard, took aim and shot her best laying hen. She turned, walked back to the hen, picked it up and never said a word as she walked off the mountain without a backward glance. She stopped on the way to church at a friend's house and told us to wait. She knocked on the door and told her friend that Pappy had shot the chicken, for her to cook dinner and they would be back by to eat when church was over.

I prayed hard that day in church, as they talked about Jesus coming into the city and all the crowd cheering him on. It was hard to concentrate on the message, because I was sure I was going to look over my shoulder and see Pappy heading for the door to get mama and us. Instead we just prayed with the congregation and tried to find some peace in the whole matter. I looked at mama though, and wondered if she felt alone now that Pappy was so different. It had to be breaking her heart.

After church was over, we headed back to her friend's house. Mother always fixed Sunday dinner, but today we ate there instead. We played for a while then left for home.

Pappy acted like nothing happened while we helped her clean up all the mess that he made. He had even used his crutch to punch a hole through her cabinet door. Mother never said a word, told us to say prayers and everyone went to bed.

The next morning when he started to leave for his office Mother said, "Milt, I want a dollar and a half for my best laying hen that you killed." He cursed and said with a stony look on his face, "I'll pay you nothing."

She had a look of disgust on her face, but said calmly, "if you don't I will come to town today and take a warrant out for you and make you pay for it." Pappy's face got blistering red with rage. He knew she meant it. He angrily tossed her the money and stomped on off down the mountain. It was never mentioned again. Mother turned to us and said, "Well, before I married your father I felt like a butterfly flying all over beautiful flowers and instead of lighting on a flower I landed on a pile of shit." It was the first and last time that I ever heard her say a bad word against my father. It made me worry about what our future held for us, with the two of them at war.

Milty Howard and Martha (his shirt collar was worn to shreds)

Time went on and Pappy just became tighter and tighter with money. A woman down in the camp sold Mother three dresses for fifty cents because her daughter had outgrown them. They just fit me, and I was proud to get them because they were prettier than any dress I had ever had. They were perfect for school.

But Aunt Susan never did get a chance to talk to Pappy about his ways with money. Late one evening, Lloyd Lankford, who had been made Deputy Sheriff after the election, again brought us bad news. Aunt Susan had fallen and broken her hip. One of her neighbors found her lying on the floor and maggots were in her side from being there alone for days. Dallas was staying with her at the time, but had left for several days to visit friends. They didn't find her until days later and late up in the evening.

Mother left immediately. She told Woodrow to help watch the children and asked me to fix supper. Everyone was scared. As I fixed supper I thought about all the things Aunt Susan had done for me, all the things she had made. There were school clothes and hats, meals and lots of love. But it had been some time since Uncle John and passed, and she really hadn't been the same since. Now it looked like she would be going to meet him. Woodrow and I talked about the meals she cooked and the gentle way she disciplined us when we threw the corn all over her yard.

"Woodrow, I hope Aunt Susan will be alright. Do you think she will be okay?"

He said, "Well, Pappy will see to it that she gets a good doctor and people do get over having a broken hip." He sounded sure, but I had such a bad feeling about it. That night we had beans, fried potatoes and baked corn bread with fresh milk and butter. When Murphy came in he said, "Pappy and

Mom will stay with Aunt Susan. I won't be going to work in the morning and I will help look after things."

But Aunt Susan didn't make it through the night. Dr. Cawood said it was too much on her heart. She was in shock when she was found and just wasn't strong enough to pull out of it. She had fallen onto the floor and lay there several days. She had even dragged herself across the floor and had tried to eat, but could not get up.

I was beside myself. Dear sweet Aunt Susan, who had cooked and fed hundreds of people, raised and mothered so many children, who had such a great big heart of love was gone. "I will never get to snuggle up to her in her big feather bed again," I thought. "I won't get to sit in the big chair while she cooks or eat at the long table. Now they are both gone. How could death be this bad? How could I get away from this terrible feeling like everything was closing in on me? Poor Dallas was deeply hurt. He had stayed with her ever since Uncle John passed away. He felt guilty for staying away for days without checking on her.

But Mother was calm. She said, "When God's children die they go to Heaven to always be with God. Aunt Susan and Uncle John were God's children, so they are together again." My brother Murphy could tell that I was feeling horrible, and gently lifted me in his arms. He said, "Now honey, everything is going to be alright. Aunt Susan was real lonesome for Uncle John and now she is happy again."

Murphy had a warm heart for me and just held me close in his arms. Finally I could wrap my arms around his neck and cry, even though I was afraid I couldn't stop. Murphy knew that after I cried I'd feel better, and he was right.

The service was on the side of the mountain. The rocky road made it rough to haul Aunt Susan to the cemetery as she was still a large woman. A gully wash the night before had washed the road away in places and the logging trails made it hard to travel. Sometimes the horse pulling the wagon loaded with the casket stopped. He seemed to know that he was taking her away forever. She often had given him apples out of the orchard and patted his nose while he nuzzled her face. Even that old horse would miss her. The ground was wet, the fresh earth was piled around the grave and she was swiftly lowered into the ground.

In the sweet by and by,
We shall meet on that beautiful shore;
In the sweet by and by
We shall meet on that beautiful shore.

We shall sing on that beautiful shore
The melodious songs of the blessed;
And our spirits shall sorrow no more,
Not a sigh for the blessing of the rest.

To our bountiful Father above,
We will offer our tribute of praise
For the glorious gift of His love
And the blessings that hallow our days.

After the funeral, mother told Dallas to stay on at Aunt Susan's house and take care of things. No one talked about it, but we all wondered how we'd get on without her. We had to, so we had no choice but to go on. It was the mountain way. We had to accept the heartaches, whatever they may be and get on with life. There was no time for long periods of mourning, or the family would not survive.

And Mama was there to take our minds off our loss. One evening after supper everyone was sitting around and she said, "Children let's take Polly and go possum hunting." Polly was our dog. Catching on to Mother's plan, I said, "I will go." Naturally, Woodrow wanted to go too. Mother said, "Children the moon will be out tonight and it will be a real nice time to catch a possum." So she got her lantern and put oil in it and excitedly we called Polly, a shaggy Airedale.

Off we went. Murphy laughed and said, "Don't let a bear get you." Ray came running and said, "I want to go too." We went around the mountainside and up the hill. We walked for some time when mother said, "Now this is a nice spot, let's rest a while."

She sat the lantern down and we all lay down on the ground. The night was warm and nice. We listened to the chirping of nightlife all around us. We were staring at the moon, talking about possum, when mother whispered, "Be still and quiet, I see a possum." I thought she was kidding and said, "Why Mom, you don't."

She replied, "I really do and I see its ears twitching. Look up there in that tree." Mother pointed toward the tree. We all looked and sure enough there it was. I said, "Mom, I will climb the tree and shake it out and Woodrow, can get Polly under the tree so she can catch it." Up the tree I scooted and shook it out. It hit the ground and ran to a hole under a rock. Polly ran wagging her tail and barking with excitement, just barely grabbing it by the tail.

The commotion was fierce. Mother got it by the tail then and we were all laughing and screaming. Hours later we showed up at the house with a tired, disgusted possum bundled up in a bag. We'd all thought she was taking us out for a fun evening, and she had, but no one expected to catch anything. Pappy and Murphy were surprised when we walked in with our catch. Everyone talked about the adventure in the woods well into the night while Proud Polly slept by the door.

Mother put that possum under a washtub for the night. Every day for the next two or three months she kept that possum under a washtub like a pet, fattening it up on sweet potatoes and cornbread until it could be killed. Then she'd dress it up and bake it.

Monday morning came and school time began again. I jumped out of bed excited and anxious to get started. This year my shoes had holes in the side, but they were clean and they were the only pair I owned. I wore one of the dresses Mother bought from the lady down the mountain. Thankfully it was still warm enough that I didn't have to wear my old thick stockings. I could go bare legged for a while yet. Woodrow had a new pair of overalls and a checked blue shirt. He went to school barefoot.

And that's how school began for us, walking quietly down the mountain, the fog just lifting and the ground wet with dew. We wouldn't have to stay all day, so we decided not to take a lunch. As we got almost out of the holler, Jane Orliff was waiting for me. She was one of my best friends. She lived in one of the camp houses near the holler. We talked and laughed all the way to school. When we got there, Silvia, Elnera, Ruth, and Lilly were looking for us. It was wonderful to see them again, and everyone started talking at the same time.

"Emily, have you heard that Silvia has a new sweetheart?"

"Who is it?" I gasped.

"It's Neal Harrison," sang Ruth. We all gathered around her to hear all about the date that she had gone on with Neal. She was beaming, and we were all jealous. "Where did you go, Silvia?" I wanted to know.

"We took a walk by the river and had a picnic."

"I just wonder that it was only a picnic," Elnera said. "Did he kiss you?"

"I'm not telling that." Silvia jutted her chin out and refused to talk. Just then the bell rang and we all ran to get in line. If only she hadn't cut her conversation short. I stood in line with the others and thought about what it would be like to have a sweetheart that would take me on a picnic.

Miss Nickles was my teacher. She was known to spank and be hard, but everything went off real good for all she did was having roll call and give a pep talk. We had to stay about two hours, and then were dismissed. All the girls got together and went down on the riverbank to talk and play.

The riverbank was a great place to play. The air was cool and everyone liked to gather next to the heavily rushing water and walk or play or tell all the tall tales they could before it was time to go home. I could have spent hours there with my friends. But I always had to be careful, for if Woodrow beat me home Mother would be worried and wonder where I was. They all walked with me to where I turned up the holler. My friend June walked on farther with me to where she left for her house. There was a large flat rock and we climbed up on it and sat and talked for a while.

June wasn't too happy at home. Her parents were getting old and weren't very understanding. She said she was glad that we were friends. "So am I," I said.

We were in sight of June's house. It seemed strange that her mother kept looking out at us. She soon yelled, "June you git on home." She looked mean when she screamed at June. I felt bad for June and terrified of her mother. I took off running for home.

Mother watched me coming up the hill and asked, "Where on earth have you been?" I told her I had been talking to June. She said," From now on young lady you come on home. I have enough to worry about."

Late that Friday evening, we had an enormous surprise. Grandmother Whitson slipped in unexpectedly. Everyone was surprised and real happy to see her. She came all the way from Coxton Mountain. It was the first time in years she had had an opportunity to visit because she couldn't travel very far at a time. The only means of transportation our grandparents had was the mule and sled. Sam brought her to the house and then went back. He didn't like to visit and never spent a night away from home. Grandmother Whitson had plans to stay until Sunday then Sam would be back for her.

I watched mother. I knew they were enjoying being together again. Mother fixed food then showed her about the place.

I didn't know Grandmother very well, and we'd only visited them a few times, for it was a long ways to Magazine Holler where they lived. I remembered being scared of their many dogs. When Sam opened the cabin door we would run inside. I could remember running and jumping in the bed, which tickled them. They loved to tease me. "Emily that dog won't bite such a pretty little girl. It will hardly bite a flea." But I stayed in the bed until time to leave.

My thoughts were interrupted with Mother telling me to kiss grandmother goodnight. That night I drifted off listening to their quiet gentle chattering. I wondered what my life would be like when I was old enough to have a husband and a life of my own. Would I be so far away from my mother that I almost never saw her? Would she come to visit me in my home so that I could show her how I had grown up? Would I find a man who loved and cared for me the way that Pappy cared for Mother? How big would my own family be?

All the next day they cooked and sewed and walked around the garden and the woods, talking and laughing and telling each other secrets that only mothers and daughters can share. The rest of the family kind of took care of themselves while they caught up on all the news they could not share while they were apart.

"I came as soon as I heard about Susan," Grandmother told her. "I was so sorry to hear about her going down like that. She was such a good woman."

"Yes she was," Mother said softly. "I'm not sure what we will do without her and John. There have been so many winters when we surely wouldn't have made it without them. I am a little afraid for the family."

"I thought that Milty was making regular money now that he's Magistrate."

"He is making regular money, but he won't share it with us at all. I have to scrape by worse than before. He drinks a lot of it."

Grandmother seemed to fret over this. "I never expected him to get a taste for liquor. We will have to pray about that situation, my girl. I wish I had more to offer you. I wish my Sam and I could afford to help you the way John and Susan could. But all I have to offer are my prayers."

"Your prayers are enough; I have faith in God's goodness. He will not leave me without His divine help."

We ended the evening with fiddling and the banjo and the boys dancing so much that Grandmother laughed and laughed. Before we went to bed, she brushed each child on the cheek with her hand, leaned up close so we could feel her breath on our ears as she said, "I will always love you, even if I never see you again. You are that special to me. Your mother is like the moon, and all of you are like the stars. I will always know that you are there, and will always be praying for you."

The night flew by and I woke to the sound of Grandfather Whitson leaving for Coxton Mountain. I ran to say goodbye and watched as her as she climbed onto the flatbed hitched to the mule. Sam yelled, "giddy up, giddy up." Grandmother Whitson would have a rough, rocky ride off that mountain. They were soon out of sight, and everyone went about getting ready for school.

It was a typical Monday until I walked home with June and she said, "Anna Bee is back. I heard that they got back sometime this morning."

Mr. and Mrs. Steegeal had moved from Sanduskey, Ohio about two years ago. Their daughter Anna Bee and son Creed had become real good friends. But they had left to find work elsewhere. This was pretty common for people in our area. When times were hard you had to go where the work was. "June, I wish I had of known, we could have went by and saw them." June said, "I figured they were real tired after their trip." "Yes," I said, "I guess you are right." When Woodrow got home I told him that Creed was back and would be in school the next day. We were eager to see our friends again, but the next day they weren't back in school. During lunch we ran over to their house to see them.

We were all happy to see each other. Mr. and Mrs. Steegeal hugged us and invited us to dinner but we said we wouldn't care for any. I was feeling hungry, but too bashful to eat in front of them. I was sure they could hear my stomach growling. Mr. Steegeal brought us a nice bowl of hot tapioca pudding and said, "You may not be hungry but I know you can eat some of mom's good pudding." He left us and went back to the table. We ate the pudding and scraped the bowl it was so good. Creed and Anna Bee weren't going to school today either, so we got ready to go back. Before we left though, Woodrow said, "Why don't we just stay and play with Creed and Anna Bee this evening? No one will find out." That scared me. I'd never skipped school. Woodrow had played hooky before, but he said it was only for the afternoon. It sure sounded enticing. Finally I agreed.

The day was ending and it was time to go home. We had to walk past a colored school and I was afraid of them. As we rounded the hill a colored boy followed us up the hill. He started hitting Woodrow with a basket. Woodrow did not act scared and told the boy in a rough voice to leave us alone. The boy hit again. Woodrow grabbed his basket and smacked him across the head. The boy ran for his life. We both stood and laughed. I was always safe with Woodrow. Or so I thought.

But that night I had troubled dreams about what Mother had said about Aunt Susan, and how it meant that our family might have some real tough times ahead. I just couldn't go to sleep at all, and I got up the next morning cranky and miserable.

To top it off, the next day the teacher kept Woodrow after school. When I was alone an older girl bullied me. The girl watched daily for me to be alone. She knew she was too large to fight. I tried to run away from her, but the girl hit me and kicked me in the shins. Every day she caught me alone was miserable. So when Woodrow was kept after school I decided to wait for him and not be caught alone with Polly. "Emily, I want you to stop running from Polly," he told me days later. "I know if you will try you can whip her." "She's bigger than I am. I can't whip her."

"Yes, you can," he said. "Take her by surprise and when she starts slapping you around; just go right into her with everything you've got. If you don't she will just keep right on beating on you. Now this evening, you go on ahead of me and I will be watching and if you don't whip her, I am going to whip you." He had never threatened me before and I thought about what he said. The more I thought the angrier I got. "Well, I'll surely not take two whippings."

I took off for home thinking of what I would do if Polly were waiting. To get home, I had to cross a hanging bridge. Polly had to cross the bridge and turn to the right to go home, while I turned to the left. Right at the bridge Polly was waiting for me. She stood there looking making a face and showing her nails as if she were going to scratch me. I looked into her face and remembered all the times I had been kicked and slapped by her and the anger welled up in me. I dropped my books where I stood and tore into Polly, scratching and hitting her like a wild child. Polly started screaming and ran as fast as her fat legs could carry her across the river into ankle deep water. I screamed, "Polly, you better never jump on me again. If you try I will beat you to a pulp." Woodrow was behind me laughing. Tears were running down his face. "See there, I told you that you could do it." He said, "Emily don't ever let anyone get their bluff on you again." I felt better than I'd felt ever since my worries started about my family. I was wrong to be afraid of the future. If Woodrow couldn't look out for me, I could always look out for myself.

CHAPTER 15: School Yard Games

School was a wonderful thing, in my opinion. I could get a break from all the chores that we had at our house. I could be with my friends before and after school, and when I was in the one room schoolhouse, I could learn all kinds of things.

And I think our schoolhouse was fine. There was a warm wood heater in the middle of the room, and students in different grade levels were grouped in different areas around it. We all sat on split logs that had legs on them to keep them steady, but the teacher had a pretty little desk from finished lumber. Near the door was a little water shelf that held the bucket for water, and when we were thirsty we could ask for permission to go over and dip a drink out with a little dipper made from a gourd. We also had to raise our hands and ask permission to use the bathroom, which meant going into the woods.

Being in a room with so many different grades was very exciting, because if your class was boring you could listen to what the others were doing, because everything was recited. There were many times after I got the hang of school that I would quietly answer questions that the teacher was asking another grade.

There were those times when I didn't feel so good about not having good clothes to wear, but I was more than a match at anything I set my mind to in schoolwork or in the playground and I didn't have to worry about not keeping up in other areas. I was proud, and besides that many others came from poor families too, so what meant something to mountain people was if you were strong, if you stayed out of trouble and if you were honest. I was all of those things. I was also known for my legs.

I remember playing on the playground. Some high-school girls were watching. They yelled for me to walk over to them. I joined them where they stood by a rock wall. They lifted me up on the rock wall and one of them said, "Just look at her legs, they are soooo beautiful. Why she has movie star legs."

Emily grew up with those beautiful legs.

One of the girls said, "She has dancing legs." Another of the girls had slipped her hose off and said she wanted to see how I looked in them. She said, "These will be too large for you but we just want to see them on you."

They slipped them on and raved about what pretty movie star legs I had. One of the girls said, "She ought to be a cheerleader."

Oh what magic words! I had always dreamed of being a cheerleader, but knew Pappy would never hear of it. But we did practice dancing. There was a small building in back of the large school building and it had a flat top. The backside was built close to the bank of the hill, and they could climb up and that's where they taught each other how to tap dance, Charleston and buck dance. There were other games too. We often had foot races. I would win over everyone except one girl, Lillie Broyles, who was a great friend. We always tied even though I tried hard to outrun her.

Those were great memories that I keep with me, but others weren't so positive. I remember one day the teacher said, "When school turns out for lunch go home and take a bath and get all dressed up." There would be lots of visitors at school in the afternoon and a play in the gymnasium.

When school turned out for the morning recess, Janet Lay asked me what I was going to wear. I knew that she was making fun of me. Janet knew I only had two or three dresses. Janet sneered as she laughed and said, "I have two brand new dresses and I haven't decided which one I will wear." I replied, "Well I haven't decided what I will wear yet." She laughed and took off to play. She knew very well that I would wear a faded dress that Granny had made from feed sacks. I had no other choice.

When school let out for lunch I took off running for it was a long way home. I ran most all the way home, told Mother why I was there, rushed around carrying water and took a bath in almost cold water. I put my faded dress on, brushed my hair, grabbed a little old worn brown jacket and took off running back to school without eating anything.

I was out of breath, but made it back just before the bell rang. Janet came over in the loveliest brown silk dress trimmed in pink. I knew it was the prettiest dress I had ever seen and it looked like it could have been made for a princess. Janet said, "See my new dress, my other one is just as pretty. Emily why didn't you wear a new dress?"

I choked my words. "Oh I didn't care about a new dress. I just put on the first old thing I came to." Janet laughed and said, "I know why, that's all you've got," and ran to get in line.

I told myself,"You just wait Janet Lay, I will have pretty things to wear." I looked down at the dress and it didn't look so good, but I thought, "Well it's clean anyway."

So I tried to put aside her terrible words and enjoy the day. I settled comfortably in my chair to watch the play, but my mind was on Janet and her dress and how much all the boys must like it, and how all the other girls must be drooling over it too. When the play was over, I walked home with my own thoughts. I daydreamed of one day owning pretty clothes, a beautiful white frame house with a white picket fence and lots of food and suckers.

But my real friends really didn't hold my clothes against me, because like I said they were as poor as I was. The next day, even though I had thought about that dress most of the afternoon, most of the girls hadn't noticed anything different at all. So I put the thoughts of jealousy aside. Playing games was more fun anyway. Some of the girls were in the swings out on the playground. Ruth Farmer and I took turns pushing. Ruth had a sister named Frances who was older, who liked to bully us. She got in the swing next to us and one of the girls began to push her.

She said, "Emily I bet I can go higher than you can."I said, "No you can't." Ruth began to push me with all her strength and I pumped with my feet. Frances did the same but I went higher. Frances stood up in the swing and so did I. Frances went so high that she got scared. But I went even with the flagpole and the swing jerked hard. That scared me but I wasn't about to let Frances win.

A large bunch of girls gathered around watching. They laughed and clapped their hands and said, "Frances, you were the one to dare Emily and she completely beat you."

I was proud that I did not give up. That was the mountain way, knowing that you had to take care of yourself or be run over by someone larger. The other girls kept kidding Frances until she became angry and said, "Oh, I could have beaten her." She looked at me and said, "I could beat you any day standing on my head."

"You just think you can."

The girls started yelling, challenging us to find out who was the best. They said, "Come on, we'll go in behind the schoolhouse where the teacher won't see us." Excitement built in the air.

First the girls pulled off their coats and tossed them on the ground. Lilly Broyles said, "When I count three go." She counted as Frances and I quickly put our hands to the ground. We flung our bodies up against the schoolhouse wall. Our dresses fell over our heads, our underwear clung to our bottoms and there we stood on our heads, baring our butts for all to see who might happen by. We stood on our heads for quite a long time, our faces getting red. The strain began to show.

Frances said, "Emily are you getting tired?"

"Why no, I could stand here all day." Of course that wasn't true for it already felt like the blood was going to burst out of my head and face just any time. My head was throbbing and I felt dizzy, but I was determined not to let her win. My friends were all yelling for me and Frances's friends were yelling for her.

It was quite a bit longer before Frances fell over. She said, "This is silly and I'm not standing like this any longer." Her face was very red. I stood on my head just a while longer then stood up and acted like it hadn't bothered me at all.

My friends jumped up and down yelling, "We knew you could do it." I saw June Orliff, Silvia Turner, Lilly Broyles, Elenore Pagett, Alma and Fay Partin, and Ruth Farmer. They sure did tease Frances. She didn't bother me after that.

I loved being at school more than I liked the weekends. Many afternoons after school let out we'd go across the bridge down to the riverbank and play games when the weather wasn't bad. Most of the time it was a nice sandy, shady place to play.

But I remember once during the flood season when the river was up. We partially crossed the bridge, stopping halfway to look down at the river. At the other end of the bridge was a telephone pole against the bridge partially in the muddy fast moving water. Someone said, "I dare anyone to climb down that pole." I felt my heart beat faster. Dares were hard to resist. Finally Alma said, "I bet Emily could for I saw her hand walk them big steel poles all the way to the top of the large set of swings on the boy's playground."

I said, "Oh Alma that wasn't anything, the water is only ankle deep at the base of the pole so anyone could wade out." But over the side of the bridge I scampered, climbing down the pole. I landed in the water and waded out. The water was brutally cold but I pretended it wasn't. It wasn't a real cold day for November, and I was used to the cold because all my clothes were lightweight.

They all began yelling and ran to the end of the bridge screaming, "We really didn't think you would do it." I said, "Oh it was no problem, anyone could do it, but no one said they wanted to."

I think my Guardian angel had patience to put up with some of the things I did, bringing me through without a broken neck.

It is important to know that my family wasn't the worst off by a long shot. Many families needed help, and more help than we did. The boys were a big help, they kept money and game coming in all the time. But some of our neighbors weren't so lucky to have large families, and even though we didn't see our neighbors every day, we looked out for them. We took care of each other, because we never knew when we would need help ourselves.

Wednesday was always our day to go grocery shopping in town. I made sure to go with Mama because she always tried to get me a treat when we went. Sometimes she also managed a few treats for the rest of the family, but Pappy only gave her a dollar and a half a week and she had to look for the best bargains to make it go as far as possible.

On one of those trips, I was reminded of how the women on our mountain looked out for one another. In Harlan, one of Mother's friends stopped us on the street and said Mrs. Jess Blankenship was very ill and asked us to stop on the way back up the mountain to visit. When we finished shopping, we did visit. As tired as mama was, she cleaned, swept and dusted, mopped and made things look real nice. Then she went into the kitchen, fixed the sick woman a plate, sat down by her bed and fed her. Mother then asked, "Now is there anything else I can do before I go?"

Mrs. Blankenship was in tears. "Mrs. Howard, you have done too much already and I can't thank you enough. If you will get my pocketbook from that drawer, I will be so glad to pay you."

Mother knelt down beside her bed and in her gentlest voice prayed for the sick lady, then before leaving she said, "You owe me nothing, but I must be going before it gets dark for I have to cook for my family. My husband will be home from his office soon. I will check again with you soon and pray that

God will take care of you." We left, walking the long walk back to our cabin on the mountain, Mother humming a song she loved.

There's a dark and a troubled side of life
There's a bright and a sunny side too
Though we meet with the darkness and strife
The sunny side we also may view

Keep on the sunny side, always on the sunny side
Keep on the sunny side of Life
It will help us every day, it will brighten all our way
If we keep on the sunny side of life

When we reached home I could hear Pappy's loud voice. After the time we spent with the sick woman, he seemed even louder and more out of place with his drinking and cursing. With just a look at Mama I went into the room to spend some time with him, because I did a pretty good job of keeping the peace in the family. I could talk to Pappy in a soft voice and after a while he would quiet and say no more.

Each night he brought the Harlan Daily Enterprise home and read it in his special cane bottom chair. Part of calming him down was spending this time with him, pulling up a heavy wooden box to sit the coal oil lamp on, and then snuggling up beside him to read with him. He knew this, often bringing the magazine called The Wild West Weekly just for me.

Let us greet with a song of hope each day
Though the moment be cloudy or fair
Let us trust in our Savior always
To keep us everyone in His care

Keep on the sunny side, always on the sunny side
Keep on the sunny side of Life
It will help us every day, it will brighten all our way
If we keep on the sunny side of life

Woodrow did not like to read, but he loved being read to. He often asked me to read to him. I read to him gladly, dramatizing every word as I read stories like, "A Trail of Blood."

Reading became very important to me. Sometimes I found pieces of newspaper along the road and would pick them up to read. It was such a treasure to me, because I knew that if I could read I could do anything I wanted with me life. It gave me power and freedom. I knew I didn't have the advantage of having things as the coal mining families had, but knowing things was my map to the world.

I had a lot of daydreams like that when Pappy was drinking. And I had strong thoughts of running away and maybe having a better life in some other town. Pappy was making life difficult for everyone and I knew one day that I would have to leave the cabin on the mountain.

When getting out of the house became my goal, walking the mountain was one of the best cures for my family trouble. I had always loved walking in the wilderness around my home. It was just that, home, to me. I knew the land like the back of my hand. I could tell you where just about every rock sat, because at one time or another I'd hidden things underneath the best ones. I knew which boards were loose in the swinging bridge that spanned from the holler into town. I knew where the water was the coldest in the streams, and where the fish rested in the heat of the day. I knew where the blueberries ripened first, and the hidden patches that others hadn't found.

I could always lose myself in the mountains during my walks, and lose my troubles too for that matter. And one time, as I was walking between the Harlan Gas camp and Harlan School, I lost myself so completely that I became Alice Ledford's sweetheart.

It was rainy that day, and before I went on a walk I put on a pair of Woodrow's overalls, his old jacket and one of Pappy's old hats. I took the path around the hill to an area that looked over the Harlan Gas camp. After some time I turned to go back, looking down over the holler, the way I always traveled going to school or town. In the distance I saw Alice Ledford going up the holler going to hunt her cows. She was about 25 years old had never been married and some called her an old maid. She was a plain girl with stringy brown hair and rotting teeth. She wore no shoes and her dresses came way down to her ankles. I stood watching for a moment, when suddenly Alice began to wave. I waved back when I realized that she didn't know who I was in my strange outfit. She obviously thought I was a boy. Just to see what Alice would do, I threw her a kiss. Alice threw one back.

For several evenings, I dressed up the same way and went back out on the hill to wave to Alice. One day Mother told me, "Well Alice Ledford has caught her a fellow." My heart pounded loud and I wondered if she knew about my game. I turned and asked, "Really? How do you know?"

Mother replied, "Well, I walked up a ways with her and she told me so. Poor Alice, I hope that she does find her a nice young man and get married." Well I never did that again. Something told me that Mother knew what I'd been up to.

Pappy continued to make life hard. We were almost barefoot that year. Aunt Susan and Uncle John weren't around to help us, and Pappy hardly helped with the family now that he was in office. Mother worried how to supply shoes. She kept saying it wouldn't be too long until she could buy nice things for us. One of the neighbor women told her the Red Cross was giving shoes away down at City Hall, so she gathered us together and took us.

All they had for me was a pair of black high top sharp-toed shoes. They were adult shoes and were way too large. Mother took them. She said, "I know you don't like them, but they will at least keep your feet warm." I hated them and was ashamed to wear them. I cried every time I wore them. I had no way of knowing they were the first of many more pairs like them. I had worn them for some time when one afternoon as school was letting out my teacher told me to stay after school.

Miss Nichols was chosen to be our teacher because she was of high moral character. She lived with one of the families near the school and wasn't even allowed to date. I knew that as a teacher she didn't make much money, so when she took me close to her and whispered, "Emily I have a pair of little slippers that I believe you can wear. Would you mind my giving them to you?" I knew that she was giving me something she could barely afford herself. She was taking them from behind her desk as she talked. I looked at them and my heart raced, for I had never had a pair of slippers in my whole life.

They were a beautiful pair of black patent slippers with a little strap and buttons up the side. I said, "Let us see if they fit." She pulled me onto her lap and gently held my foot, slipping the shoe on. I could hear myself say, "Oh they are so pretty. I would love to have them." I turned to her, reached around her neck and hugged her tightly.

She hugged me tightly and said, "Emily they are yours to keep and wear with my love." She put the old shoes in a paper bag and I took them home to show Mother.

She was pleased, and said, "I'm glad you won't have to wear those old ugly shoes, for I know how you hated them."

Going to school the next day I didn't mind my faded dress and jacket or even the little patched hole in the knee of my thick black stocking. I felt proud with those shiny new slippers. Each day after school I cleaned them and put them in a special place by my bed. I wore those little slippers until there was hardly any sole left on them. I wore them until Mother noticed them and said that I had to start wearing the ugly shoes again. There was now snow on the ground. Mother said, "Emily your feet are on the cold ground and they'll get frostbitten."

I lay in bed that night trying to think of some way to fix the slippers. The cardboard I put in them had gotten wet and had come out. I could think of no way to fix them and cried a little before finally falling asleep.

The next day I wore the old sharp-toed shoes again. Janet Lay saw them and snickered. I wanted to die. I stayed away from her as much as possible. Helen Lewallen was a good friend and she told Janet she was just a smart aleck. "You are just jealous because Emily is so much prettier than you are and you know it. She doesn't have to have fancy clothes to outshine you any day. Why, Emily is as pretty as a princess."

It felt good for someone like Helen Lewallen to stand up for me. Her folks had plenty. Her father owned the Lewallen Hotel and her mother owned a dress shop. Helen knew I hardly ever had lunch and she often brought us both a ham sandwich in her lunch. I knew she pretended she brought too much for herself when she would say, "Come Emily let's go out behind the schoolhouse." We climbed the rock wall and sat. Helen said, "My mother sure is afraid I might starve, just look what she put in my lunch. This is plenty for two people." I sure loved the taste of those ham sandwiches. It was a real treat from the biscuit and jelly mom packed.

Mother fixed a lunch, but Woodrow and I were ashamed to let the kids see us eating biscuits and jelly. Sometimes we had half of a banana and half of a nickel cake, eating the cake and banana and throwing the biscuits and jelly away on our way to school. Sometimes I just got so hungry I got sick and dizzy by the time I reached home.

Just across the road from the school, Cornett's Store sold hamburgers to the school children. I often stopped in the store at lunchtime watching everyone eat those greasy hamburgers thinking, "There is nothing in the entire world, which smells as good as those hamburgers. Oh, I wish I had money to buy me just one of them." But I never had the money, and no one offered. Many times on the playground we'd watch the kids sucking on big red luscious penny suckers. My mouth would water for one of those suckers, but I never got a penny for one. Each day I had both the pain from being teased by the big girls and the pain from hunger. My days were filled with pain from being teased by the big girls or pain from hunger. I walked home wondering if we had enough food for supper and knew I had chores and homework to do. My thoughts were of getting through my work and planning my evening pleasure walking in the woods and sitting on my rock.

Chapter 16: Dolls and Dresses

Sweet things were rare growing up and you had to make the most of them. Mountain life taught us how to do this. One year as it got close to Christmas, I told my parents that I wanted a doll.

"Emily you are a little old for a doll," Mother said. In fact I was twelve, almost thirteen. But I told her I wasn't. "I've never had a doll before, and I've always wanted one. I want to have it to make clothes for it." By this time I knew there was no Santa. But I had always dreamed a doll to keep up and take care of. But after that conversation I never mentioned the doll again because of the way Pappy was now. The truth was that with Pappy drinking most of our money, I wondered if anyone would get anything for Christmas at all.

And the idea went even further from my mind when I got home that afternoon. When I walked up, Mother was standing in the front yard crying, and a strange man was standing on the porch looking sad and uncomfortable. Through her sobs she explained that her mother caught her dress on fire and died from the burns. I knew all about Sudie, my sister who had died, and my mind flew to that immediately, because it was so strange that Mama Mary had died just like Sudie had.

She had to leave and help Sam take care of things so she left me and Woodrow to milk the cows and take care of things while she was gone. Murphy stayed to help us

Poor mama Mary, I remember the last visit Mother had with Granny. I could see her so clearly in my mind, walking down the holler with Mother as she was leaving. Strange to think that was the last time we'd see her. They had no way of knowing this and yet they both treated it like it was the last time they'd ever see each other, and I thought of how wise that was. Like was so uncertain, especially with mountain life. I decided that when it came to my own family, I should treat each goodbye with them like it might be the last as well, and tell them that I love them.

So I put aside my thoughts of running away, and the thoughts of getting a doll for Christmas, and took charge of the house. Woodrow and I were given the responsibility of caring for the family and I was going to take it seriously.

Mother returned a few days later. She and Pappy made the necessary arrangements for the burial. Grandmother Mary was carried to Kitts Holler, lowered into the fresh dug grave as the mourners sang their sad song that had become so familiar to me.

There's a land that is fairer indeed
And by faith we can see it afar
For the Father waits over the way
To prepare us a dwelling place there

It was a horrible time for my Mother to lose her mother when Christmas was so near. I watched her profile as she stood by the graveside, her lips moving in a combination of prayer and goodbye messages to Mama Mary. How old will I be when I lose my own Mother? How will it happen? Will she be alive to see her first grandchild? All these thoughts ran through my mind as we stood in the cemetery. I felt the spirits of all my family who had gone before resting heavily on my heart, brushing past all the living to welcome in Granny Whitson. They would take good care of her and keep her company, I was sure. But my mother was still alive and I worried over her. Mother had lost so many, but the sadness she felt was always the same. She blew a kiss to her Mother as we walked off the mountain.

Still Christmas drew near. Ray, Bessie and Blanche were more than excited. They shared the catalog and looked at the torn pages for hours at a time. They giggled and laughed going over and over their list for Santa.

Left-right, Blanch, Emily, Bessie

Ray (the family had few childhood pictures)

I knew just how they felt. I thought, "I wish I had a hundred dollars. I would buy them everything they wanted." The night before Christmas, Mother seemed happier than usual. She told us to go to bed early so Santa would come. No one argued as they ran to their beds. In our house, Mother slept with us girls because we didn't have enough beds for Mother and Pappy to have one of their own. I hung up my stocking and so did Woodrow even though we knew there was no Santa. I slept at the foot of our bed. Everyone went to bed except our parents.

Late in the night I lay quietly, watching mother fix the stockings. I thought, "Well I won't get a doll this time for I can't see anything else." Finally Pappy cranked the fire low and they came to bed.

In the dark I slipped my hand into my stocking searching for candy. There were more nuts and candy this time than we'd gotten in years past. I slipped back under the covers and ate some of my candy. The next morning everyone was up real early except me. I lay in bed instead, watching everyone.

Each had a toy. Mother said, "Emily aren't you going to see what's in your box?" I looked down and saw a strange box lying below my stocking on the floor. I had completely missed it because I was so used to only getting gifts in my stocking, not wrapped presents.

Excitedly I opened it and there was the prettiest doll I had ever seen in my whole life. It was a China doll with black hair and lovely brown glass eyes. She wore a pale blue dress with tiny red apples and white lace around the sleeves and neck. On her head sat a fragile yellow straw hat. She wore little black patent leather slippers with a small buckle.

I fell in love instantly. I thought I might be dreaming, and I carried her around most of the day to make sure she didn't disappear. I planned to make lots of clothes for her. I never did untie the fastenings that held her inside the box, taking special care that she wouldn't get dirty. Late in the afternoon I climbed upon some boxes and drove a nail high to the ceiling and there hung my doll out of Bessie and Ray's reach.

Bessie and Blanche also got a doll but not like mine, which was much prettier. Woodrow got a nice pocketknife he had been wanting and Ray got a truck which he could play in the dirt with.

Left-right – Bessie and Blanche –
the only picture of the two as a child

We were a happy family that Christmas. The toys were the best we'd ever gotten Later I would realize that it was because Grandmother Whitson had left Mother some money and not because Pappy was any better. At that point I didn't care though. Some would say we didn't get much, but it was probably the nicest Christmas we'd ever been able to have, if the gifts were the only thing to go by. To top it off she was able to afford some nice clothes as well, which we all really needed. Only lastly did she get something for herself, which I noticed after the thrill of having my doll had died down a little, and I was so happy that she'd thought of herself, because she almost never did.

The glow I had in my heart lasted all through the holiday, even until I got back to school. The girls were all getting their hair cut short for school and having it shingled up the back. Mrs. Sizemore, who lived down in the camp, told me that she would cut my hair if my mother said it was okay. When I asked her though, she said there was nothing wrong with my hair. I begged for nearly two weeks, but I knew Mother would not budge an inch. She finally told me she did not want to hear any more about it for it would do no good.

One day I stopped by Mrs. Sizemore's and sat talking with her sister. "Has your mother changed her mind, Emily?"

"Well, yes, she has. She said I could have my hair cut like the other girls." It just came right out of my mouth. Mrs. Sizemore sat out a chair and I hopped right in it. My heart was pounding nearly out of my chest. When the cut was finished I looked in the mirror. "Oh, what a beautiful job. I love my new haircut." I thanked her then turned and ran almost all the way home.

I slipped in while Mother wasn't looking, hurried to the back room, grabbed an old piece of broken mirror and admired the cut. I looked different, but definitely better I thought.

Then I hunted a rag and tied up my head.

Mother saw me and said, "Emily, I didn't see you come in. I see that you have already washed your hair."

"Well, yes, Mom." With that I went about my work. And I kept my head tied daily at home for a week, but finally mother caught me combing my hair.

"Why Emily, you've had your hair cut after I told you not to."

"Now, Mother, there's no use to punish me now for it has been cut for a week. You know that it looks lots better this way."

"Well, I'll have to admit that it does become you." I grabbed her and we both laughed. Mama understood how I was and didn't hold grudges with me.

I was strong willed about my clothes too. About the same time I got my hair cut, I had a new dress. It was black with little red and blue flowers. One day I was going out the door when Mother asked, "Emily where is your underwear?" I hated the long john's and felt they were meant for boys. "I took them off for they look awful stuffed down in my stockings."

Mother said, "Well, I can't help that. It is better than for you to catch your death of cold." After she made me put them back on, I slammed out of the house angrily. As I got down in the holler, I looked around me and before giving it a second thought I stripped out of them.

It was bitter cold. A light snow covered the ground. I struggled with a rock frozen to the ground and hid the underwear there. I made sure no one had seen, and then ran for school.

That evening after school, I slipped in without being seen, went into the back room and tore up some strips of rags, rolled them up and pinned them around my arms and legs. When I walked into the kitchen Mother said "Emily where is your underwear?"

I pressed the rolls on my legs and said; "Can't you see these big rolls?"

Mother replied, "You had of better not have taken them off."

That was the last pair of underwear I ever wore. From then on I did my own washing and ironing to keep mother from knowing that my old ragged underwear had been retired under a rock down the holler.

Mrs. Stokes, down in the camp, did Mother's washing in exchange for vegetables out of the garden, milk and butter, but I never allowed the woman to touch my washing. Mother teased that no one could please me. I washed and starched my dresses and ironed them until there wasn't even a tiny wrinkle left. Then I hung them on the wall with newspapers over them.

Soon it was spring again and time for planning a larger crop than ever. The family needed more now that the family growing. My brothers were big eaters. Pappy told Mother that she could hire helpers this year. The crops were planted and when it came time to hoe she hired three of John Crider's boys and a Helton boy and two Anderson boys. They were all young men and good to work. They were friends of Murphy's and Mother worked right along with them. Meanwhile, I kept the house and cooked dinner.

On Wednesdays we still went to the grocery store. Once day in the Fair Store window I saw the prettiest pair of black patent leather spike heel pumps. I went wild over them and begged mother to buy the beautiful shoes.

"Now Emily you know that you are too young for spike heels." As I pleaded and pleaded with her, I knew it was no use and I was right. Mother flatly refused, and I thought, "Somehow I will get me a pair of those pumps."

When we returned home I changed my dress and went to get my doll, but it was gone. My heart stopped with fear. I screamed for Mother and she came running. She looked at the empty space and said that maybe Bessie and Ray had gotten it down. I ran to look for them and around behind the house found my doll.

It had been beaten up into tiny pieces. I was wild with hurt and anger. I screamed, and took off around the hill looking for them. I said, "Mother, I will kill them for smashing my doll." She took hold of my arms and said, "Now honey, I know just how you feel, but I will handle this. It is not your place to punish them."

I jerked lose and ran for the woods. Tears streamed down my face as I walked and walked. I felt like someone had died. It was the only pretty thing I owned and now it was gone.

When I returned I asked mother which one had done it. Mother replied, "Emily they each say the other did it." They never told what really happened. I was sure they both beat up my precious doll. I lay in bed that night wondering where my tears were coming from. It was the last doll I would have.

But I had to put thoughts of my doll aside after a few days. It did no good to cry over something that couldn't be changed. But it was the destruction of my doll that got my mind thinking. Having that doll had been a gift from my mother and I had really loved it. But I wasn't going to wait for the next gift to come around. I knew that if I did that I'd be waiting forever, because you could never predict if Pappy was going to stop drinking or if we would ever come into the money to have nice things. But I could decide how I was going to live. I could decide to have pretty things. Soon it was summer, and summer meant blackberries.

The berries were large and sweet that year, hanging low from the vines just waiting to be picked. I decided that the way to have nice things like my doll was to make my own money.

The first day I tried this, I picked into the afternoon and got just barely a gallon, then cleaned up and headed to the mining camp to try and sell them. I started my bargaining at twenty-five cents, but as dusk came upon me, I finally gave them to a critical old woman for a dime.

That evening, June met me at the rock and listened to my troubles. June got me thinking about other things though when she asked, "What are you going to buy?"

"I'm going to get me those little black patent pumps I told you about", I said. "I'm going to save this dime and pick berries every day and sell them until I get enough to buy them."

June said, "Why Emily you know your mother won't let you wear them." I told her I'd find a way to manage that too, and smiled, thinking about those shoes on my feet. The high school girls were right, I would look and walk like a movie star in those shoes. My feet were made for them.

So every day I picked berries and saved money. Sometimes I got fifteen cents a gallon for them, sometimes a dime. All the while I'd go into the store and look at the shoes and ask how much they were. They were a dollar and ninety-eight cents.

Finally I had the money saved with twelve cents left over. I waited until mother went for a visit to Mary Miller and I knew she'd be gone most of the day. That's when I skipped down the hill to the store.

June went with me to the Fair Store. They fitted me up with a size 2. After that we went to the 5 & 10 to get a pair of socks. We giggled happily as I laid down the money for a beautiful pair of yellow silk anklets and used the other two pennies to buy a red sucker for each of us.

June said, "Emily, I could never walk in heels that high and I don't think you can either." I said, "Yes I can June. I'm going to practice before wearing them to town." When we got to my rock, I put on the delicate socks and slippers and walked up and down the rocky narrow trail.

I was right. My legs were made for high heels. I held my shoulders back, head high and body steady. I think I graced the mountain itself in my new shoes. June said, "Golly Emily, you don't need to practice, for you walk real good and they look super on you." By this time my head was just singing with pleasure.

Finally we parted and I went on up the holler and crossed the branch to the cliff where my favorite rock stood. I hid the slippers under it because I knew I couldn't hide them from Ray and Bessie at the house. If mama found them she'd make me take them back to the Fair Store.

Next I planned to buy one of the dresses I had seen in the store window. It was a handsome red and white dotted voile trimmed in blue with a full skirt for thirty-five cents. So again I picked berries to sell. I would also need to buy a pretty slip with wear with the dress.

It took two days to pick enough berries and sell them, which gave me thirty cents. On the third day, Woodrow and Dolphus Dean told me about a huge patch of berries that they had spotted when they were hunting back up in the mountains. But Woodrow wouldn't let me go by myself, afraid that a snake would bite me or something like that, so he agreed to take me out there himself in the morning. The next day we took our buckets and walked a long ways back in the mountains.

Sure enough there was a large patch of juicy berries hanging in clumps on the vines. Many of the vines had fallen to the ground from the weight of them. We both began picking and finally filled two-and-a-half gallons.

It was too late to try and sell them so we sat the buckets in the cold spring to keep fresh and cool until morning. The next day we decided to try to sell them in town where nicer people lived, so that we'd get a higher price. Soon we were knocking on doors. The second house we went to, an elderly lady came to the door. She asked how much we wanted for the berries. I asked, "What do you think they're? These are real nice berries and we went way back in the mountains to pick them."

"Berries are bigger and juicier where the soil is richer," she said as she smiled eagerly and nodded her head. "I will give you eighty cents for the lot." I smiled and accepted her offer as calmly as I could, hoping that she wouldn't change her mind. Meanwhile the lady took the berries, emptied and washed out our buckets, and handed us the money.

Woodrow looked at me before saying, "Emily, you can have it all except a dime for all I want is a good cold pop and a bar of candy." I couldn't believe he was giving me part of his money. I had the rest of my savings with me, which left me a whole dollar. I laughed out loud and said, "You just watch for I'm going to get that dress and a slip."

"Well sister, I will just have to go with you." But I didn't want to carry those buckets into town with me, because I was ashamed that someone might see them and know that I got my money picking blackberries. Woodrow offered then to carry them for me, so off we went.

So I bought the dress for thirty-five cents, and a pretty white slip. Then we both bought a grape pop each and a bar of candy. When I was done, I still split what was left with Woodrow, which left us fifteen cents each.

We were both up in the clouds that day. I knew that mother had promised that I could go to the movies Saturday, and the money left over would give me a dime for the ticket and a nickel for popcorn. On Friday I took my bath, washed my hair and sat in the sun to let it dry. Then I heated the poker in the coal stove and curled my hair, tying a cloth around my head to keep the curls in.

Saturday quickly came. I was full of excitement and got my chores done quickly. The movie didn't start until one o'clock, but I wanted to leave and be there early for because my friend Howard would be there. Mother also made me promise to beat Pappy home after the movie.

I dressed up in my new red and white dress, put on my old tennis shoes and took off down the hill to my rock. When I got there I removed my new slippers and put them on over my new yellow silk anklets. Then I hid the tennis shoes and walked very carefully down the holler to keep from scuffing them against the rough sandstone.

Oh, I felt so pretty as I walked along. Several boys whistled at me along the way, and I tossed my head and smiled. It sure was nice to be so dressed up.

When I got to the Margie Grand, a large line had already formed. I looked for Howard, but he wasn't there. Finally the doors opened. I bought my ticket and went up into the balcony. In a little while Ed Partin came in and sat beside me. I liked him too, but I would have rather been with Howard. Still, the movie had started before he walked in. I had saved a seat for him in case he arrived, but he gave Ed a dirty look before sitting down with me. I knew he was just joking though, he and Ed were real good friends. We made small talk before the main attraction until Howard said, "Emily I'm walking you home." I told him that I'd like that.

But then Ed said, "As you know, I go the same way so we can all walk together." Howard again gave him a dirty look again and said, "Well, we'll see." I felt like a million dollars having two boys getting angry over who was going to walk me home. I wondered if they'd fight when we got outside.

I was having such a good time I forgot the time. We watched the double feature over twice and the boys bought candy, pop, and popcorn. I was having a ball with all the fuss being made over me.

All at once there was a commotion downstairs, the lights went on and suddenly I heard mother's voice asking loudly, "Is Emily Howard in here?"

I nearly died. I jumped up and ran to my mother. She immediately fussed. "Don't you know it is getting dark and your Pappy will be home right away?" I was sure that everyone could hear us and I told her this as quietly as I could. But she replied that she didn't care. "Young lady I have been worried sick and you know how your Pappy is."

On the way home I told her how sorry I was and explained that I had lost track of the time. Mother soon quieted down and wasn't angry anymore, saying, "Well I guess it would be easy to let time slip by in there. I know you were having fun, honey, but you must never do that again or we will both be in trouble."

She was right, but it was hard to explain to my mother, that my first and last doll had shown me what it was like to have pretty things, and all the fun you could have when you finally got them. I would have to be more careful in the future, but I wasn't going to stop wanting those things. I was meant for a different life and I meant to have it. Wanting good things made it easier to live with the bad things at home.

CHAPTER 17: Movies and the Clark Gable Look Alike

Summer soon came to an end and it neared school time again. It was also getting very close to my thirteenth birthday. My friend, Lillie Broyles was twelve days older, and her mother let her buy a bra and a pair of silk hose. Neither of us had a thing to stuff into a bra, but since she had one, I had to have one too.

Lillie and I had been great friends as long as I could remember and had gotten even tighter during the summer. We had spent all our free time together. She lived near the river, and we would go down to the river bank, pull off all our clothes in a secluded area, swim and play and then head down to a tomato patch owned by a little old man we didn't know all that well. Lillie would slip a tomato from those bushes and we'd sneak back to her house, get a salt shaker and eat until we were full, laughing all the while.

But that was kid stuff. Now the summer was over and we were growing up. Bras and silk hose were serious business. I began pleading with Mother to buy both for me too. "Mom, it will soon be my thirteenth birthday and that is all I want. I have never gotten a gift for my birthday before so please, can't I have this one thing. Please, Mother, please."

This went on for a few days, until it was two days before my birthday and I had to go with Mother to buy groceries. In town, Mother agreed to get them for me. We went to the 5 & 10 store and she bought me a bra and a pair of hose. These were real thick hose but much nicer than the ones I had been wearing.

On the way home we met Lillie on the bridge. I showed her the new treasures and Lillie felt real pleased that we both had a real bra and new silk hose. We really felt grown up.

That night when Pappy came home he yelled, "Emily, come here." I was in the kitchen and ran to see what he wanted. He smiled and handed me a package. I tore it open and there was a blue and white dotted dress and a pink pair of silk panties edged in blue. Oh, I was pleased, for Pappy had never bought me a birthday gift before in my whole life. I knew Mother had something to do with it or had gotten someone to buy them, because he would have never bought a pair of panties, but I didn't care where I got them, and I didn't ask.

I tried the dress on quickly. It was a bit longer than any I'd ever worn before, but that was the way the high school girls wore theirs, so I decided not to hem it up. Lillie and I planned to dress up and go over to the school and walk around on Saturday when I would be thirteen. With Lillie already thirteen, we were really feeling grown up. Lillie's Mother bought her a pretty straight knit dress. She said, "Emily it comes down below my knees and I feel tacky in it that long."

"Well, Lillie, that's the way the teenagers wear them and I have decided not to hem up my dress. If we are going to be grown up we are going to have to change our ways and dress like a teenager." She agreed that if I was going to wear it long then she would too.

Saturday was a warm and breezy day, and as I was getting dressed Mother said, "I have to pick some greens to carry to one of my friends and I will walk down the holler with you." But I didn't want her to walk with me. I still had to make a trip to my hiding place under my rock, get my shoes and meet Lillie at twelve. Mother hadn't seen the shoes when she came for me at the movies and still didn't know about them. When I told her that Lillie would be waiting on me she gave me a look, but told me to go ahead.

So I made the change, just like Cinderella, and made it to Lillie's house. When I got there her mother said, "Emily you sure do look nice." That made me feel good, but I also felt a little guilty because it would make mother feel good too to see her daughter looking so fine and grown up in her new shoes. Lillie had on a new pair of heels too and she said, "Mother look at Emily's heels they are higher than mine."

Mrs. Broyles said, "I already noticed and she walks beautiful in them. Maybe later when you learn to walk in your shoes as well as she does you can get a pair that high too."

I knew Lillie felt a little jealous that I had higher heels and could walk like a grown up, so I changed the subject quickly, telling her mother that we were going off the mountain to see friends. She told us to stay out of trouble and we were on our way.

Outside Lillie asked, "do you have on your bra?"

"Well of course I do," I said. She giggled and said, "Me too."

We walked down to the school. When we arrived, there were several boys playing on the playground. We wiggled our hips trying to look all grown up and were rewarded with whistles and compliments. From there we went to the swings and some of the boys came over and began to push us. One even asked if I would go to the movies with him, but I said no.

We were having an exciting time when I noticed a strange boy talking to an Owens girl. I had never seen him before, and I knew that if I had I would have remembered him. He was a handsome boy, and I thought to myself that he looked just like Clark Gable. Just as the thought came to my mind he looked at me and smiled. My heart turned flips.

Lillie and I continued to walk around with friends, but I could not get the stranger out of my mind. None of the gang knew him and I wondered how old he was, because I could tell by his dignified ways and his fancy straw hat that he was older than the boys that I knew.

Soon we started back across the hanging bridge for home and Howard and Ed Lawson caught up with us. Lillie liked Ed and had claimed him for a boyfriend for some time even though they weren't allowed to date. Howard said, "Boy, Emily, you sure do look sharp today." He leaned over and whispered that he thought Lillie's dress was just a little too long. We laughed, but my mind was only half in the joke, still thinking about the good looking stranger and wondering if I would see him again. Howard wanted to walk with me for a way, but he knew as well as I did that I wasn't allowed to date and could not walk me all the way home.

We talked as we walked along the railroad though and as we approached the turn to go up the holler I was suddenly face to face with mama watching us. I turned calmly to Howard and said, "Howard, you can't go any farther." He knew exactly why and took off.

But strangely Mother was smiling. "Well, where did you get those fancy shoes?" I explained that I had bought them with my berry money. She sounded amused and I hoped that I wasn't about to get into trouble. After a pause she said, "Emily, you mean you've had them all this time?"

I nodded and suddenly we were both laughing. "Well, I upon my word and honor if you don't beat all. When you make up your mind to do something, nothing will stop you. I don't see how you've kept them from Bessie and Ray all this time."

"I'll show you," I said and off we went to my rock where I pulled my old shoes from their secret hiding place. I back into them, but this time I carried the slippers home. Mother laughed and said, "I should have known." She looked at me carefully then and said, "Your cheeks look pinker. Do you have rouge on?"

"A tiny bit, Mom, but don't you think it makes me look healthier?" Even with this she didn't seem too angry. "Well, just a speck won't hurt, I guess. Where did you get it?"

"I also bought a little box of powder and rouge with some of my blackberry money. I had them hid in an old suitcase away from Bessie and Ray."

My mother seemed different in that moment. Her eyes didn't seem sad, but they lost the amused twinkle they had down by the hanging bridge. "I know you, Emily," she said quietly. "You are the most responsible child I have. You take real good care of anything you own." She stopped for a minute and looked into the woods before adding, "Sometimes I wonder if your Howard blood will lead you off this mountain. I sure wish we could give you more, child. I want you to go if that's what you want. But your father is just meaner than ever and there's not a lot I can do for you. I think you're going to be okay though. You don't have a lazy bone in your body, honey. You're a survivor."

Without warning I was almost in tears. I think that was the most Mother had ever said to me about Pappy, or how we lived, or what she dreamed for my future. My mother wasn't cold hearted by and means, but it just didn't do to walk all day with your dreams out in front of you, there were too many things to do and you had to keep your hand at your work or you'd never survive. My mother was a practical woman. But she had dreams for me, and that showed me how much she loved me. My heart just burst with love for her, and as we walked back to the house I slipped my hand in hers. Today, the world felt full of possibilities.

When we reached the house I ran to get the old suitcase to show Mother my treasures. I stopped in shock when I saw the suitcase sitting on the floor, laid open and pulled apart. I looked everywhere, but could not find the powder or the rouge.

Mother and I both knew what happened. Finally, outside we found the rouge and power box in tiny pieces. I cried, "I hate them, Mother, I hate them. They are the meanest kids in the whole world. Why do they get my things?" After our talk, I could see that Mother was hurt for me. She fetched a switch and went to look for the two criminals. Soon I could tell that she had found them from the screams and the swish sound of that switch. I didn't wait to see my brother and sister come back though. I didn't want to have to talk to them.

I changed back into my regular clothes, walked around the hill and climbed upon my rock. There I sat for a long time crying for the things I had worked so hard for. It didn't take long though for my mind to turn to the things that had happened earlier in the day, to my mother's words and to the vision of that stranger. Soon I had forgotten all about my anger.

The weekend ended too soon. Monday morning came quickly and it was time to go back to school. I loved school, but by this time Woodrow hated going. He often played hooky, but last year he had not gone at all. He kept his secret from everyone, but as the New Year came up, he finally told me, "Emily, you know how I hate going to school and keeping it from Mom. Well, I'm not going back. I'm going to quit."

I was heartbroken. I wanted my favorite brother to stay in school and continue learning how to read, write and do math. School was important if you wanted things in this life. Without book learning you could have nothing. I pleaded for him not to quit school, but I could tell his mind was made up.

Soon our parents were told that he had quit school. They tried to get him to go back too, but I knew they really didn't care whether he went or not. This made me realize that I needed school more than ever. Learning became the most important thing to me that year, so that I could take the path to what I wanted in life.

But there were other things going on in the mountains. One evening after school the girls met at the giant rides and sitting on the steps of the school watching was the handsome stranger. I stared at him and like he did the last time, he turned and caught my eye. And just like the last time, my heart did flips. After that I caught him watching me many times, and each time he'd use that same special smile with me.

Several days later a bunch of the kids gathered around the stranger talking and laughing. This time I ventured up pretty close to watch. The Hensley twins were picking at him and singing one of the popular songs of the year from a movie we had seen at the Margie Grand called George White's Scandals. They were chanting the lyrics to "Oh, You Nasty Man" when he looked around just in time to catch me staring at him and smile. But this time I didn't look away at first, so that I could see his deep dark brown eyes. After a few seconds though I was blushing right to the roots of my hair and I could feel my face burning. I turned and walked away to the playground where June and my other friends were playing. My heart churned with excitement as I wondered who he was.

But I didn't see him every day, and time flew by. Days were fun with school and my friends and evenings were taken up with driving in the cows. Ed Partin often helped. One evening after the chores were over, I realized that Ed was still at our house. When I asked what he was waiting for, he said, "Emily, come sit on this rock and let's talk a while. You know I love you and I want you to marry me." I wasn't surprised, but I wasn't really sure that I wanted to have this talk. "I like you to a lot, but I don't know," I said.

He kept talking and finally I agreed to marry him. So we called ourselves engaged and I began to think of Ed as a way of getting away from home and

Pappy's drinking. By this time, Mother was threatening to take him to court for enough money to live on, because we never had enough money for food or clothing and he was mean and hateful, screaming foul language at the whole family. Pappy had definitely changed. Everyone dreaded seeing him come home. All these things played on my mind when I said yes to Ed. We sealed our engagement with him giving me a kiss on the cheek, and the next day I told Lillie.

Lillie said, "Emily, you are too young to be engaged. You have your whole life to get married." By this time I had thought about it some and said, "Well, I'm not getting married right now, maybe after my fourteenth birthday."

The days that followed made me realize that Ed did not have the same idea. I also realized that getting engaged was no fun. Ed did not want me to speak or be friendly with the other boys. By the end of the week I finally told him that I didn't want to be engaged anymore. I was relieved when he stomped off down the mountain. After he'd gone a few steps he turned and said, "Well, if that's the way you feel it's okay with me."

"That's just the way I feel, it's no fun being engaged," I screamed back. I stomped across the bridge, going down on the riverbank where the gang was playing ball. It was a beautiful day and almost the end of another school year.

I screamed to the top of my lungs when I saw Lillie and June. "I'm not engaged anymore!" They yelled at the gang, "Emily is not engaged anymore." The boys yelled three big hurrahs and someone yelled that it was the best news he'd heard in days. Everyone ran over laughing and hugging me as if I had been away for a long spell. Howard said, "From now on, I'm keeping a close watch on you to see that you don't become engaged to anyone else unless it's me."

It felt good not having Ed watching me every minute. My thoughts immediately turned back to the stranger and I wondered if I would see him when the school year ended. He spent a lot of time sitting there on the school steps watching the kids play.

I had the strangest feeling that he was only there to watch me.

But there was only one week of school left and I still didn't know his name. And for three days he did not show up at all.

But finally there he was again. I was holding the rope while the girls jumped and suddenly I felt someone staring at me. I looked up and saw him.

I jerked the rope and made Sylvia miss.

Oh but the bell rang and inside we went. The next day we only came back for report cards. I told myself I wouldn't see him there, and I was right. He was surely gone forever, and I was sad.

But summer was a busy time for the family, and I set thoughts of him aside when I could for the garden and milking the cows. I also decided to do something about the way our house looked. I knew that Pappy would never hear of buying paint for the walls if he wouldn't buy food, but down in the camp, one of Mother's friends papered her walls with newspapers. They had plenty of papers, for Pappy bought a paper home every day and stacked them in the back room. I asked Mother if I could do it, promising to do the work myself.

"Well, if you want to, but it will be a job." I ran out the door telling her, "I'm going to get Cassie Turner to help me," over my shoulder. I owned a dress that I had cut down too tight for me. I was going to give her that dress as payment for helping me. It would just fit her.

I ran all the way to the Turner house and asked Cassie's mother if she could come help.

When we got back to the house, I made thick flour starch with water, flour and a little salt, cooking it to the right consistency. We worked hard the rest of the day papering the living room, even matching the print to keep the news going in the right direction to read. When we finished, we stood back and admired the beautiful job.

It made the house look fresh and clean. I gave Cassie the dress and walked her part of the way home thanking her for her help. The rest of the week I worked on the house, cleaning windows, scrubbing floors and then turning to the yard, raking and sweeping where no grass grew. I got great pleasure making everything look nice and clean.

Mother's church group met weekly for fellowship and dinner. They took turns meeting at one of the church members' houses, but she had always been too embarrassed to invite them to her house. After I papered the wall, she decided to have the group over.

I helped cook dinner and clean the house. Everyone seemed to have a good time, but before leaving they got down on their knees and began to pray.

I watched as they began to speak in other tongues and noticed the happy look on their faces. It was strange, but their faces seemed to take on a beautiful glow as they leaned back in the spirit and spoke words I did not know. Some got happy and danced and shouted and their long lovely hair came loose and fell down over their shoulders. I experienced something good and wonderful even though I did not understand it.

The Spirit died down and they all hugged, told Mother what a wonderful time they had and left. After they were gone, she turned to me and asked, "They enjoyed themselves didn't they?" I nodded and told her that they'd be coming back often. She smiled and I realized that this was the first time I had ever seen Mother do anything with friends. That old dress I gave Cassie was worth that, and I smiled.

The weather was turning hot again and the blackberries were ripe. I found another dress I wanted in the Fair Store window and decided to pick berries again for it. It took several days of working in the hot sun and scratches all over my fingers, but I got it.

It was white, form fitting with a kick pleat in the back showing just enough of my legs to make me feel beautiful. It also showed off the tan I had gotten picking all those berries, and when I got it I dressed up to show Mother.

When Mother saw it, she stood there for some time before speaking. "Well, my little girl is growing up and you sure do look pretty," she said. I gleamed with pride. My mother approved.

I could hardly wait for Saturday. Friday I washed and set my hair, and worked on my hands and nails trying to get rid of the blackberry stains. Saturday I hurriedly did my chores and then set off down the holler feeling like a million dollars.

On the way down I met up with Lola Crider, and we walked along the railroad track together. Lola was a pretty girl with thick red hair. When we reached the bridge we met a boy Lola knew and stood talking for a while before he asked me to the movies. I said no, but he tried to get fresh with me, taking my hand as we crossed the bridge and repeating his offer. I jerked away and said, "I told you I don't want to date you or go to the movies."

We turned, crossed the bridge and met up with Lillie, May, and June on the playground. When they saw me they went on and on about how neat I looked. We all left for the 5 & 10 to the sound of the boys yelling and whistling at us.

It seemed that I was getting lots of the attention, but that day my mind was only on the stranger. I was too dressed up to go to the movies where I'd sit in the dark. I wanted to run into him. I wondered if he'd whistle when he saw me.

I kept my eyes peeled for him, for it would soon be time for Pappy to close his office and head for home. I would have to hurry to avoid meeting up with him. When I could wait no longer, I turned for home.

It was a disappointing day not seeing the stranger, but when I got home, Mother greeted me at the door. "Emily, I want to show you something." There hanging on the wall was the most beautiful yellow silk dress, with black butterflies and flowers and a full skirt with short sleeves. I hugged it to me and asked her where she had gotten it. Mother explained that one of her friends down in the camp gave her the dress for work she did. I had never had a silk dress, but when I tried it on, it fit like it was made for me. I could hardly wait to put it on with my black velvet weskit, which Ruth Miller had given me some time before.

I was truly a princess.

Time flew and there was little to do for entertainment during the summer months other than going to the movies or walking or going to the school playground. I was anxious for school to start again. Again my thoughts turned to the stranger. Would he return?

This picture was found in an old Bible. Emily was about 14 Calvin about 20

CHAPTER 18: Turning Fourteen

Before I knew it, I was turning fourteen. Birthdays growing up were simple. They weren't about gifts and parties, they were mostly just another day. I always had school to concentrate on, which began soon after my birthday and was always very important to me. This year though, I was hoping that the start of school would bring back the stranger. Seeing him again with be enough of a birthday gift for me.

June was still my confidante that year, and we spent lots of time telling each other our secrets. June was still thinking of running away from home, and I really wanted to leave also, even though I didn't want to marry Ed to do it. Pappy continued to make things rough on everyone. If it weren't for mother, I'd never have the chance to do anything, because he never allowed me to go anyplace except to school and Sunday school.

But I was able to have fun with Mother at church. On this particular Sunday I had a pretty dress from Mother to wear and a date with Taylor Nunnelly. If I could talk Mother into letting me go to the Crossing Church for Sunday school and then to the baptizing at Kitts Bridge afterwards I'd have it made.

So Sunday morning I got all dressed up and brushed my hair. I dusted a tiny bit of rouge and powder to my face and pinched my lips and touched them with Castor Oil to give them a shine. Then I stuck my finger into the bottle and greased the inside of my mouth to make it easier to smile.

"You look pretty this morning, Emily," Mother said. "You are dressed to kill." I grinned my reply and we headed to the church. On the way there, I asked for permission to go to the Crossing Church of God and to the baptizing.

"Please, Mother, it is a good church you know. It is the Church of God and lots of young people go there."

"I know that but I would rather you go with me." Finally I convinced her to let me go when I promised to meet her back at Maggie Moor's when the baptizing was over. I know that Mother always stayed for the preaching and then sometimes she's stop and visit a while with some of her friends before going on home. It would give me a fair amount of time. I quickly made the promise and hurried on.

I felt on top of the world. It was a beautiful day, I was all dressed up and I was nearly fourteen. It was only a short ways to church, and as I neared the Harlan depot I spotted a man taking pictures. He asked if he could take my picture to use as a sample. I agreed and waited patiently for him to cover his head with a dark cloth and take it. He told me that I could see it if I came back about an hour later. I thanked him, then hurried to the church, which was just across the railroad tracks from the depot.

I sat by Cassie Turner and told her excitedly about the man taking pictures. We decided to slip out after a while and go see it. Then Sunday school got underway.

After a bit, Cassie looked behind us and nudged me excitedly. She whispered, "there is the best looking boy in the back I ever saw and he flirted with me."

"Where?" I tried to glance over my shoulder without looking too obvious. Cassie lowered her head and whispered again." Over your other shoulder. He's in a white suit and white straw hat. He has the blackest hair I've ever saw. He'd about make me faint just looking at him."

"Cassie, stop looking back," I told her. "The preacher will call you down." I turned face forward at her description and wouldn't look back again. I didn't dare to hope that it was my stranger. Soon Sunday school was over and when we headed for the depot to see the picture, he was gone. Disappointed, I walked on to the baptizing. Cassie and I had walked a little ways when she said excitedly, "that good looking boy is following us. I'm gonna to wait on him."

"No, don't let him know that you are interested in him," I said. "Just pretend that you're lacing your shoe." I hadn't looked until then to see who the boy was, but when he caught up with us, I almost passed out with relief, because it was the stranger, just as I had hoped.

He grinned a pearly white grin and asked, "What are you two good looking girls doing all by yourselves?" Cassie said, "We are a going to the baptizing up there at Kitts near the bridge."

I didn't say a word, but I knew that he'd been following me all along. As we continued up the path, we came to a place called the cows crossing, which was a large iron contraption with spikes to keep cows off the railroad tracks. There he took my arm and helped me across. Cassie followed by herself, looking a bit angry.

He said, "My name is Joe Romine and I know who you are. You are Emily Howard and your father is Justice of the Peace." I was surprised by this, and happy to finally learn his name. I asked him how he knew me and he said, "I haven't been watching you all this time without finding out something about you. Say, how about me carrying you to the movies so we can get to know each other?"

I wanted to say yes like you wouldn't believe, but there was no way. "I can't today, I have a date. He is meeting me at the baptizing."

He looked real disappointed and said, "Well, how about Saturday?"

"I also have a date for Saturday, but I'll tell you what. I'm supposed to meet him outside the New Harlan Theatre and the first one who gets there will be the one I will date."

His brown eyes sparkled as I told him this, and he said, "I'll see you Saturday then," with a laugh. "So bye for now." He touched my hand briefly then walked away.

Cassie said real huffy-like, "Well I never saw the like. I sure do hope you're satisfied Emily Howard. Why you knew he was a following me."

I said, "Now Cassie, you know very well that I didn't do anything. Anyway do you remember the handsome stranger I've been talking so much about?" She nodded. "Well, you know very well that was him and you know that he was not following you." Cassie looked real sheepish and said, "Well you can't blame me for trying."

We both laughed and went on to the baptizing. When we arrived, Taylor was looking for me. He was all dressed up and was a very good looking boy, but I had completely lost interest in him.

River baptisms have been held in the mountains forever, and everyone knew what to expect because most everything was done the same way every time. By now the singing had started and most everyone joined in on the song, "Shall We Gather at the River". And huge crowds had gathered to see people come to the Lord. Several people had guitars and songbooks. The minister waded out into the water by himself at first, testing the river bottom as he went. You never knew from one rain to the next how the bottom would be, and he liked testing the spot for holes or rocks that would trip people up.

Next came one of the elders from a local church. It was the deacon's job to line up all the people for baptism. All those who wanted to be baptized were standing in a line at the water's edge dressed in white. They held hands and walked out into the water as the three of us looked on from the bridge.

Slowly the singing stopped as the minister had a quiet word with the first person in line, to make sure of her repentance and willingness to follow the Lord. I watched as he showed her how to hold one hand over the other and then cover her nose with them. Then he placed one hand over her hands and the other he lifted toward Heaven. When all was quiet, he said, "This my sister I do baptize in the name of The Father and of The Son and of The Holy Ghost." With that he placed his other hand on her shoulders and dipped her into the water.

The woman came out of the water shouting and jumping around. She fell over and the preacher had to pick her up so she wouldn't drown. The deacon led her out of the water and handed her a towel to dry her face, but she was caught up in what had just happened, shouting, "praise the Lord, praise the Lord."

His words repeated again and again, rising from the river up to us at the bridge. Over and over people stepped into the water to turn their hearts over to the Lord. The people on the bank below us started to sing again and weep and praise the Lord. As the deacon led the newly baptized up to the riverbank again, people from all around would walk down to them to shake their hands, offering them the right hand of Christian fellowship.

After the baptizing I told Taylor that Mother was waiting for me and that I'd have to hurry home. I don't think he was expecting for our date to be over that quickly. I had planned on talking to him longer too, but that was before I learned that the Clark Gable handsome man I'd been dreaming about so long was named Joe.

For the rest of the week I daydreamed about Joe. I could hardly believe that I really and truly had a date with the handsome stranger. I wondered all week how I would manage to dodge Ulysses Floyd or get out of the date with him.

Friday, I washed my hair and curled it with the poker. I had now mastered the art of using the poker without burning my scalp like I did when I was younger.

When the night of the big date arrived, I went down the mountain toward the depot. As I approached, I saw Joe standing there with a big smile on his face.

"I knew you would come by here so instead of waiting at the theatre I thought it best to wait here."

I laughed. "Aren't you cheating a little bit?" He shrugged, and instead of answering me, he asked what movie I would rather see. There were two theaters in Harlan, and I know that Ulysses would be at the New Harlan, so I decided that we should go to the Margie Grand.

"All right then, that's fine with me."

Sure enough, we had to pass right by the New Harlan Theatre and there was poor Ulysses standing in front all dressed up. I made sure that I walked close enough to Joe so that Ulysses wouldn't see me as we passed. We got to the Margie Grand just as it opened. Joe bought our tickets, popcorn and cokes and found a seat almost in the back. We held hands for a while and I soon felt his strong arms easing across my shoulders. Every once in a while he'd pat my shoulder and smile deeply into my eyes.

I thought I was going to melt.

After quite a while Joe said, "I really don't care for this movie do you?"

"No, I really don't."

"I'll tell you what. Let's run over to the restaurant and get us a bite to eat and then maybe go for a little walk so we can talk." I thought about this for only a second, then said yes. I had never eaten in a restaurant before and was far too bashful to eat in one with Joe. As we walked out of the theater, I wondered how I was going to get out of it. But the problem solved itself as we got to the restaurant. I told him I wasn't that hungry and he ordered cokes and sandwiches to go.

We walked outside of town and over to the hanging bridge. Joe spread his handkerchief on the end of the bridge and we sat down.

He handed me a sandwich and we began to eat, but with the first bite I got a bit of fat. I was so embarrassed that I didn't say anything, but I looked around me trying to figure out a way to get rid of it without him seeing.

But he did see. He looked at me and said tenderly, "what's the matter honey? Oh, I see. You got a bit of fat." I nodded and smiled sheepishly at him before I spit it out. "I'm so sorry, I just can't eat fat meat." I felt myself turn red.

Joe laughed and said, "Here take this one, and I will eat yours. I don't mind it being fat."

"No, I've bit on it." But he took it from my hand and said, "That's okay. I don't mind you biting it. Here, this one is all lean." He took the rest of it and finished it with no problem. But he laughed and cupped my chin in his hand and said, "you sure are a bashful little thing. Gosh, you look so cute blushing like that."

At that I just blushed more.

After we ate I told him I would have to be going to get home before Pappy. He said he would walk me home, but I said no quickly and explained that I wasn't allowed to date. He said, "I really didn't think you were. Will I get to see you again next Saturday?"

"Yes," I said without delay. He stood as I left and watched me head back for the holler.

That night lying in bed I tried to think of everything he had said. He worked at Verda and roomed at the clubhouse. He was raised in Alabama where his folks still lived. He had traveled riding the trains. He was mysterious, exciting and fun. Imagining that I was the luckiest of fairy princesses, I drifted happily off to sleep.

Though I didn't see him again for a few weeks, the days were still blissful. Sometimes I would go around the hill and climb upon my big rock and sit and watch the little birds sail through the sky, or listen to them singing in the trees. I felt lucky just to be alive. My body was full of happiness and I felt excitement running through my veins, as I never had before. And I could still feel the touch of his hand.

Then school started and quickly got into full swing. My buddies were happy that I was dating Joe. Joe and I were now seeing each other every Saturday and Sunday. We also wrote each other twice a week. He was even kind enough to keep me with stamps and envelopes when Pappy never gave the family spending money.

Then one day, all this changed. On Saturday, Joe and I were to meet at the New Harlan Theatre. I arrived a few minutes ahead of Joe and started talking to Margie Short's mother. We were having a nice conversation when Joe appeared. I saw him glance over at me, then just walk on past like he didn't know me.

I felt slapped and stricken. I had no idea what to think. Before I had time to worry about it, George Brown walked up and asked to take me to the movies. George was a real nice boy who had wanted to date me for some time, so I quickly said yes. I'd show Joe. If that's the way he felt, I could get another date.

Inside we went to the balcony, sat down and had just gotten into the movie when Lola Crider came in looking for me. She got my attention and pulled me off to the side.

"Joe is waiting in the hall and he wants to talk to you real bad," she whispered.

"He'll be waiting a long time, for I'm not going to see him anymore."

Lola said, "Emily, please go see him. He is real upset. He paid my way in to get me to hunt you up for him. He knows that you are not allowed to date and he thought that was your Mother that you were talking to outside. I told him that it was Margie's mother. Please Emily, at least go speak to him."

I was still hurt and angry, but said, "Lola, you go tell him that I am going to see the rest of this picture with George and if he wants to wait I will see the next one with him and if not he can do what he wants."

She left and I walked back to sit with George. By the time I got back to my seat though, I was over my anger at him. And when Lola came back a few minutes later and whispered that Joe would be waiting for me, I even felt bad for him. I told George the fib that my brother was downstairs and that I would have to leave when the picture was over because I wasn't allowed to date. He was very nice about it and said maybe we could get together another time.

Joe was waiting. He did some tall talking. Of course, he had no way of knowing what Mother looked like. He had never met her. We didn't know at the time that he'd meet my mother sooner than he had expected.

By the time he'd explained himself and I'd forgiven him, it was too late to see the next show, and I had to get home anyway. He wanted to walk me partly home, and I agreed. As we got almost even with Maggie Moore's house, I looked up and there stood Mother. My heart jumped into my throat. Mother had never seen me with a boy before and I had no idea what she might say. As we passed, I avoided looking at her, hoping she wouldn't say anything. Luckily she didn't, and we walked past her as quickly as I could manage and still look casual.

Further up the path, Joe pulled me aside where there was a large tree root to sit on. We talked there until it was about time for Pappy to be on his way home. As I stood up to go, I looked up and suddenly there was my mother again, walking into the holler. I stood still, fearing that she would jump on Joe and run him off.

Instead she came right along smiling. Relieved, I introduced them. I could tell after only a few seconds that they'd hit it off right away. We all talked for a bit when she said, "I must be going. Emily, you better hurry on in a little while for your Dad will soon be on his way home." She then made her way on up the holler.

Joe took my face in his hands and looked into my eyes and said, "That was your Mother that we passed on the railroad a while ago and you didn't even speak to her. Why?" I blushed and said, "I was afraid that she would jump on you and me." He smiled before pulling me into the curve of his arm and holding me close in a hug. "I think you have a swell Mother," he said.

"I know I have." We talked a while longer before I turned to leave. "I'm sorry Joe. My pappy wouldn't be so sweet if he saw us together." He gently lifted me off the tree root and set me on the ground, holding me a moment before releasing me. Then said, almost in a whisper, "You are so tiny" and he kissed me very lightly on the lips. Then said, "I'll see you tomorrow my pretty little green eyes."

My heart was pounding, "Yes, tomorrow." I then took off up the holler.

Life flew along on a whirlwind that year, full of the pleasure of seeing school friends during the week and seeing Joe on the weekends. But things would soon change.

One day at lunch hour several of the girls were together and someone said, "Why don't we just skip school this afternoon? It's such a pretty day. Let's go up on Ivey Hill and play ball or walk in the woods and just have fun for a change."

Everyone began to yell. "I'm game," so I joined in too. They asked if there was anyone who might chicken out and everyone promised not to. So off we went to that beautiful place to play ball, climb trees and run through the woods. All that could be heard was a brisk breeze blowing through the trees and everyone's laughter.

After a while though, someone noticed that Lillie Broyles was missing. One of the girls said, "She has chickened out on us and she's sure to tell." Everyone got scared, but decided to stay anyway.

We were playing ball when Woodrow and one of his friends came by and asked what we were doing. I said, "Oh, we came up to play ball," but he thought nothing of it because he had been out hunting and didn't know what time it was.

Sometime later we saw the school janitor coming. One of the girls yelled, "Run, Lillie's told on us." We all took off running just as fast as we could. My friend Silvia dropped her nickel and ran back to get it. "Let it go," I screamed, but she ran back to where she dropped it, so I ran back with her. As she grabbed the nickel off the ground I grabbed hold of her coat and pulled her along as I ran.

We ran all the way around the hill through the woods and onto the highway. By this time, June was upset because she knew her parents would kill her over this. I had the same fears about my Pappy.

There was a skating rink just a little ways up the road and one of the girls suggested that we go watch the skating until time for school to turn out. We agreed, but as soon as we got inside, I spotted Murphy on the floor skating. He saw me her right off and skated to me.

"Emily, where have you been? I was just fixing to go look for you. I know you skipped school and the teacher sent word to Pap." I thought I was going to pass out when I heard this. Murphy saw how shook up I was and too me by the arm. "Hey honey, it ain't that bad, but he does have two of the men from his office out looking for you. You go on home and I will go tell him where you are."

We all took off. I crossed the hanging bridge with June and we headed back into the holler. June was really scared by then. "Emily, as long as I live I will never do that again," she said. I couldn't agree more.

But as June turned around the hill to her house, Mother was coming down the holler looking pretty upset. She got up close to me and said, "I want to know where you have been young lady."

I told her everything, but it didn't help much. Mother listened to my story, then said, "I have been scared almost to death. Your teacher sent me word that a bunch of you was absent and one of the girls said you all had skipped school. I just don't know what your Pappy will do when he gets home."

When they got to the house I quickly changed clothes and began doing the chores, all the time thinking, "If I get out of this I will never be disobedient again."

In short order it was time for Pappy to come home. I decided to make myself scarce, hoping he wouldn't call me in. When he arrived, Mother fixed his supper and afterwards they talked for a long time. I couldn't tell what they were saying, but I could tell that they were arguing and that he was very angry.

After quite a while their voices quieted down and Mother got up to finish the dishes and get ready for bed. I couldn't figure out why they didn't call me in to at least chew me out, but I decided not to question it. While Pappy was reading his paper, I slipped very quietly into bed. I wanted to read the paper with him, but I was afraid to get near him. It was very late before I drifted off into a troubled sleep.

The next morning I got up early for school. Mother looked at me for a moment with such sadness and pity that I stopped where I was standing.

"Emily, honey, there is no need for you to get ready for school. Your Dad says you are not going anymore."

About that time Pappy walked in and said, "Em, as he sometimes called me, I don't want to ever hear of you being off the place." I started to cry and begged, "please just beat me if you like or punish me anyway you want to, but don't make me stay out of school. Honest Pappy, I will never, never skip school again. I promise. Please let me go on to school for I do love it." He let out a string of oaths and said, "I mean just what I said, and you had better not disobey."

He wheeled around and strode off down the hill on his way to the office. I sat down at the table and imagined the world closing down on me. I looked up at Mother after a second or two and said, "Surely he can't mean this. I made one stupid mistake that I can't undo."

Mother said, "I know how you feel and you know that I don't go along with your Father. Maybe after he cools off he will change his mind and let you go back." But those words didn't give me much hope, for I knew that secretly, Pappy didn't want any of his children to receive too much book learning.

I spent the day in deep remorse. I really tried to help with the work, but my heart just wasn't in it. Finally I went around the hill and climbed upon my familiar rock.

Now what was my life going to be like, without my friends or my school? There sure wasn't much too look forward to. Then another thought came to me. What would Joe think? I decided that I would write him tomorrow and tell him what happened.

And so I did. I wrote out everything. Thankfully he wrote back quickly and told me not to worry, that I didn't need much book learning because I had plenty upstairs and would get along fine. He wrote that we would talk about it Saturday.

I felt better after reading his letter. No matter what Pappy said about staying home, I knew that I would see Joe. I was in love with him.

CHAPTER 19: The Picture That Changed Everything

The days at home dragged by and Pappy was as firm as the mountain about his decision. No matter what I said, no matter what Mother said, he would not budge.

I was starved for school and missed my friends badly. I read the newspapers that I had papered the walls with so many times that I could just look at the wall and tell what each page said.

Sometimes June or Ruth would tell me about their lessons. The gang was also angry with Pappy and talked about what a mean old man he was and how he was drinking heavily.

When I thought things couldn't get worse, they did. One Saturday I was walking with Joe up Bailey Hill. He had been very quiet, and I guessed that he wanted to tell me something, but I had no idea what. We continued walking out of town and sat down under a large tree. Finally, after minutes of silence, I said, "Joe just tell me what is on your mind. I will understand."

He looked at me and I could see his doubt, but he went on. "Emily, honey, I've wanted to tell you for a long time, but I was afraid of losing you and I know that you will find out sooner or later. So please hear me out before you say anything."

"When I was seventeen I made a big mistake. I got married. I married a girl I didn't even love because my Father told me that I couldn't. It was a very foolish and stupid thing to do. The marriage didn't last but I have a small boy named Herman. He is almost five years old.

I never stayed around very much. I took off for California and stayed around for three years. Then I hitched trains all over until I landed here in Harlan. I am divorced and I hire a lady to take care of my son when I'm not there. So now you know."

My heart felt like a rock. Finally I said, "Joe, why didn't you tell me all this at first?"

"I couldn't tell you honey. I knew if I told you that you wouldn't date me and I just couldn't take that chance. There is a little something else I have to confess."

I thought, "Lord, what else?" He smiled this time though and said, "My name is not Joe, it's Calvin. I told you that so you wouldn't find out about me before I could get up enough nerve to tell you myself. Everyone calls me Calton."

I didn't say anything for some time and then found words to say, "Well, if I had of known I would have never dated you at all, for I've always said I would never date a man who had been married. I guess if I decide to see you again I will be calling you Calvin for I never liked Joe and I surely don't like the name Calton." He laughed at me and seemed more at ease now that he had told me his secret. But he quickly left me alone to my thoughts.

"Well that is that. I probably will never see him again," I realized. It was so sad. I knew I had feelings for him, and they were deeper than I wanted to admit. Was there such a thing as love at first sight?

As I walked home from our talk, I thought back to that first day on the playground. From that point on he had never really left my thoughts. I realized that I could not stop feeling what I felt for him, no story would ever change me. He was too much a part of my heart to let him go.

He was also a big part of my thoughts at the time, which involved getting out of the house and leaving Pappy's harsh discipline that kept me out of school. In my mind, Joe was a big part of my plans to leave home. I had no way of making a living and my education boiled down to what I could read on the wallpaper and the papers Pappy brought home, so I wanted to keep him in my life to help me leave home as well.

That wasn't the main reason though, and I knew it. I had to be honest with myself. I loved the man, whether I called him Joe or Calton or Calvin. He was part of my heart and I wanted us to spend the rest of our lives together.

So Calvin and I continued to date secretly, often meeting on the road and driving to an old swimming hole down at Dayhoit on the Cumberland River where we swam most of the day. I even bought a black bathing suit with some of my berry money and I loved stepping out of the bushes and wearing it down to the cool, clear water. When we left I would hurriedly dry my hair and race home before Pappy got home, laying the wet suit near my rock to dry before hiding it. I knew it was best this way, as Pappy would never accept an older man in my life.

Late one Saturday afternoon, while we walked the streets of Harlan a photographer approached us. He asked, "Would you mind if I took your picture? You make a striking couple." I giggled for this was the third time I had been in someone's picture. We agreed and he snapped away.

Oh but little did I know how that would change things. Days later one of Pappy's friends stomped in his office smirking, "Milt, I didn't know your daughter was seeing an older man." Before my father could beat the man, he explained that my picture was in the window of the Wainscott Studio.

And so off he went, out the courthouse door, down the steps, up the street walking as fast as his crutches would carry him to the window of the Wainscott Studio.

Pappy was so mad that he raced home to find me. As he got to the house he screamed, "Em, Em come here immediately." I knew I was in trouble for he never called me Em unless he was mad.

"I want to ask you a question and I want you to tell me the truth. Are you seeing an older man?"

"No, Pappy."

"Emily, don't you lie to me. I saw your picture in the Wainscott Studio window as big as day. Don't you think I know my own damned daughter when I see her?"

"Pappy, really, it wasn't me."

"Well, I'm telling you girl, you are to never see him again for I will kill him if I see this man. I understand his name is Joe. Is that true?"

"Really, Pappy, it wasn't me," I insisted.

Pappy would not go back to work. He lay on the porch, sometimes half in and half out of the front door watching for Calvin with his shotgun by his side. Days went by this way and one of his friends from the courthouse finally came to the up and said, "Milty, if you don't come back to work you are going to lose your job."

He called for me. "Em, I'm going to lose my job if I don't go back to work. Will you promise me that you will never see that man again if I go back?"

"I promise, Pappy. I won't see him again."

"I know, Emily, if you promise me you will keep your word for you have never lied to me before."

He left for his office and I was out the door almost right behind him to meet Calvin. I knew right where to find him too, but as I headed down the street of Harlan I looked up and there was Pappy. "Oh, God," I thought, "He will kill me."

Keeping my head down I walked right past him.

I never looked up, and he never said a word.

That evening he called me. "Em, what were you doing in town today?" Again I played dumb. "Pappy, I wasn't in town." I held my breath until all I could hear was the sound of my heart slamming inside my chest.

"Why, Em, don't you know I know my own damned daughter when I see her face to face? I knew that was you in the studio window, but hell, Em, when I walk right by you and you say it's not you, do you think I am crazy?" I stared at him but he was the first to look away. He said nothing else to me.

The picture that caused hell to break loose. Emily just turned 14. (Wainscott Studio/Harlan, County, KY) Calvin was 20.

I felt bad for him and bad for myself. I knew though that things were coming to a head and that it was time for me to make a decision about leaving. I went to my rock and wrote my heart out to Calvin.

Dear Calvin,

I am lost on this mountain without you, and I don't know what to do. My pappy is in an awful state, and I am afraid of him. Not only has he seen the picture of the two of us together, be he knows that I would lie to be with you. He spent the last two days sitting on our porch with a shotgun, waiting for you to come up the hill. I am not afraid for you in that way, I know that you wouldn't come this way without permission. I am just terribly afraid that he will not let me go. Haven't we already seen what he does? Am I not already kept from going to school, which I loved? Imagine how much more I love you, and then imagine him keeping me away from you until you leave me for someone else with a nicer family than I have. I am heartbroken without you, darling. Please help me find a way for us to be together.

Your love,

Emily

He wrote back immediately and asked me to marry him.

For us it had been love at first sight and we both knew it. The only thing to worry about now was how to get away without anyone knowing.

But Pappy still searched for the man I was dating, and he drank even more than usual. It got so bad that Sam had to get away from Pappy too, and he married his girl, named Vesta. Mostly because of this, Sam agreed to help me. He said, "Vesta will go to the house and help you pack your things and then we will go to the courthouse and get the clerk to give you a marriage license. We will have to be careful that Pap doesn't see us."

It was a dark night when Vesta and I hurriedly packed my few things, slipped out the window, and ran as fast as our legs could carry us down the holler. I felt bad not leaving any word with Mother. That night I spent with Sam and Vesta.

The next day I dressed, put on makeup, fixed my hair and met Calvin at the courthouse where we applied for a marriage license. The clerk asked if Pappy knew we were getting married. I stood as tall as possible could and said, "Oh yes, he knows."

The clerk replied, "Well you must get him to write a note saying that it's okay.

I bravely said, "Well, I will be right back, for it is okay with my Pappy." We walked into the hall and I turned to Sam. "Now what do we do?"

"Emily, just write a note and say it's okay for my daughter to get married and sign Pappy's name."

He handed me pencil and a piece of paper and there I stood and wrote out the note. ***"It is okay for my daughter, Emily Nancy Howard, to marry."***

I signed it with my father's name and took it back to the clerk and looked him straight in the eyes. The clerk looked at me strangely for a moment and then issued the marriage license. Sam signed as the witness. We were married by the Justice of the Peace on October 2, 1934, just a month after my fifteenth birthday, and spent our wedding night with Sam and Vesta.

**The wedding picture – October 2, 1934 – (Emily turned 15
September 3, 1934, Calvin was 21)**

When it was time for bed, I had no fancy nightgown to wear. I put on the
only thing I owned, which was a long outing gown and slipped into bed next
to Calvin, pulling the gown all the way down under my feet and tucking it
tightly around my legs. Before the night was over, he gently held me in his
arms and we consummated our marriage vows.

We moved into a small frame home with two rooms in Verda. The
bedroom and living room were combined with a very tiny kitchen. Calvin was

still working in the coalmines and he'd come home from work looking blacker than black.

The first night in our new home, Calvin woke early and asked me to get up and build a fire. I refused, saying that the man should be the one to start the fires and the woman's place was in the kitchen doing the cooking. He wouldn't budge. We were both so stubborn that we stayed in bed until noon when finally Calvin gave in and decided to get up and start a fire. I immediately got out of bed and cooked breakfast.

Several weeks after we were married I asked Calvin to walk with me to the courthouse. He knew I was lonesome to see my Pappy, and he said "Well, that's a good idea. Let's go right now."

We got to town and walked up the courthouse steps. We walked quietly down the hall together until we got to Pappy's office door. I eased it open a bit to see if I could see him, but Calvin was right behind me and gave me a big push. Into the office I went.

I was scared to death. There he sat behind his desk. He looked up and said, "Why Emily. I am so happy to see you." He was smiling and I knew he meant it.

"Pappy, I want you to meet my husband, Calvin." I felt myself beaming. I couldn't help it. And I could tell he was pleased to meet Calvin and his face showed his happiness at our visit. He even asked us to come by the house that afternoon. We didn't have time that day, but assured him we would visit soon. I sent my love to Mother and the family and we left.

"Isn't it the strangest thing, after all that trouble?" I said to Calvin as we left the building. "I'm so glad he isn't angry."

"Me too," he agreed. "I was hoping he wouldn't meet us at the door with his shotgun. But you know he loves you, Emily. He didn't want someone coming in and taking advantage of you. I think the marriage is what settled it all in his mind. You're my wife now."

Calvin's wife. He was right. I was still my pappy's daughter, but I had a family of my own now, and it was the best feeling in the world.

A few days later we made the trip up that old familiar holler. Everything felt a little different now, and I felt a little sad as I looked at my rock, remembering the place I hid my first shoes.

Mother was glad to see us, I could tell by the way she looked at Calvin. They were friends immediately. He was as gentle with Mother as he was with me, gaining her confidence and trust as he locked his arms around his new Mother-in-law and gave her a big hug.

Several days after the visit, the bus stopped by our little house and there was Pappy. I smiled at him, for I knew that he was checking to see how Calvin was treating me. I ran to meet him, flung my arms around him and invited him into my home. He said he just wanted to stop by and would have to catch the bus back out of the holler to get home before dark.

It was a small home, but I kept it clean and I could tell that he approved. We talked for a short time and soon the bus came back and he left as quickly as he had come.

But he left me happy. He knew now where I lived, and I knew that he felt welcome to return.

As I walked back into my house to begin making Calvin's supper, I found myself humming.

Ere we reach the shining river
Lay we every burden down
Grace our spirits will deliver
And provide a robe and crown

Yes, we'll gather at the river
The beautiful the beautiful river
Gather with the saints at the river
That flows by the throne of God.

It seemed like the right thing to sing, because I had just passed through my own troubles, but had now reached the shining river of my new life. I was Calvin's wife, and I was like a new creation.

CHAPTER 20: Surviving the Winter

As I sat next to my handsome husband in the car, I memorized his six-foot four-inch frame and wondered about his childhood. It was truly amazing the twists and turns that brought him into my life, and now we were on our way back to where his life had started.

My husband was the toughest man I had ever known, and I would soon meet his family for the first time and see where he came from. For our visit I had packed a lunch of fried chicken and chocolate cake, which we ate on a little picnic between home and Walker County Alabama. And as we drove and picnicked, he drove me down his own memory lane.

He had told me only after we were married that his birth name was Calvin Columbus Romine and that he was born March 2, 1911. His grin went crooked as he explained that he got the nickname "Calton" because his younger sisters could not pronounce his real name.

And there the entire family would be waiting for us - his parents Luther Napolean and Mary Matilda and the eleven other children. Two of them, Nettie and Silas, were children from Mr. Romine's previous marriage to a woman who died in childbirth. Mary raised the two stepchildren and had 10 children of her own. Howard, Grady, Allen, Elbert, Charles, Gracie, Ollie, Naomi and Ruth, I was going to meet them all.

Luther Napolean Romine – Emily loved the Romine family from the beginning and they, in turn, loved her...

It was a long, long drive to Alabama, and my first trip out of the Appalachian Mountains. Calvin had gotten a used car right before we were married, a 1928 Roadster. It was the first car I had ever ridden in and I thought it was so sharp and smart looking. He always kept it clean and shining. But this morning I was so excited and twisted up inside wondering if his family would like me that I could barely enjoy the ride. I think Calvin realized that I was nervous and kept me listening to him talk most of the way. He had me staring out the window, explaining that when we got there, I'd know it was Alabama because the dirt was red. I laughed at him but didn't believe him at all. Who would believe that?

We finally arrived in Townley, Alabama, in the late afternoon, and sure enough, there was red dirt everywhere, even leading up into the driveway of the Romine house. I turned to him, about to tell him he was right, but he had his sights on other things and pointed before I could say anything.

"There they are, Emily," he said with quiet excitement throbbing up in his deep voice. And there stood his family on their home's rocking chair-lined porch. They were smiling widely as they greeted me.

I stared up at them, amazed by their size. Where my parents had always struggled to keep us fed in the tough winters, this family just radiated sturdy, well-nourished health and sunshine. I stepped shyly down from my seat and stood on the running board, but Calvin's brother Grady paid it no attention. He got to me first and lifted me into the air, hugging me and kissing me on the forehead. Everyone else followed, gathering around me like they had always known me. Suddenly a plump, smiling woman with white hair up in a bun stood next to me. Calvin grabbed her by the hand and said, "Mom, I want you to meet Emily, my little wife."

We made our way to the house, and they made me feel at home in short order. The house was just enormous to me, cool inside and clean. Tired of sitting, I felt like dancing around the giant house so that I could see everything at once. This was a place of giant people and giant houses and they were now my family.

Even the girls where tall and lanky, just like Calvin. I smiled as they talked about how tiny I was, and they were right. I was tiny compared to them, and I felt very young when Mother Romine suddenly sat down and pulled me onto her lap while the others got things ready.

The sisters seemed just as interested in me as I was in them. I had to admit to myself that they were lovely. Ollie was sweet, with a beautiful smile. When she laughed with her other sisters, it made me smile. Naomi was tender too, and spoke very quietly to her brothers and sisters. Ruth had a special twinkle in her eye that reminded me of Calvin and told me that she had his sense of fun and probably liked to tease just as he did.

Oh but the smell of food took over and I was so hungry. They led me to the kitchen, and in the middle of a large room sat a table with benches on both sides and chairs at each end. A sideboard with dishes sat against one wall. A coal stove laden with pots of food sat in the far corner and a square table with wash basin sat under the window overlooking the road.

Mom Romine sat at one end near the stove so she could serve from the pots and Father Luther sat at the side next to her. He was a strong looking, lean man with no extra fat on his bones, and he was every bit the head of the house. I could tell that he was the man in charge, and I liked him instantly. He hugged me before I sat down and I knew then that he liked me as well.

As we ate, me seated between Mom Romine and Calvin, I was entertained with stories about their farm. They explained that the Romine farm was an original land grant of 600 acres. The property had been divided between two families, leaving them 250 acres, which the family farmed through sharecropping. Cotton and corn were the principal crops, but most all their food was also homegrown.

The table seemed loaded with food. There was a large platter of fried chicken, a bowl of black-eyed peas, fried corn, mashed potatoes, fried okra, biscuits, gravy, sliced tomatoes, slaw, green onions, and a dishpan full of fruit cobbler pie. Iced tea was at every plate, which was something new to me. They had no refrigeration, but ice was kept wrapped in a white sheet with a quilt wrapped around it in the middle of the wide hall that ran the length of the house.

Dad Romine prayed a prayer of thanksgiving and the hungry group filled their plates. After eating and with the dishes done, I played in the front yard jumping rope with the children. We began a popular song to keep time with the jumping feet and the twirling rope.

"Cinderella dressed in yella, went upstairs to see her fella."

I was still a child. Still, I had my fella. He sat with the other grownups on the front porch in the rocking chairs, enjoying tobacco. They watched as I played.

Our first visit came to an end too soon and we were back on the way to the mountains, complete with a little handful of the red dirt that I could show to my family when I saw them. I knew more than ever that I had married a wonderful man who was the member of a clannish family who loved each other relentlessly.

Being there set his memory off, and he shared his life stories with me on the way back home.

"It would shock you to know what I've seen riding the rails, Emily," he laughed. "Hard headedness led me there, and I got a full dose of hard living. I had been nothing but a roaming man in my younger days. I married against my parents. But then I divorced her and left them both in Alabama to find a better life. That's when I roamed the country, avoiding the rail guards who were hired to keep hikers like me from using the boxcars. Those are bad men, Emily, just looking for an excuse to kill or disable men. I've had some really close calls, dodging those bulldogs."

During one such narrow escape, he told me how he entered a boxcar and found a black man riddled with machine gun bullets. Calvin was scared he was next, and stood still, frozen in fear as the lifeblood flowed out of the man and trickled across the floor of the boxcar. The guards came in then, and Calvin thought he'd had it. Apparently though, they had been too excited to catch the guy to spend much time on Calvin. They even took the time to explain as they were pulling him out that he had raped a white woman in the town back, and had tried to flee. They left the boxcar as quickly as they had come, leaving Calvin shaking in a corner.

"That's the life that led me to Harlan. When I arrived, I had accepted that I needed a break from that kind of adventuring, so I headed out to all the nearest mines, asking for the foreman and a job.

"Buddy, we don't have any work here," the foreman told him. The mines aren't booming." But Calvin wouldn't give up and asked, "Well, where do you live?" The foreman told him where he lived and turned to leave.

"Well, I will be sitting on your front porch when you come in from work this evening and I will sit there until you give me a job. I know there is always work for one more good man."

The man laughed and walked away. Calvin made his way to the man's house and when the foreman arrived from work there sat Calvin talking to his wife. "Well, a man that determined to work would have to be a mighty good man." It was his first work in Kentucky's "black diamonds".

Harlan rests in the heart of the mountains. The roughest and highest parts of the state are in Harlan County. Coal seams weave around the Cumberland

River, and they produce some of the highest grade of bituminous coal in the country. Harlan began scale mining a few years before I was born, and the first railroad brought in the first train to carry large boxcars of coal out of the mountains. When the First World War increased the demand for fuel, mine owners were in a perfect position to cash in. Not only did coal business boom, but the lumber made the town a big shipping point.

Lives, not to mention entire towns were built around coal. The coal portals drew people out of the mountains into settlements complete with merchants and sheriffs and doctors and stores. During the 1920s, many people could make a good living at working in a mine. Many say though that the mine owners got fat at the worker's expense, and kept their money at the cost of workers' lives. Tempers flared and the United Mine Workers Association fought the Harlan County Coal Operators Association. Add to that the fact that coal mine owners were hiring armed thugs to beat up men, kick them out of their house and blacklist them if they tried to organize, and you're bound to have bloodshed, and that's just what Harlan got.

I was much younger in May of 1931, but Johnnie and Dallas were working in the mines by then trying to make a living and help out the family. They were careful to keep some of the more terrible stories from me, but Woodrow did find out things, and that's how I knew about the Battle of Evarts a couple miles from Harlan and even less from Verda where I now lived with Calvin. Carloads of company men and their hired thugs were racing down from Black Mountain to Evarts when unemployed miners waiting on the roadside confronted them. Not hard to imagine what must have happened, but the end result was that some people were dead and many others were shot up pretty bad.

That brought troops into Harlan just to keep the peace, along with writers and politicians and everything else. If you wanted to be against the coal owners, you met at Evarts is what I heard from Woodrow, and men all around seemed to flock there. Still others felt like the angry ones were just looking for a handout, when all they wanted was to work, even though it was a hard life with lots of dangers. They were no strangers to any of it. When Dallas and Johnnie spoke to Pappy, I often heard Dallas say, "It's too bad that speeches don't put food in people's mouths, or no one would be hungry."

And he was right; it was still so hard to earn a living. The coal companies would cut wages down to nothing, and take money from the men's wages before they were even paid, subtracting for rent in the camps or repairs on tools. Then, instead of issuing money they were issuing scrip. When I had been a child I'd had no idea that the scrip Woodrow and I used to buy an extra dollars' worth of candy wasn't actually money at all, but credits issued by the coal company, which meant you had to buy food at certain stores. I also didn't realize that the coal companies owned the stores themselves, and that the prices there were higher than at other stores.

As the miners tried getting help for themselves, both sides resorted to more violence. Many miners were beaten and almost a dozen were murdered, with no witnesses to the crime. Newspaper people who came to Harlan to tell the miners' story were in real danger. No one ever found out who beat the Union organizers and ran them out of the county. No one ever found out who shot the reporter of *Crawford's Weekly*, or who took the reporter from the *Federated Press* for a ride out on a lonely road and shot him. But everyone knew. Everyone was supposed to know.

The nickname Bloody Harlan was well deserved, and Calvin had been in there like my Dallas and my Johnnie had been, just barely staying safe and out of trouble. But despite being careful, there was just no protection from Black Lung, which seemed to start in everyone who had first the terrible cough and

247

then the slow suffocation that would eventually kill him. No amount of hard work would keep a man free of the disease, because it just didn't care who it attacked.

The stories convinced me that he should come out of those mines, and I did everything I could to help us get by without depending on them. Much of keeping that promise to myself depended on gardening. Just like my mother before me, I learned to keep a good garden, and Calvin had learned farming as a child. So we worked hard as a team on our first one.

So that year Calvin bought a pig, built a pen and fattened him on corn for slaughter in the fall.

Hog killing time is well known in regions where people raise their own food. You have to have to wait for the first cold snap of November to start it, because without refrigeration you need a collection of cold days to cut up all that meat without it spoiling. So when the cold weather hit and all the flies had flown, Calvin hired two black men to help build the tripod that would hold the hog. Then we walked to the pen, he put the barrel of his shotgun on the pig's head and "whap!" Quickly he grabbed him by the legs, flipped him over and stuck him clean with a knife, straight to the heart. When the heart was hit, the blood drained away like the Cumberland at high flood. When he bled out, we lifted him, hind feet first until the head cleared the ground.

Earlier we'd gathered water from the well and filled a large black kettle over an open pit, stoking it so that it would boil. When it was ready we would use it to scald the pigskin. The ham we ate was cured with the skin left on, and because you did that you had to take all the hair off the skin before you started curing. Removing the hair was tough unless you scalded the pig. So after the pig was dead I stood next to the fire while Calvin raised him up on that tripod and lowered him into the boiling water, left him in a few minutes to boil and then lifted him out again with pulleys. Then we dragged him over where all the hair could be scraped off using tin cans, taking care not to make any deep gashes in the skin.

Then we pulled him up again, and split him open from tail to top. His guts rolled out with a soft plop and an awful smelly steam rolled into the air. As messy as that was, it was easy compared to getting rid of the head, which needed a few twists of a handsaw from Calvin. As night came to a close, the inside of the big old thing was opened up and washed clean. Once that was done, we left him hanging by the tripod for the night, to cool off. Then we hauled ourselves into the house and collapsed, exhausted and bathed in sweat. I was too tired to even worry that I had just tracked a big mess into my house.

The next morning I was up before the sun. There were little things I needed to do that took an extra dose of courage. First was cleaning up the intestines to put to good use. Using a knife, I removed all the fat from them to render later. The intestines I turned inside out and scraped clean. Then I put them in a bowl of salt water to prepare them for stuffing later when we got ready to make sausage.

We didn't eat the head; it went to the black men who'd helped Calvin with the tripod. I had wanted to save the jowls, but he said those should go to them too. When the men took the head home they might use it to make headcheese, or they'd make scrapple from it by cooking the head in a big kettle until the meat fell off the bones. The meat would then be ground up and put back in its own juices. Cornmeal could be mixed in with this and cooked some more, until the meat started to float. Then it would be poured into pans. As it cooled, the fat would rise to the top and seal it. Later it could be sliced out and eaten cold or fried for breakfast, served with applesauce.

But I did make a meal of the heart and the liver for Calvin, as I wouldn't eat it. He had them for breakfast that morning before we started up again. First the hooves were cut off. An axe was used to get the ribs and the backbone free from the rest of the body to be salted down. That left the hams, shoulders and sides, which had the most meat on them. I put some of the trimmings aside for sausage, and some on the stove for the evening meal.

Before the meat could be smoked, it had to be salted down for about a month. Then it would be washed down and hung on poles to smoke until it turned a deep dark brown. After it was smoked, it could be packed away and used as needed, or traded later in the year for things we did need.

So while Calvin did all the chopping, I took all the lard, cut it into cubes and rendered it. The lard that came straight from the hog was the best, the fat from the intestines was also rendered, but it wasn't as good. All was stored in tight lidded jars though, to use through the winter. By this time we were tired again, and it was the early hours of the next day.

The next day we worked on the last of the meat, grinding up the trimmings for sausage, mixing it in a big washtub with sage, salt and pepper, frying up small batches to test. Then we stuffed the meat in the casings I'd saved, then fried up. The leftover grease from the frying was poured into the jars and sealed tight. A few of the casings we looped on a big pole to go in the smokehouse too. When we ran out of casings, we fried the rest of the meat as patties and sealed them in containers too.

From one large hog there came buckets of pure lard, shortening, hams for curing in the smokehouse, quart jars of canned sausage and cracklings for crackling cornbread. By the end of the third day, we were both pretty proud of our efforts. We sat on the porch and stared at the sun setting on our first big effort together, something that would keep us alive during the cold winter months. Calvin knew this too and said so as he rubbed my tired shoulders and kissed my forehead. He was proud of me, I could tell from the look in his eyes and the crooked smile he gave me. I read in his tender expression that I had pulled my own weight.

"We're a good team, little one," he said softly, and I had to agree. I knew then that with Calvin I would survive. We were a stronger team than either of us had bargained for.

Emily and Calvin at the old train depot in Baxter, KY

CHAPTER 21: What the Day Brings

And the early seasons of my marriage went along in a joyful rush. Before two years was up I was with child and we needed more room for the baby. Mining camps weren't the best place to raise a child. We left a miserable camp in Verda to move to a little community called Harlan Gas, and into a white frame house with two bedrooms a living room and a kitchen.

I loved my front porch with large rockers for the baby. I had dreamt of a house like this and now it was a reality. I would catch myself patting my belly with contentment. The months had been long and I was sick most of the time like Mother had been, but I had the feeling deep inside me that it was all going to be worth the pain and the wait.

My labor pains started in the late afternoon of August and increased during the night. I knew I was in for hard births if my mother was anyone to go by. I was right. The labor was rough and long. But I had seen many of the women down in the camp having their children, so I knew what to expect when my time came, unlike my mother did when she had poor Sudie. Nonetheless, Woodrow sat on the porch listening to my screams and wondering if I would survive. An old country doctor was called. In the wee hours of September 1, 1936, they laid my beautiful baby girl in my arms.

"Let's call her Shirley," I said, "after Shirley Temple." Shirley Temple was a very popular star at that time. Calvin also wanted to name her Jean, after Jean Harlow. So she was named Shirley Jean Romine.

Their first baby, Shirley Jean Romine – September 1, 1936

Woodrow helped care for me as I had done for him through typhoid fever. During that time he grew very fond of Shirley. Everyone doted on her. She was a beauty with brown eyes and shiny brown hair. She had lots of aunts and uncles who smothered her with attention. Woodrow in particular always brought special gifts, letting her stick her small hand into his pocket to find candy or a small toy. It reminded me of when Pappy brought me candy and Mother called him down for spoiling me. It was a special contentment for me to know how deeply my brother loved my baby girl.

The only shadow on my days was the troubles in and around the mining towns. Everyone carried guns to protect themselves, and Calvin was no different. He always wore a gun in a holster attached to his belt. Many times he would disappear in the night to go on what he called the raids, to break up fighting that took place between the company's hired thugs and the out of work miners, and that's when I always worried that he'd be hurt. The only real fights we ever seemed to have would be over those raids. I kept trying to convince him to take me with him, that way he'd have one person devoted only to keeping gunfire from catching him unaware. Of course he'd refuse, he wouldn't have me running around in the dark with only the moonlight to guide us, and that would have us both standing toe to toe with each other, and then hours of stony silence.

But there were other things to tend to. Soon the first day of school approached for Shirley and we were both so excited about it. It all felt so familiar to me, remembering how Aunt Susan held my hand and took me to school. It was amazing how the years had flown and it was such a sweet feeling getting my own precious daughter ready for that first day. We shopped with the money I had saved and bought some new dresses and shoes, as well as pencils, crayons, paper, a ruler and a lunch pail.

On her first day, I watched Shirley hurry through her breakfast, dressing and getting ready for school. We laughed together as I walked her to school, and then stood outside watching the other kids as we listened for the school bell to ring. We met her first teacher together. I left her with the instruction that she should walk home by herself. I felt a little uneasy about this, but it was the mountain way. Children learned early to care for themselves.

My baby really seemed to love school, and I loved to be at home waiting for her when she returned. Unfortunately she found another love in her walks home that wasn't so special.

Shirley loved animals, especially cats. On that very first day of school she picked up a stray cat along the railroad tracks and brought it home. The poor thing had diarrhea and messed all over her. I had to strip her in the yard and bathe her outside. Later that same month she brought home a puppy. I had a hard time explaining not to bring home stray animals. "You never know what they might have," I said, "some have worms and you may get worms from these animals. Do not bring anymore home." This didn't make her first year of school too easy I have to say.

Shirley loved animals and brought many home.

But I was also having my own first year, really, which was being alone in the mornings without husband or daughter to look out after. And during the day I was following in the footsteps of my mother, keeping the house as clean as I possibly could and working in a garden of my own, so that I would have food to can for the winter months. Every day I knew I was doing something that would make it easier on Calvin so that we didn't have to depend on work from the mine. I was very happy with my life.

After a bit we moved again to the community of Baxter, about a mile away, on the mountain people called Sookie Ridge. The property had chicken houses on it and a large garden area. The only real downside was that the outhouse was a ways from the house. "Just a nice walk," Calvin laughed and gave me his crooked smile. There was a small pigpen behind a smokehouse. The first year we housed two pigs for fattening.

I taught Shirley how to feed the animals. She often scratched their backs with a hoe. As she grew, one of her first chores was gathering eggs, and again she once got the opportunity to put her own special mark on her chore. It started because Calvin made homebrew behind the coal stove. Shirley loved the homebrew, and would slip behind the stove to get just a touch without me knowing. One day she had a touch too much and when she went out to gather eggs, she crawled right into the hen's nest. So instead of pulling out one egg at a time, she sat perched in the nest, dropping them like rocks into the bucket that she'd left on the hen house floor.

Soon I heard the commotion. When I ran out, there sat Shirley all giggly, quietly dropping the eggs one by one in the bucket.

"What are you doing, Shirley Jean?" I asked softly. She smiled an angelic smile, giggled and rolled back on her haunches. She turned and looked at me as she dropped the eggs one by one in the bucket, watching as they splashed and screaming with laughter.

"I see," I said, picking her up out of her spot with the hens. Gently I sent her home so that I could finish her chore that day.

My days as a mother were filled with sweet moments. As a young girl living at home I often thought my mother worked too hard and sacrificed too much and I always wondered how she could stand it. It seemed to me as I did the cooking and cleaning and washing that it was all just one chore after another and though I picked up what I needed to know, my favorite place was the rest that school gave me.

But now I discovered as I took over the running of my own house that it was different now. My family needed me like they needed no one else. I was the mother. I was the wife. And I stood either for their happiness or their misery. Mother was like that to me too. Like her mother before her, she taught me how to be in charge of a house, how to cook and garden and tend to the farm animals. And she taught me how to make the most out of what each day brings. Either we were going to have enough eggs or we weren't. Either we were going to have a clean house or we weren't. If the day brought enough time to collect flowers or it didn't. If it did, it was a day to enjoy and remember for its sweetness. If it didn't, sweetness must be found even in a chore. When a crop came in and it was time to put up for the winter, the sweetness was knowing that my family would have at least one meal in the winter that they wouldn't have had before.

My life made a difference in the life of my husband and my daughter. My husband could be the man he was because of who I was. I realized in those early years just how much my mother must have loved being my father's wife, and even in spite of all the hard work and all the hard times, how much sweetness could be discovered in keeping a home.

One sweetness I enjoyed most came pulling practical jokes. I always kept Calvin wondering what I would pull next. One morning after Shirley left for school, he came in from the mines covered with coal dust. He pulled the tub from back of the house and filled it with warm water. I waited patiently until he stepped in the warm sudsy water, lathered up with a bar of Life Boy Soap and covered his face with a thick lather of soap. Then I quietly sneaked up to the tub, placed a long string of firecrackers there and lit them. Then I ran as fast as I could.

Calvin thought someone was shooting and nearly broke his neck getting out of the tub. Woodrow and I laughed until our sides ached. Luckily Calvin never became angry with me. He was a man with a wonderful sense of humor anyway, and I think he understood that I was still a bit of a kid and growing up too. When I hid in our trunk, wondering what he would think if he came home and I was gone, he would just laugh at me.

Calvin loved to pull practical jokes too though. Sometimes as we went fishing, Calvin would lift me up and carry me through the water to keep me from getting wet. Other times he would pretend to slip on the rocks, dunking us both. This made any offer to carry me a gamble, but one that I always took. The spirit of open laughter in the house was new for me since Pappy had gotten so caught up in his drinking, and I think Woodrow enjoyed it as much as I did, as he was always with us.

Make no mistake. My husband was also a tough man. He carried a .45 and nothing scared him. He spoke very little about what was happening with work in the mines, but I knew from talking with the other women in the camp and from witnessing things with my own eyes that times were dangerous. Calvin was always reading the papers for news, and when there were radio announcements from WHLN in Harlan, it was suddenly quiet time in the house no matter what was going on. A lot of arguments went on in the mining camps, about what was the right thing to do. Men wanted to work, to raise their family and keep them fed. But they wanted to work safely too, and they wanted a fair wage for their work. Wanting both of those things sometimes meant that you were targeted by company men, and as a target you could watch your house and all your worldly possessions go up in flames. Your wife could become a widow.

I knew that if it came to it, I'd kill for my husband as surely as he'd kill for me. He found out pretty early on that I was capable of it. During a visit to Alabama, Calvin's brothers did target practice from the top of the barn. One day they carefully pulled me to the top and watched as a dog crossed in the distant field. His brother Elbert teased, "Emily, I bet you can't shoot that dog."

"Oh yes I can." I took aim and downed the poor dog. Until we left, I was scared to death that the owner would catch me. "I had no idea I could shoot that far," I said. We all scooted off the barn and never told anyone.

But living with those facts of life was easy after a while. You accept that there are dangers, and in your mind you decide what you will do when and if those dangers come. Then you put the thoughts to the side and you live your life. Knowing there are snakes in the woods doesn't mean you never go outside.

But our lives were always on the edge, always shifting around on us. Without warning, everything would change in a way we couldn't predict and still catch you off guard. That's what happened late one Saturday afternoon after a day of shopping in town. We returned to the house to find Herman sitting on the porch. Herman was Calvin's son, and he was five years old. While we were gone, his mother dropped him off and left him alone on the porch with a small pouch of clothes.

I immediately took to Herman. He loved Shirley and she thought the world of him. She now had a brother and he now had a sister. We quickly became a happy family.

Eventually though, Calvin's parents asked to take Herman. "Son," Mary said to him, "Herman will fare better on a farm for he needs to learn the ways of farming. He can learn the ways of the land. We will love him and be good to him and he does want to come live with us." I think this was one of the hardest decisions Calvin ever had to make, and he stalled his mother for a long time. But she continued to ask, and he continued to think about it. As much as he wanted Herman with us, and as much as I wanted him to stay with us, he agreed that the boy would learn how to farm and make a living with his grandparents. With us, it was likely that Herman's future would be in the mines. And the mines were terrible for Calvin, as I knew they'd be terrible for Herman. So why doom our Herman to a life he didn't need to live? I loved Alabama and felt it was the right decision. Finally Calvin agreed, though it really made Shirley sad to see Herman leave.

It was a strange life we led, that all the time we were together I worried about the thugs at the mine when it was the Black Lung that did the most damage. After a few years, a deep cough developed in his lungs that shook his body. He could no longer manage the long hard days. At twenty-one, the doctors forced him to quit. Without the miner's wage, Calvin knew we'd be in for hard times.

But he never gave up going from place to place asking for work. He landed a job with a dairy driving a truck making rounds in the county. But not long after going to work he had an accident while driving that almost killed him. Woodrow drove me to the hospital, where Calvin was unconscious, with a broken nose, concussion, internal injuries and broken ribs. Both of his eyes were black and his face was swollen beyond recognition.

The nurses explained, "You cannot spend the night with him. Women are not allowed in the men's rooms for other men are sharing the same room."

"I'll whip every damned one of you if you try to keep me away from him," I explained. We did not discuss it again.

I stayed with him for days, and for days he did not improve. I told Woodrow, "If he stays here he will die. He needs my care. I know he will be better off at home than in this hospital."

"Emily," he began, but I wouldn't let him continue. "When he hears Shirley's voice it will help him get better."

"Emily," he started again. I slapped my hand against his chest and stopped him again. "I can cook special meals that will help him heal. You must help me get him out of this hospital." With that, Woodrow put his hand over mine and said distinctly, "Emily, I agree with you. How could I argue with the sister who nursed me back to health when I almost died? Do you want my help or not?"

That night, very late, he drove the car to the back of the building. We both slipped up the stairs and stood quietly in the dark while the nurse made her last rounds for the evening before heading back to her desk and her book. I knew she wouldn't come again for another hour unless she heard a patient in distress, so we both walked as quietly as we could into the room and without a noise, lifted Calvin out of bed and down the stairs into the waiting car.

Woodrow was good not to question me. I think he was just as worried as I was that Calvin would die. And the truth of things is that hospitals then weren't like they are now, and I was right. He needed the care I could give him. Sure enough, he soon improved and within weeks he was up and about. Shirley's smiles and my care had done the trick.

When he was well enough to look for work he quit his job at the dairy and went to work as a police officer. Woodrow also landed a job with the police department and they both worked patrolling the rough streets of Harlan. I wasn't happy.

"This is a dangerous job. I try to get you both out of the mines and you have to pick the job more dangerous than working the mines. Don't you realize how many people are going to want to kill you both?" Calvin smiled his quiet smile at me over the table while Woodrow tried to talk me out of being mad.

"It's a good job, Emily, it pays better than I've ever made. And you know something, the work does dry up and leave me out of a job or without any pay but that scrip I can only use in the company store. People need good order around here."

"People don't want law and order around here. They're too busy bootlegging. You're going to have to bust up those stills and take away people make a living, you're going to get shot at."

"They all know me, Emily, I'm not going to get shot at."

"Of course we'll get shot at," Calvin said smoothly, which didn't help my mood. "Shooting is the way people always settle things." I stood up then because even though he knew it, he didn't care. He didn't care that people carried guns strapped to their body and openly carried guns in holsters and that now they'd be aiming them at my husband and my best brother.

So now I had both brother and husband to worry about. I started trying to follow them out at night, and every night Calvin would catch me before I got very far and send me back to the house with a swat on the butt. I was sure that if I went with Calvin I could keep him out of trouble, since I could talk people out of things where he'd just count on his strength to get him out of trouble. Still they wouldn't let me go, and the best part of my day became the second I saw Calvin turn up the drive to our house.

This routine began to shape my life. Then came the night that changed everything. Early in the year, Woodrow befriended a black man who often roamed the streets of Harlan drunk. Woodrow locked him in jail many nights to keep him from freezing to death. One evening as Woodrow left work to make the long walk home to Baxter, the black man passed him alongside the road. He had picked up an old black preacher.

The preacher later testified in the trial that the black man passed Woodrow, drove up the road a bit, turned around and drove back without saying a word. The preacher explained that he'd told the man that he'd hit something, but the old man said, "I didn't hit nothing but the curb in the road." But he had purposely driven back and run Woodrow down with his truck. My brother died there on the side of the road.

So that night when Calvin turned into the house, my feeling of relief was quickly blown away when he walked slowly up the stairs to our door. He looked tired like I'd never seen him before, and I realized that it wasn't just any other day where my husband would come home safe. His face was white, and I asked him what was wrong, but he wouldn't explain. Wordlessly he drove me out to the place where Woodrow was run down. When we arrived at the spot, we sat in the car and he held me around the shoulders while he quietly told me what happened. I couldn't contain myself and jumped out of the car and ran to the spot where he'd been hit. There on the side of the road I looked for proof that he'd even been there, and I found blood and what could have only been parts of his brain.

"Oh, God, not Woodrow, not my sweet, sweet brother!" I screamed and dropped to the ground. Calvin grabbed me then and held me tightly. I would never forget that night. It was February 6, 1940. My brother was twenty-four years old

Then came one of the toughest things I'd ever done. It was my task to arrange for a funeral. I cleared one of my bedrooms to be used as the parlor and there we had Woodrow placed, surrounded by low lights and waxed flowers. The scene was a familiar one, but it was so hard to come to grips with it being Woodrow. I stood looking at his handsome face and thought of our childhood, with all its laughter and fun.

Woodrow had been my buddy. We'd ridden the cow's home together. We'd fought over the size of a Christmas peppermint. We'd eaten candy together until we were sick. I stroked his brown hair and thought about the berry picking and how he shared his money to buy the first dress I bought myself. We had childhood secrets we'd never shared with another soul. And I remembered how proud he was when he twisted his first rabbit out of its hole with a stick. I tossed him a biscuit as he lay in bed with typhoid fever. I'd taken care of him then, but not now.

There was nothing I could do to stop the wheels of a truck from taking his life. And in his lifetime he'd loved my daughter as much as he had loved me. She would grow up without knowing how deeply he cared for her. Oh God, how could I stand to lose my precious brother?

When Shirley was brought in, she could not understand why her Uncle Woodrow could not smile. I could not put the reality of death into words for her. I just stood looking sadly at my family, knowing that she would have to figure all that out for herself. And there was my mother. I reached out to her with a look that I hoped showed her my understanding. We were now both mothers, and this hit us both the same way. Again I watched my sweet mother rub those worn fragile hands as the crow sang that old familiar song, "In the Sweet By and By. I smelled the waxed flowers and felt a sick quiver in my stomach.

So many children already gone.

Woodrow, Emily's favorite brother. Her childhood companion and lifelong friend until his unexpected death so young without a chance to defend himself. Gone at 24 years old – February 6, 1940.

CHAPTER 22: Sweetness and Sorrow

Soon came 1941. World War II was gearing up. In May of that year, President Roosevelt gave a speech that frightened me to my toes. He said, "what started as a European war has developed, as the Nazis always intended it should develop, into a war for world domination."

And he went on. In his speech he painted such a terrible life we would have if Hitler ever tried to take over our country. Bombs would drop on San Francisco and New Orleans. And then we would be under his control, and though his words would start off nice and sweet, our country would soon be a place without the freedom to work for a good wage, a place where we could not worship as we wished. Our entire way of life would fall apart, all because Hitler wanted to control the world.

And the president told us over and over again of the bravery of the British who had been fighting so bravely to keep Hitler from doing all that he wanted to do. For days after this speech I thought about those brave soldiers and all the sacrifices they made. I thought about all the sacrifices that I would make if I were in their shoes. His words made sense to me, like President Roosevelt said, if you waited until you saw the whites of their eyes, you would never knew what hit you. You had to run out there and meet the challenge and hold Hitler and his soldiers back, and devastate them.

And in June he took measures to show just what he was willing to do. We all listened as he ordered all German diplomats in the United States to leave our country. The Germans answered back though on the battlefield, and we listened to the accounts of German troops overtaking the Russian army.

The radio spoke of places far off, but weekly they sounded closer and closer. Many days as I worked around the house, I imagined German fighters storming up our hill and hauling me away to meet Hitler.

As the year wore on, July had been extremely hot and I was pregnant in the middle of it. I wanted to have this second child yesterday. I had been sick for months, my feet were swelling and the backaches never let up. I could hardly walk from the weight of carrying the baby.

Shirley looked forward to having a brother or sister. The nursery held a new bassinet and we were living in Baxter. This was particularly nice because we had Mother and Pappy close by.

After years of waiting we now had our dream home. It was a new large house painted white trimmed in red with an "L" shaped porch. It reached around the backside and just off the kitchen was a separate wash house. The yard sloped off in the front with a breathtaking view overlooking Baxter. The trains could be seen snaking their way out of the opposite side of the mountain, their spirals of smoke trailing into the air and the sound of the whistle echoing through the trees. The land was rich for gardening. We owned one horse for plowing. We had all the comforts of home with lots of space.

Calvin saved enough to pay cash for the place. He could not get insurance. City water had yet to be run that high on the mountain. We had planned to raise children in the safety of the mountains, high away from floodwaters where they could run and play through the woods.

And along came that familiar feeling. The labor pains started coming and on July 20, 1941, another daughter made her grand entrance in the wee hours of the morning.

We named her Joyce Ann Romine. I wanted to nick name her "Joe" from the name Calvin had used when we were dating. She was somewhat of a runt, but strong and determined.

Joyce Ann Romine – July 20, 1941 – a happy family photo, Emily, Joyce, Calvin and Shirley

The very next day, President Roosevelt asked Congress to extend the draft. Less than a month later, his measure passed in the House by one vote.

And in October, when Joyce was just three months old and we were constantly being told about our navy ships getting torpedoed and sunk, I took Typhoid Fever. Calvin was beside himself and called his mother in Alabama for help.

Mom Romine left on the next train to care for the new baby and me. "Don't worry, son," she assured him. "I will take care of her and Joyce. You have to work to care for the family and I will not leave her side until she is up and about. Now you be off to your work"

But Calvin did find a cow with a calf and this provided Joyce's milk during my recovery time. Mom Romine cared for me daily. I had lost so much weight that you could see my bones. She was a stepmother to me and to the baby, and she had to do many of the same things for us both, like bathing and feeding. I worried the family with thoughts that I would die as my delirium continued for weeks.

Calvin began bringing me milkshakes every day and soon I started gaining a little weight. He was excited to see me improving and begged just to take me for a ride. "Please, Mom, can I just take her for a short ride. I promise to be careful with her."

Mom Romine padded the car with pillows and I was carried out to the car. It felt like Heaven. I had been in the bed for weeks and the fresh air was so wonderful. The ride turned out to be really good for me. I had feared that I would never hold my baby again or hug Shirley. It was a wonderful day to be alive. I had enough strength to sing lullabies to Joyce. I cuddled her and was soon acting out the lyrics to "John Henry."

John Henry was a very small boy
Fell on his mammy's knee;
Picked up a hammer and a little piece of steel,
"Lord a hammer'll be the death of me,
Lord a hammer'll be the death of me."

Joyce and Shirley were soon laughing loudly at my game. Soon even Calvin forgot his worry, and I could see his hand relax on the wheel. I smiled at him for a few seconds and in response, he changed to "Casey Jones."

Come all you rounders that want to hear
The story of a brave engineer.
Casey Jones was the rounder's name,
On a six eight wheeler, boys, he won his fame.
The caller called Casey at half past four,
He kissed his wife at the station door,
He mounted to the cabin with the orders in his hand,
And he took his farewell trip to that promised land.
Casey Jones mounted to his cabin,
Casey Jones with his orders in his hand
Casey Jones mounted to his cabin,
And he took his farewell trip to that promised land.

Oh how I loved my family that night. So much had happened. I had lost my dear Woodrow and there were days when I missed him deep in my bones. My husband faced danger every day of his life. Most people don't understand living like that. They plan for tomorrow and see nothing that stands between them and reaching it. They know they live in safety and security.

But mountain families live differently. They don't take life for granted, because they understand better than most that they aren't promised tomorrow. And in many ways, this is the only way to live. To depend on the things of this world was to gamble on air and fog. I loved my life dearly, and I missed all those people who brought sweetness to it. But many of them had been taken away from me. That evening in the car with my lovely daughters and my handsome husband was a perfect evening. It was not an evening to dwell in my sorrows. It was a gift from God.

If the events of my own life did not convince me of this, the world events did. Later that year, to our amazement, we heard that the Japanese attacked Hawaii in the early morning of December 7, at Pearl Harbor. At just before 8:00 a.m., the Japanese planes flew in from six aircraft carriers and attacked our boys in the harbor in two bloody waves. Suddenly we knew all about Wheeler and Hickam Fields. Suddenly we knew about Battleship Row. Suddenly we knew all too well about the U.S.S. Utah, the Oklahoma, the Nevada, the Arizona, the Maryland, the California, and the West Virginia and all our war dead and wounded.

The country was grief stricken with the loss of over two thousand men. Harlan had sent their share of boys to fight and die, and would lose almost two hundred men during the attack on Pearl Harbor and in the battles that followed. The Harlan Daily Enterprise headlines brought news of tragedy and fierce fighting daily. The Courthouse square was full of mountaineers sitting, spitting streams of spit from their wads of tobacco and talking about the war. Times were hard and people were nervous about this war.

Life on the mountain was not simple. We faced our own wars every day, fighting to stay alive and keep our families healthy and safe. But this was an enemy we didn't know how to fight from home. There was no way to lock out the frightening thoughts that came to us over the radio, telling us of enemies we'd never seen killing boys we grew up with.

All the talk of war convinced me to make Christmas special that year. Heavy snowfalls began near Christmas and I planned toys for the children. We popped popcorn and strung it to decorate the tree. I hunted the woods for mistletoe to hang over the door and I picked fresh holly to decorate the house. Black walnuts were gathered early in the season ready for shelling for my famous "Black Walnut Stack Cake." I stuffed a large hen with old-fashioned corn bread stuffing I mixed by hand.

My brothers and sisters gathered in for the big day and lots of food was prepared for I wanted everyone to have a grand Christmas. The radio was turned on to my favorite station, WHLN Harlan, playing all the Christmas songs while everyone sang along and laughed. I made sure there were gifts for everyone. My brother and sister's laughter filled the house. My parents smiled. It was another perfect day.

While we had our minds on the war, things were still hard in Harlan too, so we had to keep working like we'd always done. Seasons came and went. The girls found ways to entertain themselves, sometimes walking the railroad tracks to the carnival in Harlan and other times just taking long walks into the mountains. They loved cardboard sliding down the mountainside in the leaves or cracking different nuts they found in the forest. They had plenty to choose from, with the walnuts, chestnuts, hickory nuts and beechnuts. Each had its own unique flavor.

In their early years we marked the passage of time with birthday celebrations. I tried to make their birthdays exciting so they'd always remember them. Baking a six layer chocolate cake and topping it with candles became a tradition, and so did filling the old bathtub with water for bobbing apples. I made sure the children came first. Family was the most important thing in my life and taking care of them became my joy.

Again I felt a familiar feeling in my belly and knew there would soon be three children to care for. My mother had sixteen, but as I rubbed my swollen belly I knew I would never have that many. I began praying that this baby would arrive safe and sound.

Carol Susan Romine was an unusual baby, born at home on Sookie Ridge on February 2, 1944. It was a cold Groundhog's Day, and Doctor Parks delivered her as I struggled. She arrived with a head of blonde, curly hair, and hazel eyes. Her blond hair turned light brown, as she grew older, hanging softly around her beautiful face in delicate ringlets. She had fine olive skin and high cheekbones like her great-grandmother, Mary.

Carol was a happy baby, always laughing and full of smiles.

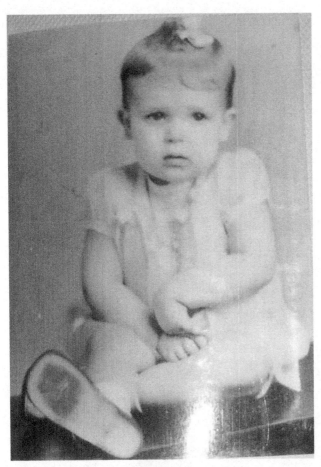

Born on Groundhogs Day, she would always remain "the baby."

She was a good baby and rarely cried. And her middle name was Susan, from Aunt Susan..

Enter the "Romine Family." Joyce, Calvin, Shirley, Emily and Carol.

But as God granted us a gift of new life, the whims of this world dealt us another blow. When Carol was barely three months old, I smelled smoke and soon found flames in the kitchen. Joyce was just two, Shirley was in school. The flames were shooting to the sky. I could feel the intensity of the heat against my skin. I picked Carol out of her crib, grabbed Joyce by the hand and screamed, "Help, help! My house is burning. God, please someone help me!" I ran to the front of the yard and screamed to the mountains for help, the echo of my voice trailing over the mountain. I stood helpless wondering if someone would help.

The reason that Calvin couldn't get that insurance was suddenly a reality, because there were no fire trucks to aid us on Sookie Ridge. Calvin had taken Shirley to school, stopped by the grocery store and someone told him his house was on fire. He drove as fast as he could to get back up the mountain. By the time he arrived there were people everywhere, and I was screaming hysterically for neighbors to get the clothes, the bedroom furniture, anything they could.

The flames engulfed the house.

I ran both the children to the next door neighbor and ran back to help. As I looked over my shoulder one last time I saw the woman holding Carol in her arms. Joyce stood beside her clad in her white panties and tee shirt. Their home was burning to the ground and there was nothing I could do to stop them from seeing it. My dream home would soon be gone.

A thought suddenly hit me. "Calvin, where is Penny?" I screamed. Penny was Joyce's dog. She was nowhere to be found. I knew this would just break Joyce's heart and I cried some more. Later, her charred body would be found under the floor where she went to hide.

What little we salvaged was carried down the mountain to Mother and Pappy's shed and stored. Most of the furniture had heat blisters. The house stood in ashes, the only structure left was the brick foundation. Melted glass of different shades of blues, greens and red could be seen scattered inside the remains of our once perfect home. Clouds of smoke rose over the maple tree. The grass was burned black and the mountain breezes carried the smell of smoke.

We had no choice but to live with Mom and Pappy until something better came along. I knew it would be hard to live with my parents, partly because Bessie and Blanch were still at home.

So we all crammed into that house and made the best of it, and I have many memories of that place. One beautiful Sunday morning, Shirley begged me to go to the store. "Please Mother, let me walk Joyce to the store to buy the paper. I will hold her tight and take good care of her." After some hesitation I gave in with, "Alright, Shirley, she can go, but you must hold her hand tight for Joyce is quick. She can be out of your sight quicker than you will know."

Shirley took the hand of my baby and they giggled away down the mountain. When they reached the bottom, Shirley looked both ways, then turned toward the main road and attempted to cross over the railroad tracks. Trains could be heard blowing their whistle a far distance away. Suddenly Joyce jerked loose, ran ahead of Shirley, across the tracks, down the steep embankment to the road and into the path of an oncoming car.

A sailor and his fiancée were on their way to get married at the Harlan Court House. He swerved his car desperately trying to miss hitting her. His car knocked her off the road, down the bank and almost into the river. Shirley watched in horror, screaming and crying. Joyce lay motionless near the water.

The man from the car ran towards her, picked her up gently and sped away with her in his car.

"Oh God," Shirley thought, "She is dead. She ran back up the mountain repeating in high tones, "Joyce is dead, Joyce is dead. Mother, Dad, Joyce is dead."

I came racing out of the house, figured out what had happened, then asked, "Who hit her? Shirley, honey where did they go?" But Shirley had no answers. She stood there shaking and crying. She only knew a car hit Joyce and someone picked her up and left with her.

Calvin was already starting up the car. We flew off the mountain across the tracks, to the Harlan Hospital. As we stepped out of the car, we could hear screaming from somewhere inside. I turned to Calvin with relief. "Thank God, Calvin, she's not dead. I'd know that scream anywhere."

The accident worked out pretty good for Joyce, who was treated and released the same day. She spent days recuperating in a dark room for the cut over her eye and enjoyed treats of candy and fruit brought by the polite sailor. Given the sorry state of the economy, it was a real luxury.

Soon though, Calvin was able to buy another house opposite the one that burned. It was a modest house, but we were glad to be able to move into it and give everyone in the family a little more room. The girls were growing up so fast that we needed it.

As her first day of school approached, I was worried about Joyce, who was small like I had been and wondered if she would suffer the same fate. But we bought school clothes anyway and dressed her in a new pair of emerald green corduroy pants, white tee shirt and bows in her hair. On the first day I combed her hair, kissed her sweet lips and told her she was the prettiest girl in the world. Then I watched my girls walk off the mountain together.

Shirley had learned her lesson about Joyce and held her hand tightly as they left to catch the early morning school bus. They stood in line to load the bus. They sat by the window as they made their way along the riverbank parallel to the narrow road to the school.

Loyall High School had grades 1 through 12. The grade school classes were on the lower level and the high school classes were on the second floor. Shirley held her sister's hand, walked through the big double doors and up the stairwell to the office. There she registered Joyce for her first day of school.

She took her to her classroom and introduced her to Mrs. Lay, the first grade teacher. Joyce sat in her chair and never said a word.

That is, until she came home that day. When they came up from the bus, Joyce ran to me, spilling her heart out about the horrible day she had. I held her tenderly in my arms, caressing her and telling her it was okay. Unfortunately, her first day of school wasn't as pleasant as mine had been.

First, the bus ride to the school had been awful. The driver had stopped along the way picking up other children, but she got stuck with a dirty, snotty-nosed, bare footed boy that continually passed gas.

Then the morning hours went on forever. She felt far too shy to raise her hand to go to the bathroom and sat there until it was too late. Her pants were already wet when she got up enough nerve to raise her hand, and she held back tears of embarrassment. The teacher nodded and off she went to the bathroom wondering if anyone noticed her wet seat. She cried in shame, dried herself best she could and returned to class and her wet chair. She picked up her crayons and resumed coloring.

The bell rang for lunch. The teacher lined up the children single file for the march to the cafeteria where the food was nothing like home. She ate little and could hardly wait to play on the playground. Soon she was swinging, having a good time and walking dangling in mid-air hand over hand on the hand walks.

But even then she wouldn't be able to enjoy herself. As she hung onto the handwalks the same dirty boy from the bus ran up and pulled her pants right off down to her ankles. Now she hung upside down in her white underwear.

She dropped to the ground and yanked her pants back up. Then she ran to the teacher crying and told her the situation, but instead of getting sympathy the teacher laughed. What humiliation! The torment grew worse as her laughter grew louder. First she had wet her pants and now they had been yanked off and this teacher thought it was funny. "This was nothing like the school Mother told me about," she thought. The teacher already had her favorites.

The bell finally rang and the dreadful day was coming to an end. She lined up again at the school bus, boarded and took a seat by the window up front. There she waited for Shirley. The high school was having a pep rally in the gym and she knew they would soon be out to board the bus. While she sat looking out the window, that same dirty boy who passed gas and yanked her pants down now knocked on the window. As she raised the window to see what he wanted, he stood on his toes and spat in her face.

She fought to get off the bus for she could hear her Daddy saying, "You never let anyone run over you. If you do they will continue to do so."

Off the bus she tore and into the dirty boy she went, never giving a thought for what he could do. They fell into shrubbery as they fought and he soon overpowered her, choking her with all the power he had. She decided that she was indeed going to die on her first day of school.

Suddenly someone pulled him off, took her to the gym and explained to the principal how the boy had choked her. Joyce stood there in the middle of all those people, neck throbbing, wanting only her sister. She cried again with shame. Shirley was soon by her side and the principal expelled the dirty boy for three days for choking Joyce.

They again boarded the bus taking them back to Sookie Ridge and to the safety of their home on the mountain.

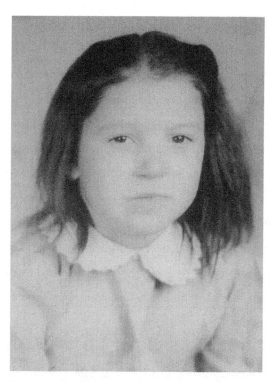

Joyce, her first grade photo the first day of school – 1947 – not a happy camper.

I cradled my daughter in my arms as I listened to her passionate saga. It wasn't hard to remember my own early days in school when I too had to defend myself from a bully. Oh how Woodrow would have laughed when I told him, giving me that look that said, "Well, the nut doesn't fall far from the tree, sister."

But Joyce got past her early school day dramas, and I got the chance to relive my own childhood in the lives of my children. Each day it was something new, and when they got together with their cousins, it was like watching one of the picture shows at the Margie Grand, because I could see the faces of my brothers in the faces of their sons. As my girls grew, they had free range of an entire mountain. Nothing would keep them away, not poison ivy, stinging nettles, chiggers or snakes. They traipsed through rocky areas and climbed onto the tops of cliffs, barely escaping death as they scaled the ridge to top a narrow ledge. They hunted for arrowheads and caves. Their playground was endless acres of ridges, hills and cliffs.

Still, the loss of our home seemed like the first in a string of terrible events. Less than a year after the fire, Murphy was badly hurt at work.

Murphy had married Calvin's sister Naomi and moved to Michigan to work in one of the plants. It was during war times and the mines were all but shutting down, leaving little work left in Harlan.

A telephone call brought bad news. Murphy had finished his shift and was talking to the plant manager when a steel ball attached to a cable accidentally fell loose from the ceiling and knocked Murphy to the floor. He suffered serious head injuries.

I had to be with my brother. "We'll go on the next train. He may need blood," I said, feeling a panic in my heart. I packed quickly, leaving the two older girls with family and taking Carol and Calvin with me on the train to Michigan.

When we arrived, Murphy was still unconscious in the intensive care unit. On May 2nd of 1945, Calvin wrote to my parents.

Dear Mr. Howard & Folks:

Will take time and write you a few lines this cold morning. Murphy is awful low. They are giving him blood transfusions. I talked with his Dr. late yesterday eve to find out his condition. This is what he said. He operated on that puncture in his right temple and that after he cut into his head found it to be worse than he expected. He said he had a blood clot and brain hemorrhages besides his fracture. He said they were having to give blood and it was very, very serious. He told me to get blood donors over as soon as possible. Emily went gave a pint and this man that looks after this rooming house gave him a pint. I'd give anything if I could give some. But with low blood pressure and asthma you can't give. I'm trying to get hold of Murphy's Union Headquarters for blood donors. I'm telling you the truth from what the Dr. has told me that it looks just as bad as can be. The Dr. told me over the telephone yesterday eve. He just had a very slim chance but they were going to do everything humanly possible to save him. Emily and the baby doing just fine. Made the trip all right. Emily said she was awful sore over the big needle they put in her arm. I'm just about sick with the flu. I've took the worst cold I've had this winter. How is Joyce and Shirley making out? You all do your best to take care of everything for us and we will write you every day and give you the latest details about Murphy's condition. As soon as it is dry enough get Clem to plow my Irish potatoes & get someone to hoe the rest of my garden. As soon as he makes a change we will come home. So ans. Soon. Yours truly, Calvin, Emily & Ground Pig

P.S. I called to have Sam come over for blood I haven't heard whether he came or not.

He was never the same again, and he lived for years in pain. His left side was totally paralyzed, he had partial brain damage and he walked with a cane. Naomi was pregnant when the accident happened, but she could not care for the baby and for Murphy, who needed nursing home care for the remainder of his life. Their marriage eventually ended in divorce.

So I was appointed his legal guardian, and I fought hard with the system to get his disability. It was a difficult decision, but we decided that he'd live in the Danville Nursing Home in Danville, Kentucky. I hated for him to be there, and made sure that I never missed a birthday or a Christmas or any chance to go up there to visit him and bring him small gifts, or just gum or some other treat. I wrote him when I couldn't be there. I took the girls as often as I could go too, though it was hard for them to see him depressed and with a shriveled body. But I had to be there for him because without us, he had no one.

I honestly think that it was this added strain of his illness that dealt mother a fatal blow. She was so full of grief that she couldn't fight off the stomach cancer when it attacked her.

Cancer for us in that time always meant death. I often wonder why we bothered going through the treatments, which were worse than the cancer in my opinion. First came the surgery, which never seemed to help. Then came radiation therapy, which is the worst torture I can imagine. It literally burned her from the inside out. After each treatment, I was the only one of the family who could stand to care daily for the horrible radiation burns, so I walked down our little lane to their house and tended to her.

"They're burning me up, Emily," she would say to me. "The pain is almost unbearable." Then she would fade out, only her lips moving in prayer and I knew that she wasn't with me, but somewhere deep inside herself, pulling on God for strength to stand the pain.

When I wasn't with Murphy or my own family I was in the hospital with my mother, standing by helplessly while she screamed in pain from the second floor of the old Harlan Hospital. When she didn't improve, she was taken to a hospital in Knoxville. She never recovered from her last surgery. She died late in the fall just when the leaves began to turn.

Pappy was completely devastated, so I made the arrangements for the funeral. First she was laid out in the home for three days of mourning, and then she was carried to the top of Kitts Holler.

There's a land that is fairer indeed

And by faith we can see it afar
For the Father waits over the way,
To prepare us a dwelling place there.

In the sweet bye and bye
We shall meet on that beautiful shore.
In the sweet bye and bye
We shall meet on that beautiful shore.

Pappy had finally mellowed through the years and before she died, my parents had forged a bond that was stronger than ever. He was lost without her. "Em, I'm so scared. Martha is the only life I have had. What will I do without her?" he cried.

"Pappy, I will always take care of you, I promise." And so I was good to my word. Every day one of the girls or I took a meal down to him. He spent days at a time making his guns and whittling on the porch.

In a way, it was nice to have Pappy around. The girls got to know him as they became adults and I was especially glad of that. Pappy had been so special to me when I was growing up, and then had gotten so bad with his drinking. Now I was able to see him as my father again and our relationship really improved. I think the fact that we had both lost family made us realize what was most important in life.

CHAPTER 23: Sookie Ridge Spit Sisters

As a call to my spirit, God also showed me the hope of new life through my girls. They were blooming like sunny spring flowers.

Shirley was a bookworm and still loved sneaking into Calvin's homebrew. She was good with her sisters for she was the eldest and felt responsible. She also still loved the animals and did her best to take care of them in her own special way.

Carol was the quiet one. She loved her dolls and often begged Joyce to play house with her. She never needed spanking. I saw Pappy in her sparkling eyes and Mother in her high cheekbones, a hint of her Indian heritage. When she sucked her thumb and twisted strands of her hair, she looked like a princess.

It was Joyce who had my temper. She often went to her special rock as I had gone, and as her grandmother had gone before us. She loved the high cliffs, listening to the wind sweeping through the tall trees and the sound of spring water running through crevices. She often helped Calvin clean fish and wild game. She spent every minute not doing chores wandering in the mountains.

A fun day at the Cumberland River swimming hole – Joyce and Carol sneaking a special face for the camera.

Calvin hung a swing in the breezeway of our barn by this time because we no longer had horses or cows. The girls would get very creative in their play, especially when they thought no one was around. One day they decided to have a "pooting" contest. The three sat in the swing and each had to take turns pooting until they couldn't poot any longer. Every once in a while I would overhear them doing this while I was hanging the laundry or doing something else outside. First you'd hear them poot, then they laughed until they cried and then it would be the next ones turn.

When they couldn't poot anymore they decided to change the game to a burping contest. Again they'd play until they screamed with laughter. They spent the day pooting and burping until they were called home for supper, tired with all the laughing.

The girls loved slumber parties. Their best friends at the time would come over, extension cords would be borrowed from neighbors around the mountain and the loft of the old barn soon had electricity for a Friday night party. When they were bored they'd go off to Gladys Nolan's Grocery store for cool aid, RC Colas, bologna and candy.

Since they were so much like sisters, the girls decided that all the participants in their slumber party should become blood sisters like the Indians did. So using a straight pen, they scratched their arms for a smidgen of blood. But the scratches hurt, so for fear of bleeding to death they decided it was easier to chew chewing gum, swap it to each other sharing their spit and become a Spit Sister. Carol initiated the ritual.

This was the birth of the "Sookie Ridge Spit Sisters." They were the coolest girls on the mountain. They had initiated Wanda, Priscilla, Bev, Louise, Margaret and Dot into their "Sisterhood."

And I've said before that Joyce had a penchant for excitement, but she wasn't the only one. As Shirley got older, she got into her share of scrapes. Once I happened to catch her trying out a dare from Sam's son Jimmy. By this time, Sam had divorced Vesta, who had been running around on him for a few years and had married Clara who was a sweet little wife for him and had two daughters, Joyce June and Juanita. All the children got along well, as Shirley and Jimmy were close in age and my younger girls were close in age to Clara's.

So one particular day, Sam and Vesta were visiting us. Jimmy and Shirley had gone off quietly together to get away from the younger girls. Unfortunately for them, not only had the younger girls seen them leave, but had decided to follow after them. When I saw the younger girls go, I decided to sneak after them as well, to see that they didn't get into mischief.

So off the older children went, crossing a fence and a creek up to Mallie Cooper's old well, which was flush to the ground.

"I dare you to jump over the well," Jimmy taunted. I stood back, thinking she might decide not to do it, but prepared for the worst. I didn't want to embarrass her really, not if she was going to back out. I could see the younger children in a clump of bushes a little ways off from me, and I felt we all held our breath while Shirley made her decision.

Just as I thought she would back down, she suddenly jumped.

There was dead silence. She slipped, barely clearing the well as she dropped one shoe into the well. My heart dropped into my stomach as she fell face down on the ground. I could hear the shoe hitting the water deep in the bottom of the well.

She started to cry and pleaded, "Jimmy, don't tell Mom for I will get a whipping." Well, it was time for me to make my exit. I knew that Shirley was done with her adventures for the day, and I hurried back home. As I stood at the porch, watching them pick their way back to the yard, Jimmy yelled as they went in the back door, "Aunt Emily, Shirley jumped over Mallie Cooper's well and lost her shoe in the well."

I watched Shirley turn white. She knew what was coming. I turned to her, scolding, "Shirley, you are to never to do anything like that again." She stood stock still, but I could see just a hint of relief on her face. I knew when a whipping was needed with Shirley and now wasn't one of those times. She had gotten off easy though and she knew it.

Shirley and Jimmy

My children had lots of chances to see their relatives, because my brothers and sisters visited often. Most Sundays after church Sam and Clara and their three children visited. In those early days they shared the cooking. I would wring a hen's neck before going to church and prepare it for the Sunday meal. Clara and I would stay busy in the kitchen frying chicken, making mashed potatoes, slaw, biscuits, gravy, green beans and banana pudding. Everyone loved our iced tea.

But eventually Sam and Clara moved to Cleveland, Ohio and only made surprise trips to visit. From then on it got harder and harder to enjoy them. I never knew when they were coming until I heard the sound of their car engine coming up the mountain. It also seemed that Sam never came to visit unless he had something to show off.

"He must have a new car this time," I'd tease when I saw the car drive up. "The girls will have fancy dresses and patent leather shoes, because he loved dressing his girls." On these visits I rarely had more than a large pot of pinto beans and cornbread and a hot chocolate pudding to feed the whole group. No one minded and it was filling.

Juanita loved my cooking, but would never chew her food and I sat as I watched her wolf down those pinto beans and cornbread. She chased the food with cold milk. At bedtime I made pallets on the floor in the dining room and the girls shared the beds. Carol and Joyce June slept side by side and Joyce and Juanita slept on the other side of the pallet. During one such night I heard Joyce yelling, "Mother, Mother, come quick. Juanita threw up." I raced to the dining room and there on the floor sat poor white faced Juanita. Joyce yelled, "Look Mom. She puked all over the bed and I have beans all over me." It was a funny sight looking at those little girls with Juanita crying and Joyce mad. A change of nightclothes and clean sheets settled everyone down for the night.

I also started noticing a change in the way Sam dealt with Jimmy. He often had hard words for Jimmy, and used his belt on the boy often. I don't think I ever heard Sam tell Jimmy that he loved him, and I found myself wondering if he took out his anger with Vesta on the boy, which just wasn't fair. I wasn't surprised when Jimmy finished high school and went off to join the Marines.

Jimmy had always loved being at our house and playing with Shirley, so when he left, he would write to me often and keep in touch with me more than his own father. I enjoyed getting his letters and telling the girls all about his training and his new life. That is, until the day I received a letter that really made me worry.

Aunt Emily,

I bought a beautiful new motorcycle. It's so shiny and smart. I think it's the nicest thing I've ever bought for myself. I earned the money by myself and didn't ask Dad for a thing, not that he would have given me anything anyway.

Love, Jimmy.

I felt the fear rise in my throat over that letter, and I couldn't explain why to anyone. Days later the news reached us that Jimmy died on his motorcycle in an accident. His body was being shipped back to Harlan.

Sam asked me if he could have one of the graves that Calvin and I now owned. The arrangements were made, and we sold them the plot. Sam buried Jimmy there in the Resthaven Cemetery at Loyall along with so many other members of our family. Shirley was heartbroken, for her it was like losing a brother. It was a sad funeral seeing Jimmy's picture sitting there on the casket in his Marine uniform.

Meanwhile, the shadow of Calvin's illness was slowly starting to creep up on us, quietly stealing the life from his body. The Black Lung was worsening. First he had to quit his job as police officer and take a job with a dry cleaning company owning his own delivery route. It was during those years that I became a light sleeper, always listening for the sound of his breathing, because as it worsened, sometimes he would find waking up in the morning really difficult. Other times he would lose his breath while he was awake and just pass out.

It took a great toll on his body. But he had a fighting spirit and I fought the battle with him. One of my remedies was to climb on his chest, open his mouth and stick my hand, which was very small, inside. With my fingers I could strip out strings of thick mucus from his throat, clearing the passage for more air. I had to work quickly when he passed out, pushing my panic to the very bottom of my gut as I pulled this enemy out of his lungs. But I did my best to keep this fear from him, kissing him happily when he'd regain consciousness. It was our very special kiss of life and it was the sweetest thing I'll ever remember about him.

The years passed in this way, the girls going to school and loving and teasing, and Calvin and me loving and teasing as well. Many things I learned from my mother I was happy to use with my own family, but some things I left to the past. Like the first time I tried to cook a possum like my mother loved to do. I was confident that he'd be as delicious as anything my mother would have made.

Calvin had brought the thing home, had even cleaned it for me so that I only had to place it in the middle of my baking pan, surrounding it with yummy sweet potatoes. Then I stuck the dark black pot in the old coal stove. Oh the smell was wonderful. When I took it out of the oven a couple of hours later, I gathered the girls around the table in the kitchen and we opened the lid together to see the results of all the hard work. I looked down at my girls, who were all pretty much ready to jump on the thing as soon as they were given permission.

But when the lid came off, we were all in for a shock, for all the meat had fallen off the bones and the carcass was laying there all white bones shining and the meat laying around it.

You could have sunk a boat with the weight of that silence. No one uttered a word, not one sound. I started to hear my heartbeat in my ears. Out of the roar in my ears came Joyce's small voice.

"Mother I don't think I can eat any of that thing." I heard Shirley's muffled laughter. Carol grinned quietly, then winked. That was the end of it. We all got tickled and soon were roaring with laughter.

The girls and I feasted on the sweet potatoes, but none of us could touch the possum. Calvin had one of his best meals ever that night, which I told him to enjoy as best as he could, because it was the first and last time I'd ever have a possum in my stove with all his shining white bones gleaming back at me.

Despite my fears about him, Calvin was still strong and did all he could for the family. Sometimes we'd dig a big hole out from the house, layer the bottom with corn shucks and store our apples and corn there for the winters. Later, he dug a cellar under the floor. He poured concrete for the floor and the girls were given the task of placing the potatoes in there. They had to be careful, and usually were because if any of the potatoes touched they'd rot and the girls would get a strong talking to. It was a nice cellar and we could also keep our canned foods there, lined on shelves that he'd also put up. Our lives were focused on survival, and if Calvin had anything to do with it, we were going to survive with room to spare.

There was another need I had though, and when Calvin couldn't help me with it, I found it in Dressen.

CHAPTER 24: Give me that Old Time Religion

I think of all the fresh images of my girls and how lively and lovely they were reminded me that my own beloved husband was slipping away from me, and the girls would not have their father as long as they expected to. This pushed me to my knees in prayer. I started attending a little country church in Dressen, not far from where we lived.

Dressen isn't much of a town, and no more than a curve in the road. Most people would never know it is existed. Rivers ran through the place, and near one area of rolling water was our little church. I always thought it was so lovely tucked back off the road a bit, sitting right next to the parsonage. Both of the buildings were built by members of the church community, put together by the hands that were in the building each Sunday, clasped in prayer.

The inside was simple, but it was beautiful too. There weren't any stained glassed windows when I was going there, just a plain wooden floor and simple heavy worn pews. On the small stage up front was the place for the preacher. The pulpit where he delivered his sermon was made from dark wood and tall like a big oak tree. The alter was handmade, but without paint where many knees had knelt in prayer at that little alter. Next to it was an old worn bench, and it was always being used, either by the deacon or a guest preacher. I often laugh to myself thinking about Curtis sitting next to the preacher, sometimes with one red sock on and one black sock and his little white buckskin shoes. Behind there to the right of the small platform was where the choir sat, usually about twenty people. And in the far left corner, just large enough for a piano, sat Agnes at the keyboard.

"You'd never know that Agnes was blind, Calvin," I told him one Sunday afternoon. I loved watching her. She would hold her head way back and looked to the ceiling as she knocked the ivory off those keys when she got into her playing. She wore dark glasses so you could not see her blinded eyes, except I could see them roll around in her head through her dark glasses, and she kept her hair all neat braided and pinned up across the top of her head with little combs tucked into the sides to hold stray hairs that might fall down. She sang and swayed to the music as if lost to the world. Sometimes she sang so hard saliva dripped from her mouth and she would kind of suck it back in, but kept on singing. Sometimes she would sling those combs out of her hair and someone would always pick them up and give them to her when she finished her singing and playing. She always smiled even when she sang and I often wondered what made her so happy when she had been blind all her life I guess it's like they say if you never have it you won't miss it and that's probably like Agnes. She could never miss seeing what she had never seen.

Give me that old time religion,
give me that old time religion,
give me that old time religion
and it's good enough for me.

I heard it in my head again and smiled, doing a little dance while I fixed dinner. The people in my church were friendly. The path to God was simple and strict, but the people leading me onto the path were so loving about it that I couldn't help but worship the Lord with all of my strength.

I loved makeup and high heels and showing off my legs, and he loved that I did it. I never had to worry that Calvin would run around on me like my brother's wives did. I knew how he loved me. But there was never any harm in being pretty, waiting for him when he got home. When I started attending the church in Dressen, at first alone and then with the girls, I understood quickly that everyone there dressed modestly and did not indulge in makeup or picture shows or liquor. How was I supposed to fit in with all that, a girl who'd grown up picking blueberries for pretty dresses and dating cute guys and going to the picture shows at the Margie Grand?

"None of that matters when I pray with them, Calvin." I leaned into him and took his hand so that I was sure he was listening to me. His sweet face looked down at my hand and he turned it over so that he could stroke my palm with the index finger of his free hand. "When I see them all praying, and when the Holy Spirit comes down on all us it's like being in paradise. It reminds me of my mother, and she was the kindest and strongest person I've ever known. I want the peace that she has, the peace that helps her live the way she does with a husband who isn't as good to her as he should be."

He raised his eyes to me then, and in their sparkling depth I realized that he understood what I was saying and I answered a question in my own heart as well. This God of mine was the man who was going to look after us both, and look after me when Calvin was gone. I needed to know that when Calvin took his last painful breath on this mountain that I would not be alone. "Always looking for your rock, Emily?" he whispered. I felt tears touch the back of my eyelids. He knew me too well, this man who was so much better looking than Clark Gable. "You'll have to come see for yourself, Calvin. I hope that you'll come, for I want to be with you in paradise."

The very next Sunday, he was in church with me.

God took up that opportunity to speak to his heart. I felt it in the prayers of the others, and I felt it in the songs. And when the Holy Spirit fell on me, I received Him in joy. I was transformed into someone new, singing and praying in tongues and swaying back and forth in the aisles with all the others.

Calvin was so moved by this that within months, he had accepted the Lord as his savior as well. It was one of the happiest days of my life.

297

This changed the things that were acceptable in our house. Gone was the homebrew behind the stove, and the makeup for me. I'm not sure, but I think Shirley was the most disappointed about the homebrew and Joyce was the most disappointed about the makeup. I know we all missed our shorts, but I never let on that any of that mattered anymore. It changed our life and the girls, but they could not understand the change.

But for a long time after that, one thing frustrated Calvin, and that was that no matter how he prayed, the Holy Spirit would not fall on him like it had fallen on me. I know how much he thought about this, how hard he prayed. Soon we were attending church three nights a week, and as we drove back with the girls asleep in the back car, he would tell me his fears.

"I don't understand why God hasn't blessed me with tongues yet," he'd speak into the night.

"I'm sorry, Calvin. I know how much you want it. But this isn't for you or your timing. This is God's plan, and you have to think of all the other people in the Bible and the patience they had to wait on the Will of Our Father. I can tell you though to rest assured in His love, and rest assured that I am praying for you to receive the Holy Spirit too."

Calvin prayed for that blessing from God and he was more focused on it than just about anything I'd ever seen him do. It really changed him, and it wasn't a change like Pappy. He was quieter somehow. He didn't drink at all now; not that he'd ever had a problem drinking. He watched his language. He led us all in prayer every night at bedtime. He led while everyone took turns blessing everyone and asking God's forgiveness and keeps us safe there on that mountain. Calvin now held his temper like never before. I know it was hard sometimes, the same with me, but he held in there until he cooled off.

And after some time, what he'd been praying for all that time finally happened.

I will always remember what a beautiful day it was. We walked into the lovely old building for worship service. The first thing I noticed was the smell of soap and I realized that some of the church ladies had cleaned the inside of the church just for that weekend. Today there would be a visiting black preacher, along with his congregation. He sat up front with our preacher, but his congregation sat in the very last pew in the back.

It was dark inside and we took our place on one of the sturdy, old worn benches. In front was a simple altar railing just in front of the large wooden altar. As I sat there waiting for people to come in and settle themselves, I had a quiet moment staring at it, thinking of just how many prayers must have risen to the Lord from that very place. I knew that many of them over the past few months had been from Calvin, and I rejoiced in that.

It was our first foot washing service and the ladies gathered the feet washing pans and the men brought in pails of water. Everything was set for the feet washing service. Towels were stacked on the alter and when it was time to start washing each other's feet, the curtain separating the choir from the congregation were pulled. The women sat in the choir and the men stayed in the congregation.

The preacher was already in his place in a simple chair behind the altar, sitting with the deacon and the visiting preacher. You could feel the excitement build in the sanctuary as people arrived and the pews filled with people already singing and praying.

Before he even got a sweat up, the Spirit descended on the congregation. First it fell on Mrs. Bedford, who'd been given the gift many times before. She started singing and praising the Lord and then behold of all beholds, she kicked over the pan of water and water went everyone. I almost felt like we were at a baptizing. I raised my hands to thank God for the gift, and stood up to sway to the music that Agnes was pounding out from the keys of her piano. After a few minutes had passed, I looked around and noticed everyone settling down and we pulled open the curtains. I saw Calvin sitting in his spot with his head down and his hands draped over his knees. He was deep in prayer.

I knew how he felt and knew he had taken this new form of life very serious.

Then there was the sound of a tambourine shaking in time with the piano playing.

> **Give me that old time religion,**
> **Give me that old time religion,**
> **Give me that old time religion,**
> **And it's good enough for me.**

People swayed in the pews with their eyes closed and the light of Christ shining on their faces. Still Calvin sat with his hands draped over his knees, and I wondered if he was feeling bad, or if he was about to have an attack with his breathing. I raised my voice to heaven and I prayed out loud this time.

"Please Lord, if it is Thy will."

And then, the most amazing thing happened. Calvin stood up slowly, to his full height, and he began swaying in time with the music. His hands lifted over his head, and suddenly I felt a tingle go all through me as my man started speaking in tongues. It was like drinking a pure shot of homebrew to have all that energy slide through me with warmth and love. I really felt a little tired from all that spirit and singing and washing feet.

Oh was the congregation ever excited. They were so happy that we all but forgot about the visiting preacher, who didn't seem to mind after all was said and done, and it was explained to him how long we'd been waiting on Calvin to receive the gift of the Holy Spirit. After it had passed, I cried and hugged him and he sat back down on the bench with tears in his eyes and a joy on his face that told me better than any words just how deeply he had been touched by God. I rejoiced with him.

The preacher announced that it was time for the foot washing service. The women pulled the curtain and pans were passed around. As people danced in the spirit and praised the Lord, some of the women's hair pens fell out of their hair and down came those long strands of hair. They danced and sang in the spirit. It was a service I will never forget.

Before long, there was talk that Calvin should become a minister, and get ordained. Calvin spent many nights after the service talking things over with our pastor, and reading the Word and praying. He also consulted me.

"Well I think that if you've received a call from the Lord on your heart that it would be a sin to ignore it, Calvin," I told him one night when he asked me again about going through with it. I had never spoken that plainly to him before, and I could tell that it had hit him right between the eyes.

"I want to be a good husband to you, Emily," he said softly. I could tell that he was worried that providing for the girls and me would be hard as a preacher.

"I think the best way for you to be a good husband is by following the will of the Lord, and teaching us all how to do the same," I said just as softly. I could tell that this had given him something to think about.

He didn't speak of our conversation again for several days, but I had seen a letter go out to be mailed, and knew that it had been to the Assembly Church of God headquarters. After a little while he received a packet back, that had some papers he had to get filled out and witnessed by our preacher. "You realize what this means, don't you?" he said to me, as if he weren't sure I'd approve.

"It means that I will be with you all the way," I said without blinking. He smiled and pulled me tightly against him. "The Lord sent you to me, Emily." That day he put aside any other doubts, and once the paperwork was witnessed it went back to the Assembly of God headquarters, where they made him a minister.

With Calvin as an ordained minister, we began attending church three times a week. There were revival meetings and he soon took over the Mosley Church of God across Pine Mountain. The Pentecostal Holiness church was our church, which did not believe in makeup, cutting off the hair, shorts, pants for women, going to the theatre, ball games, drinking or cussing.

The children felt like prisoners and Joyce argued with her daddy. "I don't believe that God put us on this earth to be miserable. I know he meant for us to have fun. What is wrong with going to the movies or ball games?" She lost that fight though, for they had to give up activities that didn't involve church.

But Calvin bought an old player piano for twenty-five dollars, and the girls made the best of it. Joyce began to play. She continued lessons for seven years, but finally quit because she did just fine learning music by ear. She played for the church and then finally Calvin found a place for his girls to really shine. He put them on the radio.

The local radio station in Harlan, WHLN, would feature a weekly radio show for religious shows. Calvin had a spot every Sunday morning. This was a great way for the girls to sing together, for Joyce to play, and for them to feel like they had something to do that got them involved without feeling trapped by all the praying.

Left to Right - Calvin opening his radio program on WHLM Harlan, with Agnes (blind) at the piano.

An old fashioned river baptizing, with Calvin assisting "Brother Morgan" at the Dressen Church river bridge.

The girls sounded wonderful together.

> *Turn your radio on*
> *And listen to the music in the air;*
> *Turn your lights down low,*
> *And listen to the Master's Radio.*

One of my favorites was "How Great Thou Art." Carol and Joyce sang that one without music and their voices were almost as one. That harmony sent chills through me every time I listened. I always thought they sounded like the McGuire sisters when they sang. Shirley sang lead, Joyce sang alto and Carol sang soprano. Their voices blended and rang in my ears. I knew they should be famous, my girls, but this mountain kept them a prisoner of their own talents. I watched as everyone hung onto every word.

All night, all day,
Angels watching over me, my Lord.
All night, all day,
Angels watching over me, my Lord.

Oh but it was the era of rock and roll, Elvis and the hula-hoop. It was hard for the girls to resist all that excitement. When I was feeling especially troubled by this, I put my love for them into a poem.

MY THREE GIRLS

Dedicated to My Three Daughters: Shirley Jean, Joyce Ann and Carol Sue

Some years ago, God richly blessed
Our home with three sweet baby girls
They filled our world. Our joy was full
Our darling girls, are precious jewels

Oh Lord, they are so dear to me
I only have the three you see
Now they are grown, and far away
So watch over them for me, I pray

I kneel in Prayer, and call their names

There's Shirley Jean, and Joyce Ann
And then Carol Sue, the baby one
Lord take them home, when day is done

Now here they are, my Lord you see
In prayer I lift, them up to Thee
Take over Lord, and set them free
And give them life eternally

Oh my Lord, please hear my plea
Don't let my girls, be lost from Thee
Just hedge them in, and hold their hand
Show them the way, to the Promised Land

You know this is my heart's desire
To keep them from the burning fire
So hold them fast, don't let them stray
And then some day they'll be home to stay

This old world is a dressing room
To get ready to meet Jesus soon
He's coming soon, there is no doubt
And then we'll know what it's all about

When I've gone home to be with you
Dear Lord who'll see my children through
When I'm up there, in my new home
Oh Lord don't let my loved ones roam

Now Lord you know I've done my best
To raise my girls to stand the test
I've done the very best I knew
So now I leave the rest to you.

All my love, Mother

God's gentle Holy Spirit answered my concerns. He gave my dear Shirley a man who loved her. Junior Alley was a handsome boy who enlisted in the Air Force and he was very smitten with Shirley. When she told me they'd go to the courthouse to get married, I wanted to make sure that she had family representing her, so I went along with two of our neighbors, Marie and Lottie. We made the drive to Jonesville, Virginia instead of just standing in the court house with the Justice of the Peace.

Shirley looked very smart in her outfit. It was a blue suit with a short bolero jacket, white blouse and blue pumps. She also wore a dramatic matching blue hat that came down on one side of the face like a movie star would wear. It even had a blue feather that swept down against her cheek. Her new husband looked dashing in his military uniform; it was a sight I'll never forget. At least I knew I was with her and remembered when Sam wrote a note for me to marry Calvin. They listened carefully to the Justice of the Peace, answering his questions quietly, with a lot of dignity, for they were mindful of the importance of the occasion. When everyone congratulated her, she walked shyly to me and said, "Well Mother, I love you for your understanding."

"I'm so proud of you, Shirley," I whispered, and I was. My beautiful little bookworm had shown some real spunk, taking the leap just like she'd done that day jumping over the well. It seemed only yesterday that she was small enough to get a whipping for being bad. Now she was a new wife. My biggest wish was that my mother was alive to know that her granddaughter had gotten married.

Almost immediately after the wedding, Junior and Shirley packed up to his new station in Tacoma, Washington. I was sad to lose her, but happy too, that she was starting a new life. I missed her terribly, but the church also missed her beautiful voice. She could belt out "Peace in the Valley" like Martha Carson. Oh, how I would miss my Shirley. I knew Sookie Ridge had one less of my girls, but I also knew that someday they would also follow Shirley's footsteps.

Some changes though aren't happy, and that was the case with my brother Ray. Less than a year later, life taught us that lesson yet again. It was August 17, 1954 by this time. We'd spent the night on the porch watching the falling stars. The night had been clear, and Calvin had just pointed out the Big Dipper when we heard it. The train whistle started to blow.

Everyone went quiet as the lonesome wail trailed through the mountains with a strange echo. Everyone in those days knew that sound. It meant that the ten o'clock train had hit someone. It sent a chill through me. After a few minutes of awkward silence, we all decided to get ready for bed.

Later, the telephone broke into our stillness. I answered it. It was a friend of ours named Bill. He asked tensely for Calvin.

Calvin stood up, came inside from the porch and picked up the phone. Before he could stop himself, he blurted out, "Oh, my God, Ray has been killed."

I don't remember anything after that, because I fainted to the floor. I came to as Calvin was bending over me telling me he had to leave for a while. Calvin went down the mountain to identify the body.

Worse yet, his wife, sweet Aunt Eleanor Jo, had been pregnant with their fifth child when she learned the news of Ray's death. She had given birth to Kenneth and Curtis and two stillborn babies. She fell apart as I had when I told her the news. She had been waiting for her husband that evening in their front porch swing overlooking the railroad tracks that went by their house. She knew he would never walk that railroad again. She still had pinto beans cooking on the stove for his supper. I held her in my arms and took her home with me for the night.

My brother was such a fun loving person, spending lots of time in our house. The girls loved to swing on his strong arms, which was so funny considering how weak he'd been when he was a baby. As an adult he made up for it. He worked for the railroad and had large muscles from the heavy work. But his last days in our house he spent in his casket, which was brought in and placed in the side corner of the bedroom. I still remember the sights and smells of death, flowers and candle wax. Kind words exchanged in soft whispers. Family and friends took turns watching over him around the clock.

As I rested in the kitchen, I could see Ray's casket. On the last night, when she didn't think I was looking, Joyce walked into the room to see the body. Her movements fascinated me, and I reacted very slowly, probably because I was so tired. She was curious about death, I realized, so I left her alone to examine her uncle.

She must have heard all the talk about how Ray looked, because she stared into the casket for a long time. Then she reached out to feel the lining. Slowly, her hand reached out for his face. She was my curious child and I knew she was up to something.

I had examined the body myself, so I knew she was seeing where the train hit him on the left side of his head just behind his ear. His hair was thick, brown and pretty. His skin was like a rock, hard and cold.

What she didn't see as she stretched over the body was that she was unbalancing the casket. It shifted and I stood up, about to say something as she lost her balance and almost knocked the casket over. But she quickly recovered and ran for all she was worth before I could say a word. I sagged down into my chair in relief and let her be. Dealing with his death was enough for her poor heart without getting blessed out by her mother for dumping my brother in the floor.

Joyce would soon have another close encounter with death. After the funeral Jo asked me if Joyce could spend the night with her, and since I knew she was so heavy with child, I agreed. While Joyce was with her at church the following day, Jo told her that she thought she had started her period.

"Mother, how could she have a period if she was pregnant? Even I know that much," Joyce told me later. "Then when he got up to go to the bathroom behind the church, I noticed a puddle of fresh red blood on the church pew." Then Joyce's pretty face got pinched as she went on. "Mother, I asked her about it when she came back, and she just said that she had been spotting some but didn't want to see a doctor. I know I should have made her go, but she was so sad, and I had no idea what would happen next."

I pulled Joyce to me then, and let her cry. That following week, we received another dreadful phone call. It was Jo's mother. "Emily, if you want to see Jo alive you better hurry." Off we went, Carol and Joyce and I. Curtis, the older boy, was in the yard in a diaper. Kenneth was inside and Jo was in bed. There was an old country doctor tending to her.

Something wasn't right, you could tell as soon as you walked in. Jo lay in the bedroom, her eyes closed and the doctor standing over her.

"Why have you not gotten her to a hospital?" No answer. Before Jo died, she lost the baby and bled through two mattresses. Harlan was a back woods town, but times were changing and the nearest hospital was no more than three miles away. The old doctor had let her lie there and bleed to death in bed.

Now her two boys weren't just fatherless, but motherless too.

I took Curtis that day. I tried to get Kenneth too, and adopt them both, but Jo's mother had favored Kenneth, and when I came back for him she had left Harlan, taking Kenneth with her. We didn't see Kenneth again until he reached adulthood.

It wasn't long after that, after Curtis had just settled in, when Carol came to me, put her arms around me and said, "Mother, I'm so glad that I have you and Daddy to take care of me." I could see in her soft eyes that she'd been crying, and I squeezed her to me. She walked away before I could say anything, but I could tell that the events of that year weighed heavily on her mind. She wasn't just a Sookie Ridge Spit Sister anymore. She was growing up and learning about death.

Unfortunately, some heartache was attached to growing up for Shirley as well. Within two years she had divorced Junior Alley. The one consolation to me was that she hadn't had any children with this man, and she could start a fresh life on her own. Shortly though, we all got news that she had married another man named Harold McConnell. I couldn't put my finger on it, but something in her letters to me about him wasn't right. I cautioned her about finding a man who treated her as good as my husband treated me, but she insisted that everything was fine. I prayed for her daily and let it be.

Joyce and Carol were dating too, a fine couple of boys named Tom and Alvin. Their dates were walking through the woods, target practicing or church. They weren't allowed to go to the movies now that we had religion. I often wondered if it was wrong of me to keep them from sharing in the activities of ball games and movies. My choice of religion was against these activities and Joyce rebelled against her feelings for right and wrong as the church taught. I knew she would leave these mountains one day and often wondered where her life would lead her.

Shortly, there was another tragedy to take up my time. January of 1958 was a cold winter, but the most chilling thing about it was the call we got one morning that Dallas had gotten trapped in the mines.

In those days, working conditions in the mines were still very poor. Men worked at terrible risk to themselves, and I often thought about my brother climbing around in the dark silence of the mine, where poisonous gases could creep into the shaft at any time, and where explosions could literally burn the mountain from the inside out. And that was the year when Dallas was caught by "after damp." That's what it's called when the air in the mine goes bad from the explosions that they set off in the holes. Everyone knew to get out of the mines as soon as possible, but no masks were given to the workers by any of the companies. Caught in the hole during one of those explosions, he was killed instantly.

So the roll they called up yonder added one more Howard to the list. My Dallas was gone too. The after damp that took him reminded me so much of when he got hurt playing around with those dynamite caps and had them go off in his face. Gone was my grandfather's namesake.

"He saved my life, Calvin," I explained, telling him all about his midnight trip with Murphy and my mother, taking me in a bundle of blankets through the snow to the doctor's house for the medicine that kept me alive. I quieted my tears in the other stories I had of him, from the playacting he'd do with Murphy to the potato stuck to his ear. With Murphy's brain damage and Mother gone, I was one of the last ones left to remember all his wild antics. As his casket cradled him inside, we sat on the porch, talking into the night about how our harsh life on the mountain had claimed another Howard before his time.

He had been a loving man, though he never married. He laughed all the time and loved to make others laugh. And so we carried him to the top of the mountain and laid him to rest there with the rest of the family. As the last of the earth was swept in to cover his casket, I could almost feel his spirit taking its place among all the other members of our family.

They would wait until we had finished our crying and then they would begin walking through the tall grass that surrounded the graves. In the old days I cried because I felt like I was leaving them all behind. Now I cried because they were the ones leaving me behind.

It had a deep and lasting effect on Pappy, to see his boy die like that. I think he was terribly upset by it because it could have easily been his fate to die like that if he had been born with two good legs. Of course, outlasting mother like he did just made his moods bad, and this was just another reason for him to feel that he had outlived his usefulness. It's then that he started getting a little more forgetful, which the family just took as a sign of getting older. But late in the fall, what happened to him really shook us up, and spelled the beginning of the end of his life.

Calvin and Pappy set out early one morning for Pine Mountain. They heard red squirrels were abundant and I loved to cook squirrels almost as much as they loved eating them. They left before daylight and drove across Pine Mountain to an area popular for hunting. They separated for the day, when time came for them to leave; Calvin could not find my Pappy. After hours of looking, he finally gave up and came home to call for a search party.

A large search party was organized, the television network brought in cameras and covered the daily search and people from surrounding counties came in to help find him. Everyone camped on the mountain; Joyce, Carol, Alvin and Tommie came to help.

Three days passed with no news, and the weather was not in our favor. A cold front was rolling in, and on the morning of the third day, we got news that the first frost of the season would be coming in that night. Amidst the whispers that he was doomed, I took to my knees in prayer.

It was midnight when voices brought me from the house. Searchers started yelling down the fill that they'd found him. No one could say if he was dead or alive, but I raced up the mountain as fast as I could, and when I saw the stretcher I yelled, "Pappy, oh, Pappy." His eyes opened then and he smiled at me weakly. He was alive.

The ambulance sped him to the hospital. The searchers found one of his crutches a good distance from where they found him. His gun was yet in another place. He became confused with the area when he thought he heard men talking and thought they ambushed Calvin. In trying to get out of the area the terrain was steep with cliffs and dense forest and he went deeper instead of going back to the road.

He was in fairly good shape for being out in the wilderness for three days. He spent only a few days in the hospital, but I took him home for special recuperation. After settling him in, I sat with Joyce on the porch.

"I said a prayer this morning, thanking God for finding him," Joyce said quietly after a few minutes. "I would have been so upset if that had been Daddy. I know I argue a lot about all the church stuff, but I'm so glad I have him around to argue with."

"I know," I answered. She laid her hand on mine for a few seconds, and then she was gone. Though the moment lasted only briefly, I felt so close to Joyce in that instant that I stayed on the porch to have a much-needed cry. Within six months, Joyce would leave the mountain too, for Florida. She had graduated from school in June and on her 18th birthday, July 20, 1959, she left. Calvin could hardly stand on our porch watching the car that took her off our

Sookie Ridge. He finally let go and we both broke under the pressure. She decided to live with a young couple from our church who had gone to Orlando for better wages. Little did I know that she would never return to Harlan to live. She had loved these mountains as I had loved them and I knew in an instant she would miss her rock. I could still see her bending over those beans, lifting each little leaf and picking bean bugs for her allowance. I remember her first day in school when she wet her pants and nearly died from the hands of a mountain boy. I remember when Merle Wilder, her date for the prom had died from heart problems.

Joyce and Merle Wilder at the senior prom. Merle lived less than two months after this picture was taken. (1959)

I could see her and Wanda dancing and laughing as they teased Starlete for asking me for chocolate beans, which were my pinto beans I cooked daily. Joyce was small like me, but I knew she was tough like her daddy. Within months she announced her engagement and before I realized I was heading for Florida on a bus to the wedding. Ronnie was a fine boy and they produced two beautiful children. I had the pleasure of naming Kimberly and Ronald, Jr. would take his father's namesake. Joyce was restless. It was not her goal in life to be married. She went back to work as secretary to Roy Disney of Disney World. I always knew she had a strong will. I had watched as she set goal after goal and I could see how hard she was on herself, but this child would be the one to one day care for me. She was the strength of our family. I also saw that same determination and strength in my sweet granddaughter, Kim.

So as they sang, as they teased, and even as they cried for our losses and fought against their father's rules, I savored every moment I had with them. I watched them grow up, and slowly slip from my home into the light and into the happy new world they were destined to shine in. These were my daughters. These were my very own children. These were my girls.

Dear Joyce,

Daddy is sicker with Black Lung. I have to go to the grocery store to charge food, but sometimes I am called to the back of the store and told that we are over our limit. They always let me have the groceries, but it is so embarrassing I could die. I don't know what Mother is going to do when I leave, but Doug and I are getting married soon and I hope you can come home for our wedding. Mr. Cawood loaned me a dress of his daughter's that just fit. It is the most beautiful dress in the world. I miss you and love you.

All my love,
Carol

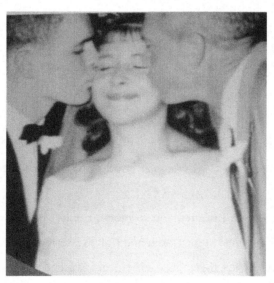

Carol's wedding day with the two most important men in her life. Doug, her new husband, and Calvin, her father. Carol and her father would be buried side by side, passing at the same age of 56 years old.

I read my daughter's mail before she sent it out to Joyce, and I felt her indecision. She wanted to stay and help out with the family, but she was so happy to be with Doug, to have found this young man who loved her so much. It was a new life calling to her, and the old life trying to hold her back.

The last few years had been a struggle indeed. Two years after Joyce had left for Florida, my father was hit by a car on the way to church. It was a blow to me, to have my father survive his battle with the woods only to lose his life so tragically within two years' time.

After his stay in the hospital, I had taken him back to my house, where he stayed for almost four months. However, he had recovered enough to go home finally and life had returned to normal. Then one night, I stopped by to pick him up for church. When we arrived at the church, I left him out of the car and drove off to find a parking place. As he walked toward the church, a car swerved from the opposite side of the road and hit him, knocking him several feet into the air.

I couldn't believe it. I barely got the car stopped before I was running toward him screaming hysterically. "Pappy, what have they done to you?" I knew even before the ambulance arrived that he was hurt badly.

Still, he lived for more than four months with me nursing him. In the middle of all that pain, God was very good to us, giving us that time to say goodbye.

"Your mother and I wanted you so much, Emily," he said one afternoon. I had set a bed for him on the porch and Calvin had moved him there, so we could watch the sunset together. As the peace washed over him, his tongue was loosened, and he told me all the things he'd held back all those years. I listened and patted his arm as my tears flowed freely.

"I wanted so much for you to have everything I never had, sometimes it scared me that I wasn't the father to you that you needed. I wasn't good enough, and I did so many things wrong."

"I have a wonderful life, Pappy. I have everything I ever wanted."

"That wasn't because of me," he sighed. I stroked his hand and shook my head. "You gave me a lot of strength when I was little. You raised me right. I wouldn't have survived without you." And then I felt sobs shake his body, and I knew that he was at peace finally. No more words were necessary.

Within a week he was rushed back to the hospital. I could see his strength fading as I sat beside his bed. Often he opened his eyes and looked up into mine, still with a twinkle and a smile. He pulled my head down to his and weakly whispered, "Em, you know I have always loved you." "Yes, Pappy, I know." I felt his hand slip from mine as he closed his blue eyes and I knew that instant he was gone. I felt myself falling. It was 1961, and I no longer had either parent with me. I broke under the strain, and nurses had to work feverishly on me this time, for fear that they'd lose me too.

Pappy wanted me to have the old house, and Calvin felt it would be a better place than where we were staying, and a nicer place to raise Curtis, so he set about to fix it up. There was urgency in his repairs to the house at that time, because he knew how short his time would be. In today's world, I suppose people would call it "getting his affairs in order." But Calvin didn't have much in the way of an estate. He had no assets that he could give to the girls and me in a Will. Instead, he worked on my house, so that I'd have a good roof over my head after he was gone.

And in that same spirit, Carol met her new life face on. Mr. Cawood was the president of the Harlan National Bank, and Carol had worked for him for quite a while now. He wanted very much to do something special for her, so he let her borrow his daughter Cecilia's dress for her wedding. Doug and

Carol were married in a church. Neither of her sisters could be there because Shirley was taking care of her first child and Joyce was working lots of hours in Florida. Despite that, it is a day that will always stick in my memory because it was the day I got to watch Carol's daddy give her away. I will never ever forget it. Soon after, they two were gone, leaving for Chicago where Doug could find good work.

So truly it was my house now. Without Curtis or Calvin there to take care of me I'd surely be alone. This really bothered Calvin, and it drove him to get the house in order. Pappy's house was brick. It was two stories with a beautiful view of the mountains. The porch was L-shaped and a swing hung from the ceiling. My kitchen was just as I wanted, small enough to be cozy but large enough to cook dinners for the family.

Those were the minor things that made me feel very special, like he had customized the house just for me, which I suppose he had. Every time I walked onto our porch, I felt happy. I loved sitting in the swing and looking out over the mountains.

But Calvin wasn't just interested in the surface things. Even before we moved in, he began to work on the house from top to bottom, repairing the roof to protect me from the rain, sealing the windows to protect me from the cold winter winds and reinforcing the flooring to protect my house from decay. He crawled on the floor nailing and plumbing until he could crawl no longer. The last thing he did was put in a bathroom a few short months prior to his death. It was the first indoor toilet I had ever had.

During these years I watched Calvin become weaker and weaker with the Black Lung. It was memories that broke my heart.

They were also part of my best memories because of Curtis.

Curtis became my unofficial son after his mother and father's death, and he was a handful to raise. I remember once how he embarrassed me in front of our preacher. It was hard for Calvin to have the extra strength to get out after working on the house all day, so the preacher sometimes dropped by for a visit. On that evening, I had baked one of my six layer chocolate cakes, dripping with frosting. It was Calvin's favorite and I'm sure it was the preacher's favorite too.

However, the quiet of the evening was broken that day by a round of barking. I ran for the door fearing an unwelcome houseguest. But there on the porch stood the preacher, held at bay by the dogs and Curtis. They were each taking turns barking at the poor man. First Brownie barked, then Curtis barked. Then Brownie and then Curtis repeated. Then Skipper barked, then Curtis again. I nearly died with embarrassment. I quickly scolded the trio and sent Curtis to his room for punishment.

Curtis, Calvin and Emily. Curtis loved "barking" with the dogs on the porch.

But he really wasn't any worse than any of my brothers, when I got to thinking about it, so I learned to roll with the punches.

And in a way I needed the girls to be away when their father got really bad. They loved their father so much, especially Joyce. I knew what going through his death journey would tear them up from the inside out, seeing him get sicker and sicker. I was well acquainted with Black Lung death, and knew what would start to happen to his body. They did not need to see this in the detail that I would see it as his wife. It was my job, I knew, to stand by this man who'd stood by me so faithfully over the years. I'm not sure I could survive the whole thing being strong for all the girls and for Calvin too. And they needed to see life and new beginnings, not death, the end of their father's life.

And so, for the next six years, we listened to news from long distances. Joyce from Florida with her two children, Kimberly and Chuck (short for Ronald). Carol had four children, Kevin, Alicia, Darla and David. She had two natural children and two adopted, but loved taking in foster children and giving them a loving home. Shirley had a boy, named Michael, but left his father when he turned abusive. She then married another man, named Cecil Davis, had another son named Keith. Unfortunately, though she would not go into much detail, she divorced again and married a man named Earl Abrams, who gave her a daughter, Shannon. Yes, my family was growing.

There were times when it was excruciating. But there were also times of great laughter, and most of that was because of our unofficial son. We suffered through having the money for food and medicine on our limited budget. We were alone for long stretches, but did not feel alone because we were so wrapped up in our time together. I will always have those memories, resting with him on our porch at the end of the day. Our hands would be softly clasped and we'd stare lazily at the view in front of us. Like the time I spent with my father, it was peaceful, because for so many years we'd been so busy just trying to make a living and keep food on the table that we'd not had time like this, just to share each other's company. I often think of how we worked together as a team. These were times that we could enjoy quiet time without feeling the need to say or do anything. I would look over and find him staring at me with a pleased little smile on his face, and I would smile back and squeeze his hand. His breathing was difficult and I had to have large oxygen tanks brought up that mountain weekly.

"You have made me so happy, Calvin." Moments would pass and he would respond with, "I had no other choice, Emily. You were the best thing that happened to me."

So I was with him when he took to his bed for the last time. I was with him when the oxygen tanks were delivered to the house. I was with him when his health failed completely and I had to call an ambulance.

The girls arrived then, when he was in the hospital, and I watched their faces when they received the news that his kidneys were failing. Shirleys' face was pinched. Carol's eyes were soft with tears. Joyce's fighting spirit wanted to find a miracle to save him. But there was nothing left to do. We all knew it, me better than the rest only because I'd been there to see how far his health had declined. The girls each had their quiet time with him, saying their goodbyes. He could barely speak to them by then, and doing so wore him out, but like fixing the house, it mattered to him that he share those important words with his precious darlings. I watched as each girl rested their soft cheeks on his rough one so that they could hear every whispered word. I sat in the hall and prayed for their peace. I listened while tubes were laced down his throat and cried listening to his screams for help, but I knew these were the last attempts for giving him a little more time.

And then we were alone again, together again, struggling to find our way, led only by the doctors and the hospital room and the bed we'd never slept in together. So I stayed by his side to remind him of our promise.

Wilt thou love him, comfort him and honor him?

I will.

I was alone with him when the breathing machines were hooked up and when the tubes were placed in his lungs again and when his screams would have filled the hospital hallways if he'd had the strength to scream.

Wilt thou keep him, in sickness and in health?

I will.

I was with him when he'd wake up out of a drugged sleep, frightened because he could not breathe. I stroked his face and spoke to him in soft words, of my undying love for him, of the love his daughters had for him, of the wonderful husband he had been, of the beautiful eternal life we'd share in paradise. I was with him when he unconsciously fished and watched as he tied the knots in the invisible line, pitching it out and yanking just a little with an imaginary bite. He reached for me, he stroked my cheek, and his eyes told me all I needed to know. I had been his partner in life. I had been his special friend. I had been his wife. I had no words to explain to him that it was the highest honor I would ever know. So I tried my best to show him with my tears.

I was alone when his time came. It was just after midnight when the nurse called and said "I'm sorry, he's gone." As with Ray, I fainted to the floor and came to knowing I was alone. Joyce and Carol had talked about how near Father's Day was, "Just two weeks away," said Carol. "I don't know if I could stand it if anything happened to Daddy on Father's Day. But just as their premonition had spoken, the day was destined for Calvin.

On Father's Day, 1967, I had to phone my daughters and tell them that their strong father, who'd been so much more precious than Clark Gable, had passed away. He was fifty-six years old.

After I got off the phone with them, I made all the funeral arrangements. I would have it no other way. Calvin would be the first of six brothers to pass. He was laid out in his best suit in the little church in Dressen. His family designed a special funeral decoration for the day, a wagon wheel with one spoke from the wheel missing. For some reason, that symbol of their loss was so striking to me that I cried til I thought my heart would break. He was my spoke missing and I knew I would be lost without him.

At the services, I sat in front with my girls and the congregation played all the old familiar songs we'd learned through the generations to contain our grief and express it as best we could.

Precious Memories.

Rock of Ages.

In the Sweet Bye and Bye.

I'll Fly Away. Calvin's favorite.

And on and on into the day. People gave testimony to the kind of man my husband was, of the people his life had touched. People came from everyone. My Calvin was so loved that the church could not hold the many who came to say goodby. The large congregation filed by his casket and then to me, to pay their respects and share their memories. The phrases floated around me trying to offer comfort.

"Such a good father, and such a caring man."

"What a compassionate preacher."

"So protective of his family". People hugged the girls, rubbed Joyce's shoulders and reminded her that he'd called her his "little chalk eye," an old mining term for an apprentice. As a child she had followed him everywhere, and had often introduced her to people that way. Obviously the name had just stuck. I could see in her eyes that she felt a new void in her life that she would have a hard time ever filling.

She wasn't alone in this. As we took that last familiar walk together, I hated that he was in his casket and not standing next to me. Fifty-six was too young to die. I imagined him holding my hand as we made our way up the mountain to Resthaven cemetery.

I, Calvin, take thee Emily.

The congregation then gathered around the cold hole that had been dug in the earth to hold him. It wasn't right that he'd be left in this cemetery all alone. I wanted to climb in the ground and pull him out with my bare hands, like Woodrow and I'd done that time in the hospital.

I, Emily, take thee Calvin.

If only I could open his mouth and pull all those strings of poison out of his lungs. Why should lungs fail when the man was so strong and healthy? I felt myself sinking as he was lowered into the ground. So tired. I felt a million years old, lightheaded and lost in my grief.

For better and for worse, for richer and for poorer, in sickness and in health, to love and to cherish.

My knees gave away and I was cradled in the arms of the people around me as I finally surrendered to my loss. My husband was gone. His fight was over and my fight to stay alive without him was just beginning.

Until death do us part.

Calvin

Calvin and Emily had been a team. They had been inseparable. Now she would be alone.

CHAPTER 26: Beginning Again

I know it seems odd to say this, but I handled my grief over Calvin's death. Yes, I missed him terribly, but as with my father, we'd said our goodbyes. He was a wonderful husband to me, and I had no regrets about our life together. We left nothing unsaid. There was a sad goodbye, but as always, life was moving me forward with each day that passed after his funeral. One of my biggest helps in this was living with Curtis.

Even before he was much out of diapers, Curtis was always high-spirited and found plenty of ways to get in trouble. He did finally meet his match though.

Our house was two stories, and Curtis had a bedroom on the top floor, opposite from mine. Shortly after Calvin died, Curtis had started drinking, and began slipping out at night, using a ladder hid near his window. One night he had gone out on a real tear and arrived home as the sun was coming up over the eaves. After he managed to climb on the ladder, he turned and attempted to shove it away from the window. But he was so drunk, he missed and fell out the window.

I heard him, ran to the window, looked down and called, "Curtis, are you hurt?"

When he looked up, all he saw was the sun shining on me with a strange glow. It did the trick. That was when Curtis got religion.

And Curtis was different from that day on. He didn't get a lot of school learning, for he had a learning disability which made this very hard, but he taught himself about the intricate wiring or radios and televisions. Once I thought he'd gone crazy, talking to himself in the barn. But he had fashioned a two-way radio from an old piece of plywood wires he had soldered together and he was talking to the police.

Soon though, even Curtis was gone from the house. He still lived with me of course, but he'd be gone for weeks working for a moving and storing company. Slowly I felt myself start to disappear into a routine of quiet and boredom.

Curtis and Emily after Calvin passed. He was her support.

Two years after Calvin died; I went to the post office for mail. As I was picking up my mail, I ran into an old neighbor.

"Hello there Emily," he tipped his head at me and smiled.

"Hello Frank, how are you this afternoon?" I asked congenially.

"I am doing well, thank you. Emily, I am sorry to hear you lost Calvin." I hesitated a second, then nodded. "Well Frank, I was sorry about Mildred." Frank had been nursing his sick wife for more than two years, and she had died just recently. "I have been kind of quiet these days, and I should have been around to pay my respects."

"I understand, Emily. There are just times when you can't be around other people's grieving." Yes, he would understand that only too well.

As we talked he asked what I had been doing, and then suggested that we have coffee later that evening. I agreed. It would be nice to have company again, and I was surprised at how much I looked forward to it, even as I was walking away.

Frank later admitted to me that he set our wedding date that first day. He wasted no time though, over that first cup of coffee. Before we had finished the second cup, he told me why he'd come.

"Emily, many years ago I was on my way hunting. As I passed by your house I saw you working in the garden. You had on a freshly starched dress and your beauty was such I could not take my eyes off you," he said honestly. "I sat down behind a tree and there I watched you hoe for a while before making my way on up the mountain. Before long I came across Calvin sitting under a hickory tree squirrel hunting. I sat down for a spell, we talked and I went on my way hunting. From that day I could not get you off my mind. Maybe it was wrong. I was married and had children. But there was something about you that I could not let go. I probably have loved you all these years and would not allow myself to come to grips with it for you know I have been a Minister of God and I would not commit a sin knowingly."

Two weeks later, Frank and I were married, in 1970.

Frank and Emily's wedding day.

Frank's children weren't happy about the arrangement at all, and though Shirley and Joyce encouraged us, Carol was dead set against it, at least until she met Frank for the first time. I think the minute she saw him, she knew we were made for each other.

Frank was caring, and I was giving. We made a handsome couple. We were also a good team for his church. And without warning, I was deeply in love with him. It's almost like Calvin sent him to me that day, and took me by the hand and said, "Emily, I fixed up our house to keep you safe, and now here is the man I've sent to keep you loved." Frank never uttered a cross word to me. His voice was soft, but strong.

And I have to admit, we were like young lovers. I had missed being with Calvin as he'd gotten so ill, and now my love affair with Frank was like a second spring. One day on the phone, Joyce laughed out loud and said, "Mom, you are the luckiest woman in the world. You have lucked out with two good men in a lifetime. That's more than most women get the first time around."

She was right too. Frank fit into the fabric of my life with ease, and soon even the girls were calling him Dad. I had a companion again, and I took full advantage of it. We both did, because we both knew what it was like to lose our beloved, and now we both felt like being selfish. I remember the year that Flu season hit Frank hard. He had been in bed for more than a week. I felt so sorry for him, because he couldn't even get up and make it to church. So, I decided to entertain him.

I went to the chest, pulled out one of Joyce's old hats, found a pair of long white lace gloves, put on a blond wig, put on a blazing red short nightie and black fishnet hose, put on a pair of red patent high heels and carried an old purse.

"Frank, Frank, honey are you covered up? We have company and I am bringing them into see you."

He called back, "Yes, Sugar, I am covered up."

"Frank, are you sure?"

"Yes, Honey, I am covered up."

With that I entered his bedroom, danced a little jig, and sang while twirling my purse.

He got well that very minute.

And we had thirty good years together. We traveled to all the places we'd always wanted to see and shopped for antiques and loved each other. When we traveled, we never rushed. When we were in the car together for long stretches, he held my hand. We talked about Mildred and Calvin sometimes, but often it simply wasn't necessary.

He also stood by me through other family heartaches. Five years after our marriage, we lost my sister Bessie.

Bessie had married who had a son by a previous marriage. They built a cabin on a mountain up Coxton Holler. But after a few years she realized that he wasn't a good man, prone to fits of violence, so they parted ways. As it turns out, his violence begat violence. He began seeing a married woman after Bessie left him, and when her husband caught them in bed together he hacked him to death with a hatchet.

Bessie and Ira. Ira was hacked to death.

Fortunately for Bessie, she remarried a man named Ed and they were inseparable. She sometimes helped him with his construction work, tearing down buildings. On August 28, 1974, she was doing just that. Ed was on the roof and she was on the ground at the side of the house. She began pulling nails out of the side of the house, not realizing that the side of the building had been released so that it would fall. When she pulled on it, the entire side came down on her. She was killed instantly. She was fifty-one.

Bessie was buried in the back yard of their little house. Ed couldn't stand the idea of her being too far away from him. When I looked into his eyes, I could see a man who just wanted to follow her into the grave, and within the year he did just that. At his request, I had him buried there under the tree in his backyard, right next to my sister.

And there was also Murphy. I knew that Murphy's fight wouldn't last forever, but I was still unprepared for his death March 7, 1980. I couldn't help but think back to the time when he was strong and healthy. He had been so easygoing and full of life then. I remembered once a trip to town, seeing him squatting on the street camouflaged as a beggar.

I had asked, "What were you doing in town today dressed like a beggar? You nearly embarrassed me to death. What would people say seeing my brother sitting on the street with a cup in his hand?" But he didn't care about appearances. He just said, "Why Emily, no one knew me and besides, I needed a little money and it didn't take long to get what I wanted. It would take days working in the mines for what I got in a short time. Plus, there is no risk for sitting on that street. Why, I could have a full time job sitting on the street with my tin cup," he finished with a laugh.

Would he have lived a fuller life had he stayed in the mines and away from that plant in the North? As much as I wanted to be angry at how he was injured, I knew that his odds weren't much better in the mines of Harlan. He would have surely faced Black Lung like Calvin did. He could have been trapped by a fire or killed by any number of senseless accidents.

Perhaps now that Mother was gone, I was taking on one of those moods that she had suffered from all her life. Still, I think my family had just had a lot of hard times, and it upset me to think about just how poor my brother's chances had always been. I hated the hard life and the hard choices that he had to make. I wanted so much more for him. I wanted more for all my family. I teased Frank then, telling him I bet he was sorry to have to put up with such a moody wife.

"Emily, I think my wife brought you into my life so that we could be together. I would never give you up for anything in the world." I believed him. He was so strong and such a good man. Calvin would have wanted me to be happy, to have new opportunities for our perfect days again. And so I did.

But the dark moments came to our life together too, the same as with Calvin. Early on, Frank sold his home in Loyall and moved to Sookie Ridge. But we wanted a new house together, so we soon found a large home in Evarts once owned by the late Dr. P. O. Lewis, owner of the Yokum Creek Coal Company. We sold the house on Sookie Ridge and moved into our dream home. We now had 56 acres of land, six dormant coalmines, virgin timber and a wonderful view of the mountains.

In the mid-90's, we were offered a contract for the coal to be stripped. We wanted nothing to do with the idea, and turned it down flat. Turning this down changed the course of our lives.

Early one Sunday morning we were awakened by the sound of chain saws. Our next door neighbor, who had bought his house two years prior, was cutting our virgin timber. We quickly dressed, approached him and asked what he was doing on our property. "It's my property, and you better get off my land," he told us. Apparently he felt that was the end of that.

Frank and I had worked the land, lived here for over twenty years, supplied free water to five neighboring families and now we were up against something that would not go away. We filed suit of course. We fought with everything we had. The neighbor was actually put in jail, but in the meantime, the judge awarded the neighbor our fifty-six acres of land.

"How could a judge take away something that you honestly pay for, have a deed that says it belongs to you and get away with it?" Frank asked me this over and over again. Nothing about it made sense to me either. We were devastated. Joyce helped with all the fight in her, rounded up previous owners to testify, but the judge would not accept any of our evidence. We lost nearly everything after a four-year battle.

We tried for an appeal, but the attorney said, "The judge will only allow me to present certain evidence and the judge can make any decision he wants to make. He can accept what he wants and do as he wishes. I am sorry, but he's a powerful man, and I can only do so much and still live here." We were left with two and a quarter acres of land. The same judge continues to sit on the bench.

Our once beautiful home was now our prison. After the property settlement, things were never the same. First we were harassed. Then we were threatened. Worse, we had to watch trucks stripping our hills of the virgin timber. We could no longer roam our beautiful mountains, walk along the mining trails or plant trees throughout the forest.

In our seventies by this time, our health began to fail. I developed high blood pressure and heart problems. Frank had one heart attack after the land was dissolved and developed high blood pressure as well, after years of no health problems at all. I watched this kind, soft-spoken man become tired and depressed all the time. And I had always been a fighter, but I felt beaten. There was nothing more I could do.

It was then that I started noticing that I was getting more and more forgetful. Frank teased me gently about this, saying that we were both just getting on in years, but it bothered me more and more that I couldn't remember simple things, like what I'd planted in my flower garden, or that I hadn't turned off the stove. But Frank was always patient with me and I slowly began letting him do more and more for me. I made up my mind though that I would tell something to Joyce before I forgot about it, or before anything else happened in our lives that were out of our control.

"Joyce, would you like to read the story of my life?" She had come up for a visit and I sprang this on her one evening before she left to go home.

"Would you like to read my life story?" Joyce's face looked confused, and she stared at me for a few seconds before replying, "I'd love to read your story, but I'm not sure what you mean."

"I wrote the story of my life for my girls to read, so that they'd know what it was like to grow up like I did. Would you like to read it?"

We went into my bedroom, where I opened the closet and pulled out one of our old flip top suitcases. I laid it flat in the floor and opened it. From it I produced a worn blue spiral notebook. When I opened it, I showed her years and years of entries, in my own handwriting.

Joyce begged me to let her to take it back to Florida. Then she stopped, stared at me for a second and asked, "This is amazing mother, but why are you giving it to me?"

"I'm giving it to you because you'll know what to do with it," I said quietly. This was true. Joyce and I had so much in common. I knew that she would respect what was inside, all my memories about our family and our lives, and that she would share it when the time was right. She seemed pleased, and I gave her permission to not only read it, but to copy it and share it with her sisters.

This was one of my best treasures, all about my life growing up in the mountains of Kentucky in my beloved home. She hugged me tightly, and I touched her cheek. I could relax now. My diary and my memories were in good hands.

CHAPTER 27: Fading Away

The year 2000 was supposed to be the beginning of the New Millennium. For our family, it brought new heartbreak.

January 17 was a normal Monday morning, nothing all that unusual. I had not slept well the night before, but didn't think much of it, until I got a call in the early morning from Joyce.

"Mother, I need you to sit down, I've got some bad news. Carol Sue did not report for work this morning. She's missing. The police are looking for her now."

It was too much to think about. I broke into tears and immediately began praying. Frank came into the room, took the phone and gently led me away. After speaking to Joyce for a few seconds more, he came to me and we both began to pray. After that, Frank gave me a tranquilizer to help me calm down and sleep. He told the girls that there was no way we could brave the mountains to get to Kingsport. Snow was in the forecast and the roads would be bad.

The lack of sleep I had gotten the night before suddenly made perfect sense to me now. I didn't give up hope that Carol would be found OK, but deep down I was certain that she was gone.

Carol Sue had a gentle softness, a glow around her and a smile always on her face. She loved people and always tagged after Joyce, begging her to play dolls. As she grew older they began double dating best friends.

Carol had beautiful features and brown hair so outstanding. When I look back on her childhood, I am so glad that we had no way of knowing that Carol would follow in the footsteps of so many of the women who shared her name, and of so many others in the Howard Clan.

After twenty-five years of marriage, she divorced her husband Doug, keeping custody of David, who was youngest. Kevin, Darla and Alicia had left home by this time, and that's when Carol started taking in foster children.

She took in Duane, the last foster child, against her better judgement, but the local caseworkers had begged her, "Carol, this child is fifteen years old and has been in and out of foster care all his life. He is the same age as David and if anyone can help him you can."

Obviously, there was no help for Duane Brian Brooks but the help of God himself. He was trouble from the beginning. I remember a conversation I had with her early on. "Carol," I said, "he is set in his ways and he has been problem all his life. You can't change this child. He will cause you nothing but grief."

She took him in anyway.

When he came of age, David married and left home. Carol made Duane leave to make a life of his own. Before Duane had been verbally abusive to her, but now he began to abuse Carol physically, throwing her down, slamming her up against doors, bruising her and stalking her at work. Once when she was in her car he screamed in her ear so loud that he damaged her hearing. In 1995, she called 911 for the police.

She took out a restraining order against him to keep him away, but nothing seemed to really help. She once told her oldest son Kevin, "If anything happens to me it will be Duane."

That Monday in 2000, she did not report to work at the Sullivan County Health Department. Her employer and co-workers knew something was amiss for Carol had never missed a day at work. David received the call and arrived first at the house.

When he arrived, he found little amiss, but several things made him uneasy. Her car was missing. The coffee table in the living room was scooted a bit to one side and the rug was buckled under it. He found his mother's bed unmade, a phone off the hook and another phone missing. There was a can of Campbell's Vegetable Soup sitting on the table by the front door with a large dent.

The children had been with Carol just that Sunday before. She told all of them that Duane had dropped by at 3:00 am the morning before. She told them, "I heard someone at the door, took the portable phone from the kitchen and went to the door. It was Duane. As I opened the door I pretended I was on the phone with Kevin and said, "Why Kevin, it's only Duane. I'll talk to you in the morning." With that she said she hung up, let him in and gave him a coat for it was very cold outside. He stayed a bit. She asked him to take his Christmas presents from the children, but he said, "No, I can't take them until I have something to give back."

At 10 p.m. Sunday night she called Shirley. "She was in a wonderful mood," Shirley said later. "We talked and laughed for a long time before hanging up."

The children gathered at their mother's home. Late in the afternoon Duane was found and interrogated for over three hours before being released. Once he was released, he headed straight for Carol's house. Her daughter Alicia was on the phone with me when he walked through the door. Alicia had Joyce on the phone when he arrived, and she told Joyce that it was obvious that he had been in a serious fight.

He stood at the door, insisting that he hadn't done anything to harm my child. In fact, he got her kids to walk through the neighborhood with him, questioning the neighbors. They did this only because they were waiting for the police to come. When the police got there, they took pictures of all the scratches on Duane's body, then left. Duane left too.

In the following days, an all-points bulletin was issued and all the news media covered the story. Over the following days, many psychics called and gave accounts where she could be found, from Pennsylvania and the surrounding area. Schoolmates soon learned of her disappearance and calls came from Ohio, Florida, Pennsylvania, Tennessee and Kentucky. Prayer chains began.

Still, there was no sign of Carol.

My grandchildren started to gather at Carol's house, and Joyce and some of her friends went as well, to be there for Carol's kids. It was a sad reunion and everyone feared the worst.

On the seventh day, the Monday after her disappearance, the case began turning up leads and the holes in Duane's story closed in on him. His friend Jarod started to break. Carol's credit card had been used at 6:55 am on the morning of her disappearance and some of the missing gifts from her house had been found.

After a long week of waiting for news, the detective worked nonstop on the case telling the family that things were starting to happen. "Everything I hear about Carol is good. When I stop in restaurants people come up to me and tell me what a good person she was. How she had helped so many families."

She had a black belt in judo and karate, had been a former deputy sheriff and was an excellent markswoman. She had defensive training and knew how to care for herself. She had obviously known the intruder.

The detective broke Duane down. He admitted to choking her on her sofa, wrapping a telephone cord around her beautiful neck and strangling her until he knew she was dead. She fought hard and scratched the right side of his face all the way down his chest leaving her entire thumb print in his chest. She upset the coffee table in her death struggle.

Duane asked his friend Jarod to help dispose of the body. He wrapped her in a rug, carried her to her car. He placed her in the back seat and drove her to Fort Henry Lake, pushing the car off the boat ramp into 13 feet of water. In the dead hours of that January 17, she went to her watery grave in the subzero weather.

The car was brought to the surface of the cold, half frozen water. She had been there for eight days. I can't really describe the horror we felt as the divers located the car and pulled it out on the snowy bank. They lifted her little body onto a stretcher. She was still clad in gray flannel pajamas and cut off white tee shirt. Duane had pulled her shirt up over her face before wrapping her in the rug. The coroner was waiting to perform the autopsy.

DNA was matched to Duane.

Grief hit me like a flood. When Joyce called to tell me the news, the next thing I remember was Frank holding me. I was screaming, and I couldn't make myself stop. Frank held me until I could get myself together, but I have no memory of what he said.

Instead, my mind drifted back through the years, seeing Carol as a child in diapers running in the yard. Seeing her playing with her dolls, sucking her thumb and tagging along with Joyce like one of a pair of twins. She used to love our mountains too, picking blackberries, cooking in the wild and playing with animals. I remembered her first date, and the day of her wedding.

"Oh God, how could he do such a thing to you?" I cried and prayed, speaking to her as if she was standing in the same room. I thought of her hair that I had combed so many times as a child, rubbing her head and braiding her hair. I knew every inch of that head, all of its bone structure. That bone structure was crushed by a can of soup. I wondered how quickly she died and how long she suffered. Now the rest of her family would suffer through a child with a boy Carol had believed in even when no one else had. Her warm heart and kind spirit had cost her life itself.

I knew that only God would carry me through this loss. The strain of it sent me to my bed.

Significant dates in Carol's life that year took place on holidays. Carol died on Martin Luther King's birthday. Duane Brian Brooks was arraigned on Groundhog's Day and Carol's birthday, February 2. The Grand Jury met on St. Patrick's Day.

I thanked God for Frank that year, who stood by my side, watched every move I made, and kept me supplied with tranquilizers to help me sleep. When the body was finally released, I gave up my gravesite to the family.

"She has to be laid next to her Daddy, "I told Joyce, "That spot was for me, but Frank and I have been together so long and we should be buried side by side."

Kevin was so heartbroken and in a rush to get his mother buried that I barely had a chance to see her body and say my goodbyes before she was buried.

Frank held me closely as the casket was opened there on the side of the mountain. "She's so beautiful. How sweet and peaceful she looks. I know that God has her in heaven and she is with her Daddy," That was all I could do before I dropped to the ground in tears.

Life proceeded in a blur, then days later I received a letter that gave me tremendous comfort. The letter was from Carol's first sweetheart, Tom Madon. When he heard of Carol's untimely death he wrote me.

Dear Mrs. Romine (as I knew you),

While we have not maintained contact over the years and I had not seen Carol since sometime during 1961, I can't tell you how shocked and saddened I was when I heard of her tragic death. On Sunday, January 30, my mother read to me over the phone the article in the Harlan paper. Later in the day I looked up the Kingsport times News on the Internet and read the obituary along with the various reports that were written about what happened. My prayers are certainly with you and with Carol's children and grandchildren.

Over the years I have often wished for the opportunity to tell Carol how much the ten months we dated impacted my life those many years ago. While I know very little of the direction her life took over the years since then, I am quite confident that I would not be a Christian today had it not been for the profound influence she had on my life at that time. This continues to be absolutely amazing to me even today, especially when I remember that she was only fourteen years old at that time. (Since I recall that her birthday was Groundhog Day, I know she would have been 56 this week.)

In the years I have served as a pastor and in other forms of Christian work since 1963, I have given my testimony hundreds of times to individuals, churches and other gatherings of all sizes and she was always mentioned, often by name. Let me give you the shorter version.

At the time I met Carol, my life was clearly heading in the wrong direction. I had no purpose to my life and little hope for the future. When I asked Carol for a date and she accepted I had no idea until I arrived at your home and Curt answered the door that our first Thursday night date was to go to church. Because I enjoyed being with her and your family as well, I tolerated the church and treasured the times I could spend with her. As I questioned her about the church and spiritual things that very first night, she communicated to me how important Jesus Christ was to her. While I had never heard anyone express what she did, I liked what she said. Even more, I was impressed by how her life was different and with the dating standards she set and maintained throughout our relationship. You and Mr. Romine obviously were a major influence on who she was as a person but she took her stand in a winsome way and I was impressed. While I must say that I was somewhat scared of Mr. Romine, I appreciate the way that you, as Carol's mother, treated me during those months. (I didn't like the way you would turn the porch light on and off when it was time for her to come in but I understood).

Through going to church with our family and my many discussions with Carol, God was speaking to me and letting me know how much He cared for me. I came to understand not only that I was lost but that I was loved. One night I told Carol I was getting close to giving my life to the Lord and asked her to pray that I would make this decision soon. What I was asking was that she pray for me after I left but she actually prayed for me out loud as we were sitting on the rock wall in front of your house. After heading down the hill toward my home, I began to realize that I did not have to wait until Sunday to be saved. I got on my knees on the little gravel road there below your house where I could still see your porch light through the trees. I remember telling god that I had a lot of problems and lots of questions but also that if He could do for me what He had done for Carol (and for her family), I wanted him to do it. Even though I was only sixteen years old, it was like an incredible weight rolled off my back and I knew I was saved. I went home and with tears told my mother what had happened and the next morning told my dad. The night this happened was May 8, 1958. The next Sunday was Mother's Day and I went to the Baxter Methodist church in the morning and went forward at the end of the service to let Pastor Roy Reeves know what I had done. The next Sunday I was baptized and the following Sunday I joined the church. I think I went to that church because several friends of my parents went there and I felt if they were Christians they would probably be members in that church. This is what Mom and Dad actually did a year later when they both were saved.

While I don't recall the reasons, Carol and I stopped dating early that summer. My friends did not think my Christianity would last as they felt I had made my decision only because of Carol. While she was the major influence, God Himself changed my life that night and is continuing to change me all these years later. It has been such a joy over the *years to share my testimony with others and then go on to present the life changing message of the gospel of Jesus Christ. Many, many others have come to know him as a result including some who are missionaries, pastors and who serve in other forms of Christian work. It all started with Carol's simple but courageous testimony to me while she was only a young teen. While I was never able to relate my gratitude to her, I want to share it with you. Feel free to pass it along to her family as you sense to be appropriate.*

As I said earlier, I have no way of knowing the direction Carol's life took since that time. I know we all make a variety of choices, some good and some bad. Because we live in a fallen world, we all experience a combination of joy and sorrow as well as pain and pleasure. The description of Carol's kindness in her obituary is one of the qualities that attracted me to her even those many years ago when she was a young teen. I wish I could have known her as an adult.

While I share your sorrow from a distance, I wanted to express these thoughts to you. I also pray that God Himself will be to you and Carol's family just as the Apostle Paul described Him, "the God of all comfort who comforts us in all our trouble…" A prayer group here in our church prayed for your family just this morning. The people in our church know the gratitude I felt for Carol as they have heard my testimony various times during the past fifteen years I have served here.

Finally, my faithful wife of thirty-six and a half years has also often thanked God for Carol and her influence on my life. She joins me in praying for your family.

With much gratitude and with my sincere prayers,
Tom Madon

Carol and Tommy on their first date – the date that changed his life forever.

I read the contents over and over. In some ways it was a great comfort, but in others it just accentuated our loss.

"Why did God allow me to live to be the last?"

"I don't know, Mother," Joyce said quietly. "I think we'll know in the next life." It was easier not to think about it.

For the first time in my life, the changing of the seasons did nothing to warm my heart. My child was dead, and so the garden was left untended and I sat in my chair on the porch and stared out into space. Eating held no interest for me, and neither did Frank. I felt like a dead weight, with no heart in me and no tears left to cry.

And the seasons did nothing to warm me, or prepare me for what else was coming that year. The months that followed brought more sadness. As the leaves of autumn were showing a hint of color, my Curtis was riding his bike as he always did, to visit friends on the ridge and stop by the local store for his usual RC Cola. As he jumped on his bike to ride off, he suddenly fell over, off the bike and lay on the cold hard ground. He lay there using his last breath asking his friend to get his Mommy, as he still called me. The bike ride to the small country store ended his life. A heart attack had taken him, just like that.

It was so much like when Goff and Johnny, my brothers died that I couldn't contain myself. I kept speaking to Mother, hoping she would hear me, but she did not come. "Mother, why couldn't I get there in time? Why couldn't God let me be there for my boy?"

The news spread through the mountain communities. Curtis was well liked and well known. He was a simple person but had a heart of gold and his loving ways and his kindness to others had gained him many friends.

The church was small, the congregation large. He had spent many hours at the fire departments in Evarts and Harlan donating his time doing odd jobs and helping where needed. At his funeral, he was saluted and honored as a fallen brother. Instead of the usual mourning service, Curtis had requested that songs be sung and people not mourn. Songs were sung.

I admit that it was a strange way to mourn, but I liked it somehow. The firemen were sitting around, turns were taken singing songs he loved and Kenneth sang his favorite song, "There Will Be Peace in the Valley." People took turns playing Curtis's drums. Flowers were sent from everywhere. The firemen saluted their brother, the preacher gave Kenneth his drumsticks, and he was carried to the Resthaven Cemetary and buried just above Calvin and Carol, beside Jimmy.

I had given out my last grave plot.

And still there was no peace. Less than two months later, I got news that Ruby was also dead. Ruby had moved to Detroit. To our despair, she developed cancer. She died in October, and I was in such bad shape from Carol and Curtis's death that Frank convinced me that I wasn't strong enough to make it to the services. This was devastating. I was too tired to attend the funeral of my last sister, and I just couldn't believe that it would happen without me being there.

But Frank was tired too. He was worn out taking care of me, and I tried very hard not to be a bother. I know that I worried him terribly though, because I couldn't convince myself to get out of bed, fix myself up or eat anything at all.

"Emily, do you know how much I love you?" he said quietly one afternoon as we were sitting in our chairs by the fire.

"Yes, Frank, I know. You are an angel sent to take care of me. I'm not sure what I would have done if you hadn't come to me after Calvin died. I would have never been able to really move on and have a life. You've given me a remarkable life."

"This year has been hard, I know," Frank said. "I want you to know that it has been an honor to help you carry your pain and grief. I would have been nowhere else but here."

I look back on that conversation and I know that Frank was saying his best goodbye. I hadn't noticed that he was feeling bad, and I'm not sure that he was. But in late November, he came down with a cold. I told Joyce about it when she called on Thanksgiving Day.

"Mother, how are you?"

"Well, honey your Dad is sick in bed. He's been sick at his stomach." They all referred to Frank as Dad.

"That's strange, I'm sick too. Well, maybe we have a virus from the air. Tell Dad it came all the way to Alabama and I have it too." We laughed, said our good-byes and hung up.

That morning, I woke because I heard him breathing. He touched my side and I rested my hand in his.

"I've been thinking, Emily."

"What about?"

"Well, this year has been so bad. What do you think about taking a little trip? Just something to get our minds off all the things that have happened? I was thinking that we could go up north a little and look at antiques. I have a mind to find something new for the house. What do you think?"

"I think you need a good strong cup of coffee," I said. But the idea didn't upset me as much as I thought it would. It was something to think about, something to get my mind moving again, and I really needed to do that. Carol would have wanted that, and so would Curtis and Ruby.

As I was working in the kitchen, I heard Frank get up and go to the bathroom. He was there for a long time, so I went to see if he was OK. I knew immediately that something wasn't right. Frank was resting in the tub, which was full of water. But when I touched the water to rouse him, the water was ice cold.

"He's gone, God, he's gone. What am I going to do?" I screamed into the phone.

"Mother, what is wrong. Is it Dad?" I realized suddenly that I was talking to Joyce. I didn't remember dialing her number.

"Yes, yes, I'm here alone, he's in the bathroom, and he's gone." I was screaming the words and crying at the same time. "What should I do, oh Joyce, what should I do? I tried to get him up, but I hurt myself. Help me, help me."

I vaguely remember her telling me to hang up and call 911, then call the neighbors to sit with me. She said she was on her way.

Kevin and Alicia arrived from Kingsport and sat with me until Joyce could get here. I was too dazed to function. We both went to the funeral director together.

"Now Mrs. Emily, we will need his insurance papers, do you have that?" I looked at Joyce, who nodded.

"Ok, so we should talk about the funeral service now. Did he have any medals?" Do I know the answer to this question? I can't remember. Joyce reached to me and held my arms to steady me as I picked out his casket, left his suit and asked for his favorite song to be sung.

In the sweet by and by, we shall meet on that beautiful shore.

The day after the funeral, Joyce took me to the hospital because I had terrible pain in my chest from trying to lift Frank out of the bathtub.

I don't remember a thing.

EPILOGUE

It was time to go. I dreaded the long drive. Together we bundled up for the walk out to the car. Mother did not wear her high heels that day, but I could still see them in my mind's eye, hear their click against the flagstone walk and the little feet tap dancing and doing the Charleston, moving with her body as she laughed and twirled. She loved high heels even though her feet now showed signs of bunions and the beginning of a hammertoe. I opened the car door and mother stepped in. I buckled her into place then took a minute just to stare at her.

She was still a beauty. Mother always knew she had pretty legs, and I had pictures of her shoveling snow in a jacket and shorts, but this day I tucked a quilt around her legs to keep her warm until the car heated enough to make her comfortable. Her skin showed little signs of aging. Her eyes didn't carry that sparkle, dimmed by the pain of so much recent loss, she just sat in the front seat as I prepared for us to leave. I remembered when those hazel eyes carried a lovely gleam in them, like when she was looking at my father, or when she was playing a joke on one of us.

I missed the gleam in her eyes. It made me feel lonely and sad. My heart too was breaking for her loss and knew it would be a lifetime change for my mother.

Mother had yet one more journey to take after Frank died. Her journey to recovery from all the heartbreak she had endured that year. I knew she was suffering from the early signs of dementia. The family had probably missed it especially Frank as he had cared deeply for her and protected her. Now the signs of dementia were obvious, and I realized she could no longer live alone. Mother began her simple prayer as we started to leave.

"God, help me to know what to do and help Joyce as she drives today. Take us in your arms and protect us. Please help me since you have taken

Frank. I needed him much more than you. Amen." My heart was tearing open and tears began to flow for mother.

After much of her things and her house were sold, I wanted to move mother to Alabama, so that I could watch after her. Living close to me, I could call her every day, and have lunch with her, and spend the weekends. As I spent those weeks with her preparing the house and her things, I understood a new reason behind her grief. Frank had taken care of everything. Memory loss had probably been afflicting her for quite some time, and he had shielded her from all this. He had answered her questions over and over. He had unraveled the backward and forward toss that her brain had taken through time, had turned all the circles of confusion into straight and even lines.

My thoughts were racing, "How was I going to live up to that? And how was I going to convince her to leave her beloved mountains?"

Why couldn't she remember the terrible times, the winters cold, the endless work, the seasons when they had so little to eat? Life had been hard for her growing up, and the mountains had taken so much from her over the years, but she felt safe in Harlan and I knew I was taking her to unfamiliar places. It was a scary time for both of us.

My thoughts also took me back with wonderful memories that wouldn't let go of me, like days roaming the mountains, hunting arrowheads and swimming in the Cumberland River. There were summer nights telling ghost stories and playing until dark or roasting marshmallows over an open fire. Mother was always there for us making sure we were having fun.

I continued my thoughts with thinking about when the fall came, the leaves of the maple trees turning golden red and many shades of brown and orange and how much mother would miss all the beauty of the seasons. Cardboard boxes were used as slides down the mountain through the fallen leaves. Mother had raised her family on Sookie Ridge, the front side of the Lisenbee Field, near the town of Harlan a little place called Baxter. She had raised three girls and outlived two husbands. When she was born she was so small her head fit inside a teacup and she had to be pinned to a pillow so that she wouldn't be lost in the blanket.

As I thought about these things, I shed tears for her and for all the family we had buried in those mountain cemeteries. I cried for all the memories I had made on this mountain. I also knew that my mother, who had spent her entire life in those hills, and I knew that she would never return again. It was strange that she never fought me that day as I started the car to leave everything behind and she would never realize where I was taking her. She trusted me that I knew.

Thankfully, mother did make the transition. She liked her neat little apartment. It was her first with controlled heating and air conditioning. I worked hard with her in those early days, preparing her evening meals on my way home from work, and doing things like starting her a collection of hummingbirds and dolls, anything to lift the shadow of grief that fell so heavily on her shoulders. Mother was never diagnosed with Alzheimer's, but with a type of dementia brought on by severe stress. Her sorrow was still very fresh, but the new apartment proved to be a good distraction.

In those early days she would cry at the drop of a hat, reliving the moment in the house after Frank died. However, she slowly began to sort out some of those more painful memories and shut them away in a place that wouldn't hurt her. Sometimes I wondered if this was the best thing for her, but she had enough heartaches from the past few years to last her a lifetime, and I knew I could not fault her methods for trying to forget. "I have a way of storing some things in the back of my head (as she pointed to the back of her head) and I don't want to go there," she had said to me so many times. She would then change the subject. Those are the things she will not talk about.

She continued to talk about Frank daily, which I felt was good. She would make comments about how he would enjoy favorite foods they had shared. There were days when I wondered having someone to love again would be the best thing for her. She still took pride in of her appearance, washing and curling her hair every day and putting on makeup. She no longer cooked, but she did sweep the front of her apartment and trimmed her shrubbery. I kept her in fresh flowers and she loved to water them every day.

Mom's dementia was a huge challenge. In some ways she was her typical self. She thought she was in great health and would hide her pills, but it kept me on my toes trying to watch her closely and making sure she took her medicine daily. I had found pills in her pants pocket, and under her milk glass, under the cushion of the sofa or sometimes she would hold them under her tongue, most anything to keep from taking them.

There was still a lot of pain in mother's eyes, and I felt she kept to herself to avoid talk of those things that she wanted to forget. It was becoming harder and harder to read her, but knew that being away from her little apartment home made her nervous. I had Meals on Wheels deliver to her every day but she would not eat the food. I also paid for her to go to the senior center, but it was also something she refused to do. She also did not like to go anywhere without me, and when she visited Ruth, her sister-in-law still living near Jasper, she would look around nervously and ask for me unless a video of the Gaither Family homecoming of religious music was playing.

She wanted to go back to Rockcastle where she was born and to Harlan to visit all the graves. I knew where her sweet family was buried except for Goff. For years I had searched for his grave and through the kindness of Jean Shoemaker, with the Genealogy Center in Rockcastle, KY I did visit the spring where he was killed. Jean said, "Joyce, do you know it was named The Howard Spring?" She also took me to the old school house and showed me where the Howard's had lived. There on the side of the mountain, just as mother had so vividly described stood the house with the porch overlooking the road. And just down the road as she had said, was the spring where Goff went for water. I stood looking at the spot where he had taken his last breath and looked around the area almost feeling his sweet spirit with me. Through the Rockcastle Library I found his grave, but did not get to visit. I hoped to take mother back before she faded totally away and perhaps, just perhaps it would not be too late, I had hoped to ignite a spark that would take her back home for a moment. Slowly though, I saw signs of my mother's old self, but the signs only come and went quickly only to disappoint me. I knew the she would not be with me forever.

I had gone by her house one morning to make her breakfast. She had just put on her bra and panties. I went to the kitchen to put her dinner in the refrigerator.

"Do you have your camera," Mother yelled from her bedroom.

I said, "Well, no." When I came out of the kitchen there she stood, posed like a movie star, alluringly clad in those undies. I got so tickled, and we both stood there for several minutes, laughing so hard we both cried.

Another day I took her back to her apartment, and when I turned to leave she yelled, "See you later." I turned in surprise when she yelled and when I did she kicked her leg straight up in the air above her head like a Rockette. I never knew what she would do next, but I always ended up in a good laugh.

"Why I still have all my teeth," mother would boast. "I do my exercises every morning before I get out of bed. This is what you do to keep your stomach tight." With that she would lie down, stretch out her body, and hold her hands by her side. Then she would begin lifting both her legs up and down. Her skin was still flawless. She wanted to remarry.

Against great odds, one thing about my mother never changed. She was a survivor. Slowly, I saw the sparkle in those eyes beginning to return. One rainy day in late August, she finally spoke of some of those painful memories for the first time. It wasn't a deep revelation, but it was a start. "Did Frank die," she began. I told her yes and then she said, "Did that boy do something bad to Carol?" And I said yes and she said, "Oh, I don't want to go there anymore." With that she changed the subject and the memory was gone again.

During a Sunday outing we stopped for ice-cream cones. Mother ate very slowly and suddenly she turned to me as I had inhaled the last smidgen of the ice cream down to the cone. She said, "Joyce Ann, you can eat faster than anyone I have ever seen except for Frank. I have figured out why you eat faster." I said, "Well, mother let's hear it?" She said, "Well, your licker is longer than my licker!" We both laughed til our sides hurt.

"I'm eighty-four. I would give anything to go back to Harlan and walk down those streets again," she said with a smile, "and visit Frank and Calvin's grave, also Carol and Curtis. If I could just go back to Kitts Cemetery and visit Mom and Dad and my brothers and sisters." She gazed through the window, as I realized her thoughts were up there near Coxton Mountain. This tiny woman, the last of the Howard Clan, had survived the ruthless ways of life. She had never had a fortune, but she held her treasures in her heart as she murmured, "I don't think about things that upset me, I just put those things in the back of my mind and leave them alone for I can't change what happened yesterday. I have to think about today."

If that wasn't reason enough to love her, you'll just have to forgive me. She was my precious, beautiful mother.

I did visit Rockcaste, KY where mother was born, gathering notes and taking pictures of the old home place, the coalmines, hanging bridges and storefronts. I also visited Kitts Cemetery many times. When I stood looking at the beauty of the mountains, which was still so much like my mother had described in her diary; I hoped that one day she could be buried here with her people. As she said, outsiders would not go looking for it. The people there are left alone. They continued to float above the trees and watch over each other.

After another two years passing and I began to see mother slowly fading away. She thought she cooked the things I brought her. Phyllis was her best friend and visited daily helping care for her. Phyllis fried mother's potatoes crispy just like she liked and took her for drives and walks. Mother would tell you in a heartbeat that she did all the cooking. She gave no one credit for doing anything, but Phyllis understood. Mother constantly reminded me that she had all her teeth. And she got angry if I gathered her laundry. "Why, my clothes are not dirty. I am not a dirty person. Me and dirt don't mix," she boasted. I felt she was going back in time when she was a child with no pretty clothes and afraid the ones she had would wear out if they were washed often. I often hid the clothes and took care of cleaning them without her knowing. It was the little things that made her nervous and those were the things that mattered so little.

I had come to understand dementia and the role it had played in my life. It was very much like dealing with someone who was inebriated. They could not remember what they did from day to day, what they said five minutes ago, what they wore the day before, if they ate, what day they were in as time was not a factor anymore in their lives. They became agitated if you suggested changes, which caused mood changes, but remembering 10 years ago and the list would go on and on. The hangover did not exist, but the signs of brain functioning normally were gone forever.

My mother's dementia continued to rob her of the adventures she had over her lifetime, but I felt this adventure would be her last. I would come to miss her very much, but I would not fret over her. I had the diary to remind me of her life, and I knew we would meet again one day in the sweet by and by and it would be on that beautiful shore.

Joyce Osborn Wilson is a woman with many talents.

She is first a Christian and also author, entrepreneur, instructor leader, caregiver and inventor. She was honored with Professional and Business Woman of the Year twice in her community, served on numerous boards too many to mention, has appeared on the John Stossel Show, a charter member of Leadership Walker County, Jasper, AL, and featured in the New York times in 2013. She continues to serve as President of the CCTW an organization to fight for her constitutional rights for non-teeth whitening. She made the Forbes list twice.

Other Books:

In The Sweet By and By
Take a Walk Through Life with LED Light
Copyright 2008 All rights reserved

www.booksbyjoyceosbornwilson.com

Made in the USA
Coppell, TX
17 September 2020

38165957R00203